GENERAL EDITORS
Gloria Bowles
Renate Klein
Janice Raymond

CONSULTING EDITOR
Dale Spender

The **Athene Series** assumes that those who formulate explanations of the way the world works need to know and appreciate the significance of basic feminist principles.

The growth of feminist research internationally has called into question almost all aspects of social organization in our culture. The **Athene Series** focuses on the construction of knowledge and the exclusion of women from the process—both as theorists and subjects of study—and offers innovative studies that challenge established theories and research.

ATHENE, the Olympian goddess of wisdom, was honored by the ancient Greeks as the patron of arts and sciences and guardian of cities. She represented both peace and war, the latter in its cognitive aspect. Her mother, Metis, was a Titan and presided over all knowledge. While pregnant with Athene, Metis was swallowed whole by Zeus. Some say this was his attempt to embody her supreme wisdom. The original Athene is thus twice born: once of her strong mother, Metis, and once more out of the head of Zeus. According to feminist myth, there is a "third birth" of Athene when she stops being an agent and mouthpiece of Zeus and male dominance, and returns to her original source: the wisdom of womankind.

RE-ENGINEERING
Female Friendly
Science

SUE V. ROSSER

Teachers College, Columbia University
New York and London

Published by Teachers College Press, 1234 Amsterdam Avenue, New York, NY 10027

Library of Congress Cataloging-in-Publication Data

Rosser, Sue Vilhauer.
    Re-engineering female friendly science / Sue V. Rosser.
        p.   cm. — (Athene series)
    Includes bibliographical references and index.
    ISBN 0-8077-6287-3 (cloth). — ISBN 0-8077-6286-5 (pbk.)
    1. Science—Study and teaching—United States.   2. Women in education—United States.   3. Women in science—United States.   4. Mathematics—Study and teaching—United States.   5. Engineering—Study and teaching—United States.   6. Curriculum planning—United States   I. Title.   II. Series.
Q183.3.A1R69   1997
507′.1′073—dc21   97-5935

ISBN 0-8077-6286-5 (paper)
ISBN 0-8077-6287-3 (cloth)

Printed on acid-free paper
Manufactured in the United States of America

03 02 01 00 99 98 97   8 7 6 5 4 3 2 1

In Memory of Charlotte

Contents

Acknowledgments

The confluence of the many tangible and less evident ways in which supportive colleagues, family members, editors, and staff have made this volume possible become so complex and interwoven that I find it difficult to tease apart the invaluable contribution made by each individual. I am grateful to faculty and teachers at colleges and universities throughout the country whose new ideas and pedagogical techniques inspired me to think about the impact of gender and race on the implementation of the revolution in science education reform. Colleagues, particularly Roosevelt Calbert, Daryl Chubin, Midge Cozzens, Jim Dietz, Trish Morse, and Lola Rogers in the Education and Human Resources Directorate at the National Science Foundation, in the course of their daily struggle to make a difference in science education, prodded me to think about these issues.

Without the support of my new colleagues and friends in Florida, especially Patricia Miller, Barbara Pace, and Denise Standiford, I would not have been able to complete this book during this time of personal trauma and difficulty. The staff at the Center for Women's Studies and Gender Research at the University of Florida facilitated the production of the manuscript. I am most appreciative of the work of my administrative assistant Robbie Blake and of my graduate assistants Allan Wood and Mireille Zieseniss, who wound their way through computer glitches and post-its to produce the final version of the manuscript to go to press. As always, Faye Zucker gave invaluable insights, provided support, and demonstrated her outstanding competence as an editor. Without the excellent copyediting by Myra Cleary, the book would not have come to fruition. Finally, I again acknowledge the importance and support of my family, Charlotte, Meagan, and Caitlin, who perpetually inspire and support me in my endeavors.

Female Friendly Science Goes Mainstream

During the 1980s the scientific community and the public became increasingly aware of problems with the teaching of science in the United States. International studies of educational performance revealed that U.S. students rank near the bottom in performance in science and mathematics compared with students educated in other industrialized countries and in many less-developed countries (International Association for Evaluation of Educational Attainment, 1988). Studies of educational achievement within the United States uncovered decreasing performance of students in science and mathematics. For example, the National Assessment of Educational Progress documented that the average performance of 17-year-olds in 1986 was substantially lower than it had been in 1969 (American Association for the Advancement of Science, 1990).

Faced with the grim statistics of these and other reports, the scientific and educational communities undertook a variety of attempts to study the problems and propose solutions for both the K–12 and college levels. Professional societies, government agencies, and private foundations (AAAS, 1990, 1993; Astin & Astin, 1993; National Research Council, 1993, 1996; National Science Foundation, 1991, 1992, 1993c; Seymour & Hewitt, 1994) poured considerable resources into these studies.

A growing body of research documents the need to change the way science is taught at the undergraduate level to make it more appealing to all students, regardless of gender (Astin & Astin, 1993; Astin, Green, Korn, & Riggs, 1991; Green, 1989a, 1989b; Seymour & Hewitt, 1994). For example, a recent Cooperative Institutional Research Program (CIRP) report (Astin & Astin, 1993) reveals that 40% of all students who enter college indicating an interest in science, engineering, and mathematics (SEM) are lost between their first and senior years. Other studies document that the highest risk of SEM switching (35%) occurs between the first and sophomore years (NSF, 1991).

In response to these and other studies (Astin & Astin, 1993; Seymour & Hewitt, 1994; Tobias, 1990, 1992) documenting attrition from SEM due to problems with undergraduate pedagogy and curriculum, government agencies (NRC, 1993; NSF, 1989, 1991; Neale et al., 1991; Project Kaleidoscope, 1991, 1992, 1994) and private foundations (National Advisory Group, Sigma Xi, the Scientific Research Society, 1989; NRC, 1996; Oakes, 1990; Strenta, Elliott, Matier, Scott, & Adair, 1993; Tobias, 1992) have placed considerable emphasis on curricular reforms. New first-year college engineering courses, tailored physics sequences for engineers, Chemistry in Context (Schwartz et al., 1993), and guided design calculus (NSF, 1991/1992/1993) exemplify some of the large-scale curricular reforms funded at the undergraduate level. Hands-on laboratory experiences, collaborative learning, emphasis on practical applications, and group work (Project Kaleidoscope, 1994) have been stressed as pedagogical techniques likely to improve retention of all students. Although some of the studies explored gender differences in rates and causes of retention in SEM (Astin & Astin, 1993; Sax, 1994; Seymour & Hewitt, 1994; Strenta et al., 1993), very few of the reforms focused specifically on women. For example, the Undergraduate Course and Curriculum Development Program Summaries (NSF, 1991/1992/1993) reveal that in 1991 two out of 88 new awards (NSF, 1991), in 1992, five out of 110 new awards (NSF, 1992), and in 1993, six out of 82 new awards (NSF, 1993) focused on women as a specific target population.

A study by Matyas and Malcom (1991) of over 400 undergraduate institutions revealed that of the less than 10% of programs that did focus on women in science, virtually none considered the impact of curricular and pedagogical issues in the classroom on recruitment and retention. In an attempt to increase the relatively low percentages of women in most areas of science, mathematics, and engineering, the National Science Foundation established the Program for Women and Girls within the Division of Human Resource Development, with three initiatives to increase and retain women throughout the pipeline from kindergarten through the faculty level (NSF, 1994b). A review of the Model Projects for Women and Girls reveals that only 22 of 43 projects funded between 1988 and 1993 (NSF, 1994c) targeted the undergraduate level and above; of those 22, only 11 might be said to center on pedagogy, curriculum, or classroom climate, by applying the most broad, liberal definitions of those terms. Of the 11 proposals in the Experimental Projects for Women and Girls (for which the first funding was available in fiscal 1994), only three focus on the undergraduate classroom or have a major classroom component. Similarly, of the 20 projects funded by the Women's Educational Equity Act Programs in 1993, five targeted postsecondary women (WEEA, 1993). Of those five, only one had a faculty development component to sensitize "faculty teaching upper division courses . . . to the needs of these women students and to introduce them to techniques of collaborative learning and gender neutrality for co-ed classrooms" (WEEA, 1993, p. 4), although that was not the primary focus of the project. In sum, most of the curriculum reform efforts in science, mathematics, and engineering have not focused on women, and the bulk of the newly initiated efforts centered on women in science have not made the curriculum or classroom their major impetus.

Although curricular and pedagogical reforms to attract women to science may have fallen between the cracks of both curricular reform and women in science initiatives, many of the solutions suggested by each initiative appear to be derived from, or at least compatible with, ideas championed by those of us from women's studies and ethnic studies. Collaborative learning through the use of groups, emphasis on practical applications, integration of information from the history of science, and placing science in a more holistic and social context that emphasizes dependence and connection among the earth, humans, and other living beings, were suggested by scholars from women's studies (Fausto-Sterling, 1992; Rosser, 1990, 1993b, 1995) and ethnic studies (Clewell & Ginorio, 1996) as ways to make science, mathematics, and engineering more appealing to women and to men of color. When these ideas appeared in curricular and pedagogical reforms, in women in science programs, or in other science education reform movements such as Science, Technology, and Society (STS) or undergraduate curriculum reforms (Tobias, 1992), little discussion about men of color or women accompanied them. I wondered whether the omission of references to gender and race meant that the connections of the ideas to women's studies and ethnic studies had been obscured intentionally as the ideas had become mainstream or that their origins had been entirely different.

To determine their alignment with previously proposed ideas of feminist pedagogy and curriculum reform, I compared the studies with the suggestions I had made in *Female Friendly Science* (1990). The mere fact that gender and race were not explicitly mentioned frequently in the reports and that women's studies and ethnic studies were cited barely or not at all, did not necessarily mean that they had not formed or provided foundations for the studies.

THE EVOLUTION OF FEMALE FRIENDLY SCIENCE: PHASE THEORY

In *Female Friendly Science* (1990), I proposed a six-stage model for curriculum transformation to aid in including more information on women and men of color. Built on models developed by feminist scholars working in other disciplines (McIntosh, 1984; Schuster & Van Dyne, 1985; Tetreault, 1985), the following model is specific for science and mathematics:

Stage 1. Absence of women not noted. This is the traditional approach to science and the curriculum from the perspective of the white, Eurocentric, middle- to upper-class male in which the absence of women is not noted and gender affects neither who becomes a scientist or the science produced.

Stage 2. Recognition that most scientists are male and that science may reflect a masculine perspective on the physical, natural world. A few exceptional women such as Nobel laureates who have achieved the highest success as defined by the traditional standards of the discipline may be accepted in the scientific community and included in the curriculum.

Stage 3. Identification of barriers that prevent women from entering science. Women are recognized as a problem, anomaly, or absence from science and the curriculum. Women may be seen as victims, as protesters, or as deprived or defective variants, who deviate from the white, middle- to upper-class norm of the male scientist.

Stage 4. Search for women scientists and their unique contributions. The extent to which the role of women has been overlooked, misunderstood, or attributed to male colleagues throughout the history of science is explored to determine women's scientific achievements.

Stage 5. Science done by feminists/women. In this phase, new perspectives result when women become the focus. Topics chosen for study, methods used, and language in which data and theories are described may shift and become expanded, improving the quality of science.

Stage 6. Science redefined and reconstructed to include us all.
As I worked in projects and modified the stages to describe the way I saw curriculum transformation occurring in the sciences, especially biology (Rosser, 1990, 1993b), I recognized that the phases applied to more than curriculum. These stages describe steps of personal development through which individuals progress as they become aware of androcentric and ethnocentric biases in curriculum and pedagogy. In fact, as I suggested in a much earlier article (Rosser, 1986), I believe that an individual must progress personally through, or at least to, a stage of development before he or she can develop curriculum and pedagogical techniques at that stage. For example, a faculty member cannot teach a stage 6 course in which the primary focus shifts from the white male experience to include women, men of color, and disabled persons, if she or he is only at the "add women and stir" phase (stage 2) in her or his own thinking. The syllabus and theoretical framework from which the course would be conceived undoubtedly would reflect the addition of a few famous women or a couple of examples of women's experiences to the course as she or he traditionally conceived and taught it. Without personally passing through the stages of under-

standing that the female is an exception, deviant, or anomaly when the male body or experience as a scientist is defined as the norm (stage 3), to a concentrated study of how the subject, problem, or research might be conceived if women, the female experience, or the female body were the focus or norm (stage 5), an individual could not conceive a curriculum or teach a class that was truly inclusive (stage 6).

Just as phase theory may be applied to personal development and transformation toward inclusion as well as curriculum, it also may be applied to programs, departments, institutions, and/or agencies. As is the case with individuals, even with a well-conceived (stage 6) plan for diversity and inclusion and the best of intentions on the part of all faculty, staff, and/or employees, an institution or agency cannot jump from stage 1 to stage 6 without going through the intermediate stages.

PHASES OF CURRICULUM TRANSFORMATION IN STUDIES

Most of the studies appear to articulate stage 6 as their overarching goal. For example, in the introduction to *Science for All Americans,* the first publication produced by Project 2061 (AAAS, 1990) to define what constitutes adult science literacy by recommending what all students should know in science, mathematics, and technology by the time they graduate from high school, the following statement is made:

> The set of recommendations constitutes a common core of learning in science, mathematics, and technology for all young people, regardless of their social circumstances and career aspirations. In particular, the recommendations pertain to those who in the past have largely been bypassed in science and mathematics education: ethnic and language minorities and girls. (p. xviii)

In a similar vein, Project Kaleidoscope (PKAL), begun in 1989 with support from the National Science Foundation to outline an agenda for reform in undergraduate science and mathematics education, includes the following as one of six points in the PKAL vision of *What Works:*

> Build communities of learners, in which students of all backgrounds and career aspirations are attracted to and enabled to succeed in science and mathematics. (p. 2)

These statements of goals and those made by other science, mathematics, and engineering curriculum reformers (Sigma Xi, 1994; Tobias, 1990) express clear intentions of inclusion. They attempt to attract more diversity to the pool of scientists.

Although diversity in the pool of scientists is a desirable goal that might result in an inclusive curriculum, it is not the same as stage 6, a curriculum with inclusive content. Perhaps a reason that women's and ethnic studies were not mentioned, while women and minorities (the phrase often used in the studies) were referred to occasionally, was simply a repetition of a familiar phenomenon: Men of color and women would be included in science as long as they assimilated and agreed to do science and mathematics like white men. Science curriculum and teaching would bear little of the integration of perspectives from men of color and women; they would be changed only sufficiently to attract slightly more women and men of color. Most of the reform or change was still expected to occur on the part of the new recruits to make themselves "includable" in science, mathematics, and engineering.

It would not be surprising if this "assimilation" stance for women and men of color was the expectation. Past efforts to "include" women and minority men in science have emphasized improving visuo-spatial skills, assertiveness training, and competitive sports (Matyas, 1985) as mechanisms to erase deficits and accommodate women to the culture of white male science. The belief in objectivity buttresses this assimilation model, which suggests that all of the accommodation needs to be on the part of the females. Many scientists assume that since science is "objective," gender does not influence either who becomes a scientist or the science produced by those scientists. Scientists taking such a stance suggest that science is "manless" as well as "womanless"; they are unaware of or would openly reject the notion that gender might influence the theories, data collection, subjects chosen for experimentation, or questions asked. This stance of "genderless" science represents an aspect of stage 6, in which the absence of women and men of color from science may have been noted, but is deemed insignificant or not applicable because of the objectivity of science.

A re-reading of *Benchmarks for Science Literacy* (AAAS, 1993), *Science for All Americans* (AAAS, 1990), and the *National Science Education Standards* (NRC, 1996) convinced me that the authors sincerely attempted to move beyond stage 1. For example, Chapter 13, "Effective Teaching and Learning," of *Science for All Americans* includes the following paragraph:

> *Support the Roles of Women and Minorities in Science.* Because the scientific and engineering professions have been predominantly male and white, female and minority students could easily get the impression that these fields are beyond them or are otherwise unsuited to them. This debilitating perception—all too often reinforced by the environment outside the school—will persist unless teachers actively work to turn it around. Teachers should select learning materials that illustrate the contributions of women and minorities, bring in role models, and make it clear to

female and minority students that they are expected to study the same subjects at the same level as everyone else and to perform as well. (AAAS, 1990, pp. 205–206)

This paragraph serves as a clear expression of stage 2: It recognizes that most scientists have been white and male. In suggesting that teachers bring in materials and role models that illustrate the contributions of women and minorities, it advocates the "add women and stir" approach. This stage 2 approach does not require basic revision of the white male curriculum; it simply suggests that men of color and women who have achieved similar prominence by the same standards as white men (Nobel laureates, for example) be included.

Program Standard E of the *National Science Education Standards* implies a stage 3 approach in its suggestion that barriers, or at least lack of encouragement and opportunity, may have excluded some from science.

In particular, the commitment to science for all implies inclusion of those who traditionally have not received encouragement and opportunity to pursue science—women and girls, students of color, students with disabilities, and students with limited English proficiency. It implies attention to various styles of learning, adaptations to meet the needs of special students and differing sources of motivation. (NRC, 1996, p. 221)

Acknowledgment of different styles of learning and differing sources of motivation might be read as accepting that some (i.e., females) may approach learning (and therefore science) differently and be interested in it for different reasons than others.

Chapter 13 of *Science for All Americans* contains statements that represent stage 3 in their attempts to identify barriers that prevent women and men of color from entering science.

Provide Abundant Experience in Using Tools. Many students are fearful of using laboratory instruments and other tools. This fear may result primarily from the lack of opportunity many of them have to become familiar with tools in safe circumstances. Girls in particular suffer from the mistaken notion that boys are naturally more adept at using tools. Starting in the earliest grades, all students should gradually gain familiarity with tools and the proper use of tools. By the time they finish school, all students should have had supervised experience with common hand tools, soldering irons, electrical meters, drafting tools, optical and sound equipment, calculators, and computers. (AAAS, 1990, p. 205)

Although taking an approach that in some respects blames the victim by stating that "girls in particular suffer from the mistaken notion," the authors of this paragraph clearly attempt to identify a barrier for girls and suggest solutions to remove it. Later in the same chapter, the authors remove the responsibility from girls and minority students.

> When demographic realities, national needs, and democratic values are taken into account, it becomes clear that the nation can no longer ignore the science education of any students. Race, language, sex, or economic circumstances must no longer be permitted to be factors in determining who does and who does not receive a good education in science, mathematics, and technology. To neglect the science education of any (as has happened too often to girls and minority students) is to deprive them of a basic education, handicap them for life, and deprive the nation of talented workers and informed citizens—a loss the nation can ill afford. (AAAS, 1990, p. 214)

These statements demonstrate an attempt to move beyond stage 1 to stages 2 and 3 to identify barriers and add information about men and women of color and white women to the curriculum. Since my experience with a number of curriculum transformation projects indicates that most fail to reach beyond these phases, particularly in science, mathematics, and engineering courses, the level of phases attained as indicated in these reform documents comes as no surprise. Failure to attain true inclusion (stage 6) probably should not alone be viewed as a sign that gender and race have not been considered seriously or that all expectations of accommodation should be on the part of men of color and women.

PHASES OF PEDAGOGICAL CHANGE IN STUDIES

Since curriculum transformation has proved especially difficult in the sciences, mathematics, and engineering, a look at the attempts to incorporate female friendly pedagogical techniques in these reforms might prove more revelatory. In *Female Friendly Science* (1990), I suggested 20 teaching techniques based on research in women's studies, ethnic studies, and science education that might be useful for attracting and retaining women in science. These techniques are summarized in Table 1.1.

A comparison of *Benchmarks* (AAAS, 1993), *Science for All Americans* (AAAS, 1990), the *National Science Education Standards* (NRC, 1996), Project Kaleidoscope Phase 2 (PKAL, 1994), *They're Not Dumb, They're Different* (Tobias, 1990), *Revitalizing Undergraduate Science Education* (Tobias, 1992), and other science education reforms reveals considerable overlap with the list of pedagogical techniques from *Female Friendly Science*. All stress hands-on and interactive approaches to involve students directly with experimental science. Most stress collaborative learning and group work, as opposed to competition; connection and interdisciplinarity are emphasized. Placing science in its social context is underlined through learning about the history of science, as are prac-

TABLE 1.1. Teaching Techniques

OBSERVATIONS

1. Expand the kinds of observations beyond those traditionally carried out in scientific research. Women students may see new data that could make a valuable contribution to scientific experiments.
2. Increase the number of observations and remain longer in the observational stage of the scientific method. This would provide more hands-on experience with various types of equipment in the laboratory.
3. Incorporate and validate personal experiences women are likely to have had, as part of the class discussion or the laboratory exercise.
4. Undertake fewer experiments likely to have applications of direct benefit to the military and propose more experiments to explore problems of social concern.
5. Consider problems that have not been considered worthy of scientific investigation because of the field with which the problems traditionally have been associated.
6. Formulate hypotheses focusing on gender as a crucial part of the question asked.
7. Undertake the investigation of problems of a more holistic, global scope than the more reduced and limited-scale problems traditionally considered.

METHODS

8. Use a combination of qualitative and quantitative methods in data gathering.
9. Use methods from a variety of fields or interdisciplinary approaches to problem solving.

METHODS (*continued*)

10. Include females as experimental subjects in experimental designs.
11. Use more interactive methods, thereby shortening the distance between the observer and the object studied.
12. Decrease laboratory exercises in introductory courses in which students kill animals or render treatment that may be perceived as particularly harsh.

CONCLUSIONS AND THEORIES DRAWN FROM DATA GATHERED

13. Use precise, gender-neutral language in describing data and presenting theories.
14. Be open to critiques of conclusions and theories drawn from observations differing from those drawn by the traditional male scientist from the same observations.
15. Encourage uncovering of other biases such as those of race, class, sexual orientation, and religious affiliation that may permeate theories and conclusions drawn from experimental observation.

PRACTICE OF SCIENCE

17. Use less competitive models to practice science.
18. Discuss the role of scientist as only one facet that must be smoothly integrated with other aspects of students' lives.
19. Put increased effort into strategies such as teaching and communicating with nonscientists to break down barriers between science and the lay person.
20. Discuss the practical uses to which scientific discoveries are put to help students see science in its social context.

tical uses for the theory and experimental manipulations that students have tried in the laboratory.

With the goal of scientific literacy for all Americans, the AAAS publications underscore the importance of teaching and communicating with nonscientists and using nontechnical, nonjargonistic language to break down barriers between science and the layperson. For example, the following two quotations, along with others in a similar vein, occur in *Benchmarks*: "Benchmarks avoids technical language used for its own sake" (AAAS, 1993, p. xiii), and "The intent of this Project 2061 report is to say something important about education and say it clearly, not to expand literary horizons. Since education is everybody's business, it is important that *Benchmarks for Science Literacy* be understandable by the general public as well as by teachers and educators—an admirable aim not easily attained" (AAAS, 1993, p. 316).

Science for All Americans makes similar recommendations.

> *Deemphasize the Memorization of Technical Vocabulary.* Understanding rather than vocabulary should be the main purpose of science teaching. However, unambiguous terminology is also important in scientific communication and—ultimately—for understanding. Some technical terms are therefore helpful for everyone, but the number of essential ones is relatively small. If teachers introduce technical terms only as needed to clarify thinking and promote effective communication, then students will gradually build a functional vocabulary that will survive beyond the next test. For teachers to concentrate on vocabulary, however, is to detract from science as a process, to put learning for understanding in jeopardy, and to risk being misled about what students have learned. (AAAS, 1990, p. 203)

Major methods stressed in the AAAS publications for achieving this goal include interdisciplinary approaches that demonstrate connections, global interdependence, and holism between science, living beings, and society: "SFAA emphasizes cogency and connectedness" (AAAS, 1990, p. xiv), and "A central Project 2061 premise is that the useful knowledge people possess is richly interconnected" (AAAS, 1990, p. 315).

> The common core of learning in science, mathematics, and technology should center on science literacy, not on an understanding of each of the separate disciplines. Moreover, the core studies should include connections among science, mathematics, and technology and between those areas and the arts and humanities and the vocational subjects. (AAAS, 1990, p. xii)

Benchmarks also emphasizes integration and connection:

> *Interdisciplinary.* With relation to curriculum, this term is used to refer to many different possibilities. . . . But with regard to curriculum, there are three senses in

which Project 2061 is solidly behind integration. First, integrated planning, . . . second, interconnected knowledge, . . . third, coherence. (AAAS, 1993, p. 320)

Program Standard B of the *National Science Education Standards* requires connection with other disciplines.

The program of study in science for all students should be developmentally appropriate, interesting, and relevant to students' lives; emphasize student understanding through inquiry; and be connected with other school subjects. (NRC, 1996, p. 212)

Project Kaleidoscope articulates its vision for *What Works* in undergraduate science and mathematics education.

Make critical connections between the classroom, lab, different areas of study, the undergraduate and educational community, the nation, and the world. (PKAL, 1994, p. 2)

All of the reports favor collaborative over competitive approaches and group work over solitary investigations. For example, *Science for All Americans* stresses the importance of group work.

Use a Team Approach. The collaborative nature of scientific and technological work should be strongly reinforced by frequent group activity in the classroom. Scientists and engineers work mostly in groups and less often as isolated investigators. Similarly, students should gain experience sharing responsibility for learning with each other. In the process of coming to common understandings students in a group must frequently inform each other about procedures and meanings, argue over findings, and assess how the task is progressing. In the context of team responsibility, feedback and communication become more realistic and of a character very different from the usual individualistic textbook–homework–recitation approach. (AAAS, 1990, p. 202)

The *National Science Education Standards* emphasize collaboration as integral to science itself in Teaching Standard E.

Nurture collaboration among students. Working collaboratively with others not only enhances the understanding of science, it also fosters the practice of many of the skills, attitudes, and values that characterize science. Effective teachers design many of the activities for learning science to require group work, not simply as an exercise, but as essential to the inquiry. The teacher's role is to structure the groups and to teach students the skills that are needed to work together. (NRC, 1996, p. 50)

Two of the six ideas from PKAL of *What Works* in undergraduate science focus on collaboration and community building.

- Build communities of learners, in which students of all backgrounds and career aspirations are attracted to and enabled to succeed in science and mathematics.
- Bring faculty and students together as partners in learning, where faculty are committed to undergraduate teaching as a part of their own intellectual vitality, and where they are encouraged to assume a leadership role in the process of building and sustaining a strong undergraduate community. (PKAL, 1994, p. 2)

By quoting rather extensively from the AAAS, PKAL, NRC, and NSF publications, I have attempted to demonstrate the congruence between three of the suggestions (communication with nonscientists; use of interdisciplinary approaches; use of collaborative techniques) I make for female friendly pedagogy and the recommendations made in these reports. Similar overlaps are found for 14 of the other 17 suggestions from *Female Friendly Science*, although neither gender and race nor their implications for women and men of color are explicitly considered. Only the three suggestions (formulate hypotheses focusing on gender as a crucial part of the question asked; include females as experimental subjects in experimental designs; and be open to critiques of conclusions and theories drawn from observations differing from those drawn by the traditional male scientist from the same observations) with an explicit mention of gender focus have no congruence with recommendations of the reports.

Perhaps the absence of congruence with the techniques that specifically focus on gender should not be shocking. Similarly, the failure to mention the effects of particular modifications of the techniques that would be especially helpful to people of different genders, races, and classes might not be surprising either. After all, these reports were written to appeal to all students, all faculty, and the general public. The title of one of the reports, *Science for All Americans*, reflects this very general focus. The *National Science Education Standards* emphasize repeatedly the goal of appealing to all students.

> *The intent of the Standards* can be expressed in a single phrase: Science standards for all students. The phrase embodies both excellence and equity. The Standards apply to all students, regardless of age, gender, cultural or ethnic background, disabilities, aspirations, or interest and motivation in science. (NRC, 1996, p. 2)

In contrast, I wrote *Female Friendly Science* with particular emphasis on what would work to attract girls and women, and to a lesser extent, males of color, to science.

PHASES OF CHANGE AT THE INSTITUTIONAL LEVEL

The difficulties of transformation that are encountered by individuals multiply when entire programs, departments, agencies, or institutions attempt inclusion.

Despite almost insurmountable problems, a significant number of institutions of higher education have attempted curriculum transformation projects. As early as 1987 (McMillen, 1987), over 100 institutions had received foundation or federal monies to support such efforts; since then, substantial numbers of other colleges and universities, beginning their inclusion efforts after the cutting-edge money provided by foundations had ceased, initiated their transformation projects using internal or private money. In 1995, the National Center for Curriculum Transformation Resources on Women reported over 200 projects in the United States (Coulter & Vanfossen, 1995).

Federal agencies, such as the National Science Foundation, support programs for women and girls and for minorities, in attempts to bring these previously excluded groups into the scientific mainstream. Although their focus is not primarily on curriculum or pedagogy, the stage model may be applied to examine the stages of development of these programs.

For many years, the scientific mainstream and the National Science Foundation remained in stage 1—absence of women not noted. Keller (1983, 1985), Merchant (1979), and other historians and philosophers of science have documented the extent to which notions of objectivity and masculinity became entwined and functioned to exclude females and define science as genderless.

Data analyzed by the Commission on Professionals in Science and Technology (Vetter, 1989, 1992), the National Science Foundation (1986, 1988, 1990, 1992), and the National Research Council (CWSE, 1991) revealed a dearth of women in science. Mandated by law under the Science and Technology Equal Opportunities Act (1980), the National Science Foundation must collect and analyze data and report to Congress on a biennial basis on the status of women and minorities in the science and engineering professions. This activity on the part of the NSF might be viewed as stage 2, as information on women and minorities (or data disaggregated by gender and sex) was added to the data already collected as indicators about the scientific profession.

Analyses of these data revealed discrepancies between the numbers of women and men holding degrees in science and their employment, rank, and advancement in the scientific profession. These analyses led to stage 3 definitions of women and minorities as a problem, anomaly, or deviant from the white male norm. In response to this "problem" in 1982 (NSF, 1994a), the NSF established Visiting Professorships for Women (VPW). The program announcement for VPW gives a rationale for them: "The NSF Visiting Professorships for Women program addresses the need to develop full use of the Nation's human resources for science and technology. The objectives of the program are: To provide opportunities for women to advance their careers in engineering and in the disciplines of science supported by NSF; and To encourage women students to pursue careers in science and engineering by providing greater visibility for women scientists and engineers employed in industry, government and academic institutions" (NSF, 1994b, p. 1).

Graduate Fellowships for Women, Career Advancement Awards (CAA), and Research Planning Grants (RPG) represent initiatives that might be viewed as stage 3 within the traditional research directorates of the NSF. They attempt to correct the problem of lack of women in science and deviance from the male career trajectory.

In a similar vein, in 1992 the NSF established Faculty Awards for Women Scientists and Engineers (FAW). This program attempted to recognize outstanding women faculty in institutions of higher education and enable them to advance to senior positions (tenured, full professor). All of these initiatives represented stage 3 attempts to correct the problem of women in science and bring women in line with the white male norms for career advancement in science. Part of the shift in emphasis was spurred by a recognition in the Directorate of Education and Human Resources at the NSF that a focus on efforts to target individuals in groups such as minorities and white women would not work as long as the system remained the same. This led to the development of systemic initiatives, including the Statewide Systemic Initiatives (SSI), Urban Systemic Initiatives (USI), and Rural Systemic Initiatives (RSI).

In keeping with the general systemic approach, efforts shifted from examining what is wrong with women and how that might be corrected, to comprehensive factors and climate issues that may systematically deter women from science. In a shift toward stage 4 approaches targeted toward women, the National Science Foundation established three initiatives in 1993 with a focus on women. Model Projects for Women and Girls "encourage the design, implementation, evaluation and dissemination of innovative, short-term highly focused activities which will improve the access to and/or retention of females in SEM (science, mathematics, and engineering) education and careers." Experimental Projects for Women and Girls (EPWG) are large-scale projects requiring a consortial effort with multiple target populations. They aim "to create positive and permanent changes in academic, social, and scientific climates (for classrooms, laboratories, departments, institutions/organizations) in order to allow the interest and aptitude women and girls display in SEM to flourish; and to add to the knowledge base about interactions between gender and the infrastructure of SEM which can provide direction for future efforts" (NSF, 1993b, p. 7).

As revealed by the statistics on women in science and the research beginning to be gleaned from studies examining systemic and climate issues that deter women, science, engineering, and mathematics in the United States are far from the inclusion envisioned in stage 6. Substantially more resources, more stage 4 and 5 studies, as well as continued stage 2 and 3 efforts for a considerable period of time will be needed to bring teaching and research in science, engineering, and mathematics as a whole through stage 2. Presently, only parts of the enterprise have entered stages 3 and 4; stage 5 is populated primarily by a few individuals and some departments.

For example, in a stage 5 department, the theoretical question shaping the research might be, What would be the parameters of a feminist or women-centered science? Such a science might focus on matters of particular concern to women, such as pregnancy, childbirth, menstruation, and menopause in the arena of health. It might consider the social values and significance of research for human beings in determining whether the research should be funded. The anatomy, physiology, and life-cycle changes of the female might become the norm against which variations are measured. Approaches that shorten the distance between the experimenter and the subject of study might be explored, and feelings for the organism under study would be permitted. Consideration of the parameters of a women-centered science would lead the scientist-teacher to incorporate pedagogical techniques that were more in tune with female life cycles and experiences. Exploration of socialization processes and theories of female developmental psychology (Belenky, Clinchy, Goldberger, & Tarule, 1986; Chodorow, 1978) might lead the scientist-teacher to develop less competitive models to teach science. Avoiding timed tests and competitions to see who can solve the problem first at the blackboard and encouraging cooperative problem solving where everyone "wins" might be more attractive to women students. Consideration of differences in the life cycles of men and women would lead the scientist-teacher to consider research demonstrating that many potential women scientists drop out of science because of their perception that being a scientist is incompatible with having a relationship or a family (Arnold, 1987). Scientist-teachers might discuss the role of scientist as only one facet that must be smoothly integrated with other aspects of women's lives. They would provide the class with role models of practicing women scientists who demonstrate that a successful career in science can be combined with a variety of lifestyle options.

PITFALLS OF FAILURE TO FOCUS ON GENDER AND RACE

Dangers and difficulties can arise when suggestions for reform known to be helpful for particular groups become translated as techniques useful for all students. An unfortunate consequence may emerge when the connection with women's studies is severed as the ideas become more mainstream. When the emphasis on gender and/or race is dropped and practitioners are unaware of the race and gender dynamics that cause a technique to be successful in attracting and retaining particular groups, the portions of the techniques helpful to women and/or people of color may be lost. Application of such techniques without a focus on gender and race may result at a minimum in their losing their helpfulness, or in some cases in their actually working to disadvantage the very groups that they initially were designed to attract and retain.

Use of collaborative or group work serves as an example. Because of the current popularity of small-group work in science and mathematics classes, some faculty undertake group work without the knowledge of research in gender and race dynamics necessary to make group work succeed for women and men of color in areas new to them. The *National Science Education Standards* do not spell out how race, gender, and other factors may influence group participation. The *Standards* seem to assume that the teachers will be educated as to their influences.

> *Recognize and respond to student diversity and encourage all students to participate fully in science learning.* In all aspects of science learning as envisioned by the *Standards*, skilled teachers recognize the diversity in their classes and organize the classroom so that all students have the opportunity to participate fully. Teachers monitor the participation of all students, carefully determining, for instance, if all members of a collaborative group are working with materials or if one student is making all the decisions. This monitoring can be particularly important in classes of diverse students, where social issues of status and authority can be a factor. (NRC, 1996, pp. 36–37)

My experience suggests that faculty, particularly on the college level, often do not understand gender and race dynamics in group work and the particular implications for science, mathematics, and engineering classrooms. For example, a faculty member might assume that a physics class containing 25 students (five females and 20 males) should be divided into five groups. She or he might assume that placing one female in each group would constitute gender equity. In fact, such an arrangement demonstrates a lack of understanding of the research documenting the tendency of women to drop out of study groups when they are the only female, particularly if the subject is a nontraditional one for women, such as mathematics or science (Light, 1990). Even if the faculty member had read the literature on the significance of racial groupings (Treisman, 1992) for encouraging success for African American and Hispanic students in mathematics study groups, she or he might remain ignorant of the importance of gender composition and dynamics. Connecting the faculty member with the relevant research from women's studies and on gender dynamics in group communication would be helpful in making study groups work for women in the physics class.

In a similar vein, some changes advocated as female friendly, such as more focus on practical applications, increased information from the history of science, and attempts to place science in its social context, may lose their gender appeal unless they are undergirded by serious curricular transformation supported through women's studies. For example, presentation of certain chemical or drug effects that use a 70 kg white male as the prototype, may do little to reveal side effects or benefits for women in general and women of color in particular, who may be students in an introductory biology or chemistry course. If western European white males constitute the only contributors to the history of mathematics discussed in class, students who never see anyone of their gender or race portrayed all semester, despite the fact that the mathematics course includes considerable information on the history of mathematics, may conclude that they have no valuable contribution to make to mathematics. Environmental geosciences and hydrology courses that focus on the social effects of water resource management policies in third world countries may not be perceived as female friendly if the impact on women's lives in terms of the distance they must walk each day to obtain water is not considered. Simply adding on practical applications or a bit of history of science to a course, without rethinking the structure and perspective from which the course is taught, may result in cosmetic changes that appear to be female friendly but represent superficial understanding of the changes needed to attract and retain more women in science.

What would be a true measure of inclusion? Although it is difficult to determine a fair benchmark for gender or racial inclusion, even relatively crude statistical measures suggest that we are far from equity for women in science. Females represent 52% of the population (NSF, 1994c). If science were truly gender-neutral or gender-free, then one might anticipate that 52% of the scientists would be female. Another possible benchmark might be the 46% of the labor force that is female (NSF, 1994); using that benchmark, one might expect 46% of scientists to be female. In fact, women represent only 22% of the science and engineering labor force.

Against these benchmarks, the statistics documenting relatively meager increases for women in science are placed in perspective. Women have earned the majority (54%) of bachelor's degrees in all fields combined since 1982, but they earned only 44% of science and engineering degrees in 1991 (NSF, 1994). Although women have earned more than half of master's degrees in nonscience and nonengineering fields since 1975, they have earned only 36% of master's degrees in science and engineering (NSF, 1994). In 1991, women earned 45% of master's degrees in science fields, but only 14% of master's degrees in engineering (NSF, 1994).

At the doctoral level, the percentage of women drops further. Although the percentage of women earning doctoral degrees increased from 24% to 29% between 1982 and 1992 (NSF, 1994), their proportions varied considerably by field. Women obtained 59% of Ph.D.'s in psychology, but only 9% in engineering. Between those two extremes, fell the biological sciences (38%), social sciences (35%), mathematical science (19%), and computer science (14%) (NSF, 1994). The statistical perspective suggests stage 2, rather than stage 6, gains.

When I wrote *Female Friendly Science* in 1990, the predicted shortage of scientists and engineers motivated faculty to seek ways to make the climate more friendly to attract women to science. In the current political climate of tight fiscal resources and relatively high unemployment in the scientific workforce, programs to increase the numbers of men of color and women in science are being threatened and cut. Increased financial support to move beyond stage 2 seems unlikely. Perhaps the time is ripe to assess how friendly the climate really is for females in science.

In the following chapters, I explore the curricular and pedagogical changes touted in the mid-1990s in science teaching as beneficial for students, with the objective of examining their specific impact on females. Although the mainstream of science education now advocates curricular transformations that overlap with those advocated by feminist scientists, in some cases, such as when all examples in teaching about the history of science are white men, curricular reforms represent cooptation rather than transformation. Similarly, the impact of gender issues has been overlooked in some of the current science education trends, such as the school-to-work reform movement in high school, group work in undergraduate classes, and the transition to graduate school. In other cases, such as the creation of single-sex sections in the coeducational environment, too much credence may have been placed in a single, gender-based solution.

To understand some of the reasons why these curricular and pedagogical innovations may have produced results that are not always, or only, female friendly, I use feminist theories to look at women in science programs. The theories provide a framework for evaluating specific interventions to determine which ones might prove successful in one arena, and which might be more useful for different ends. The more sophisticated theories evolved by feminists during the past 2 decades serve as a lens to focus on the complexities of science, women, and women's studies to reveal new venues when female friendly science is re-engineered.

CHAPTER 1

Curriculum Integration:
Transformation or Assimilation?

Professor Alicia Smith is eager to include more information about the history of science in general, and the contributions of women and men of color in particular, in the integrated first-year biology/chemistry course she teaches. In the wake of falling enrollments in both the chemistry and biology departments (a situation signaling impending disaster, since departmental budgets are enrollment-driven), the faculty decided that the introductory courses should be revamped and that majors and nonmajors should no longer be separated into different courses. Alicia was given carte blanche by the department to make whatever curricular or pedagogical changes would be necessary to make the course more appealing to retain declared majors and even attract nonmajors to the department. The study of falling enrollments indicated that a particularly significant group to consider for retention was female students. Although as a group the female students had higher grades than the male students in the introductory courses, a significantly higher proportion of the female students did not continue into the second semester. Further study revealed that the group of female students who dropped out of science had, on the average, grades that were as good as or better than those of the male students who continued. Furthermore, many of the female switchers had declared on their admissions form an intention to major in biology or chemistry. The women students seemed to be a group toward whom revisions might be targeted. They indicated dissatisfaction with the current courses, yet demonstrated high achievement and initial high interest in majoring in biology and/or chemistry.

This knowledge about the female switchers, coupled with a personal curiosity and growing interest in women's studies, led Alicia to attend the one-week summer institute for faculty on curricular and pedagogical transformations. She found the institute to be fascinating. In addition to providing her with some ideas about how to revamp the introductory courses, it also revealed why many aspects of her own education in science had been less than satisfactory. The phase transformation model had provided a framework that permitted Alicia to

19

question whether her extensive training in biochemistry had suffered from an androcentric bias. The very few names given in class of those who were associated with the history of biology or chemistry, or affiliated with important discoveries, always seemed to be male. Perhaps it had been her own prejudices that had led her to think that all scientists referred to by their last names were male, but she had been amazed and proud to learn as a postdoctoral student that a couple of those last names (for example, Martha Chase of the famous Hershey–Chase experiments determining that DNA *was the genetic component in bacteriophage; and Mary Lyon, of the Lyon hypothesis of genetic dosage compensation) had female first names attached to them. Although the molecules, chemical reactions, and pathways clearly were not gendered, it did seem that whenever an example was applied, the health and disease processes of the male body were assumed to be the norm. If the female body was discussed at all, it was in its aspects as deviant from, or other than, the way things happened in the male; no theory, process, or course took the female body as a starting focal point. Perhaps this explained why Alicia had sensed a connection felt by her male colleagues to the material that she herself did not feel. Was it because the men knew that the discoveries that had opened this wonderful world of molecules had been made by individuals like themselves exploring health and disease processes in bodies like theirs? Did that provide them with a confidence in their ability to become biochemists and a connection to the material they were studying that she and her female colleagues rarely experienced? More important, given her current position and the task of revising the introductory course, could these be the same reasons that women students switched while men with lower grades persisted?*

In the spring term of the previous year, she had taught a pilot section of the course integrating biology and chemistry for the first time. She noticed that all the students, and especially the female students, responded well to the bits of history of science and practical applications she had included in the course. Somewhat overwhelmed by the task of integrating the two subjects, Alicia could barely recall the snippets of scientific history she had dredged up to include in the course. She hated to admit it, but probably the names of only one woman and one man of color had made it into the course.

Spurred by new awareness from the institute, Alicia spent parts of each day during the remainder of the summer in the library, recovering the history of women and of men of color in chemistry and biology. She also sought increased numbers of examples of practical applications, to the environment and health, of the principles she was teaching.

Despite the mandate from her colleagues that she could do whatever it took to bring about increased retention, she was well aware of issues of quality and standards. She took care to select examples of women and men of color who had made contributions that were at least as good as, if not better than, those of many of the white men she had previously discussed. Contributions of the nine female Nobel laureates and several Lasker award winners highlighted her lectures. She also made certain that she did not have to deviate significantly from the course organization to include these bits of history; she certainly did not want to open herself to accusations of sacrificing traditional scientific content to history. In addition, she emphasized positive contributions by women who had positive careers and personal lives; Alicia saw no need to dwell on James Watson's treatment of Rosalind Franklin and her data (Sayre, 1975) or Ellen Swallow Richards's experiences at MIT, *where her experiments in sanitation chemistry and ecology resulted in her being honored as the founder of home economics (Hynes, 1989).*

In a similar fashion, she made certain that the practical examples appealed equally to men and women. Shocked to learn that male students often reacted negatively to any inclusion of material centered specifically on women, she sought genderless or gender-neutral examples.

At the end of the fall term, Alicia was proud of the stage 6 course she believed she had taught. She also was quite relieved that aside from the one-week institute and the several hours in the library, she had not had to spend massive amounts of time revamping the pilot course from the spring term. It was good to include information on women and men of color in the course content, and not all that difficult, compared with integrating the disciplines of chemistry and biology.

What happened in this scenario represents a frequent occurrence in curriculum transformation initiatives. Despite her best intentions (at least she was fully committed to the idea), Alicia mistook an "add women and stir" approach for true inclusion. She failed to focus sufficiently on race and gender, simply adding them to the course she previously had taught without rethinking the conception of the entire course to weave race and gender as central threads.

During the past decade and a half, I have had the opportunity to work with a number of curriculum transformation projects attempting to integrate women's studies into the mainstream introductory courses and upper-division courses for students majoring within the scientific disciplines. The focus and scope among these projects varied considerably. Many were initiated at small, private liberal arts colleges; others developed at large state universities. A few became embedded as part of statewide or consortial initiatives. Some had significant outside grant funding (more than $250,000 per year); others were supported on a shoestring, from a combination of released time and other internal sources. For some, a department in the sciences served as only one of 13 departments participating in the project, the other twelve of which found their home in the humanities and social sciences. For a few, the sciences became the focal point of the transformation effort. Some projects became ongoing, multiyear efforts;

others represented attempts of relatively short duration, such as an intensive week during the summer or one semester of monthly lectures.

From such experiences with a variety of projects and from emerging information and evaluation of curriculum transformation efforts (Project on the Status and Education of Women, 1988; Rosser & Kelly, 1994c), distinguishing the elements that result in true transformation (stage 6) from add a woman and stir (stage 2 or 3) and other assimilations has become increasingly possible. Light has been shed on the following questions that often arise during transformation efforts: Through what stages do most faculty, courses, and disciplines progress during transformation? Why do most faculty, particularly those in the sciences, seem more willing to change their pedagogical approaches than their syllabi and curricular content? Does transformation help only women students or is it beneficial for men as well? Do such projects really improve teaching and retention of students in science?

To explore these questions and others about linking women's and ethnic studies and scientists through curriculum transformation, I will provide examples from two relatively comprehensive projects with which I was intimately involved from 1992 to 1994. They used faculty development techniques to integrate women's studies into the science and mathematics curriculum. Both projects occurred at large, public universities. Since both represented system-wide efforts, they encompassed 2-year, 4-year, and research institutions and embraced a relatively significant portion of the faculty. Both of these projects focused on science, engineering, and mathematics faculty and had durations exceeding 2 years. Both received substantial funding from the National Science Foundation, which provided considerable internal and external backing and prestige for the efforts. These two efforts may deviate from other transformation projects in that they were relatively well supported, extensive, and centered exclusively on science. However, the difficulties they encountered in transformation seem likely only to be increased in projects with less extramural and institutional support.

UNIVERSITY OF WISCONSIN SYSTEM WOMEN AND SCIENCE PROJECT

The overarching goals of the University of Wisconsin (UW) System Women and Science Project funded by the NSF included attracting and retaining women students in science. The project aimed to accomplish this through faculty development to change pedagogical techniques and curricular content to make them more inclusive of women and people of color.

The Women and Science project used an intensive and systemic approach to incorporate innovations in course content, pedagogy, and classroom climate.

Although other visiting distinguished professors affiliated with the project attempted to accomplish project goals through semester-long efforts at one campus where they taught a course using changed pedagogy and curricular content and conducted faculty development seminars each month, the format that my interventions took was quite different.

During the 1993 fall semester, I worked with nine different campuses (Madison, Milwaukee, Oshkosh, Parkside, Platteville, River Falls–Eau Claire–Stout, and Stevens Point) at seven different sites, the River Falls–Eau Claire–Stout campuses functioning as a collaborative community. Each campus submitted a proposal with specific objectives and aims, consistent with the overarching goals for the project, describing how they would use me as a faculty development consultant while I visited their campus.

Each campus and proposal were unique, and the number as well as qualitative content of visits varied from campus to campus. The generic plan, however, included three 2-day visits, interspersed throughout one semester, to each campus. The major focus of the first visit typically included an assessment of the climate for women in science and of teaching techniques used to improve the classroom experience for women. Usually during this visit, I gave a presentation entitled "Female Friendly Science: Teaching Techniques to Attract and Retain Students" (Rosser, 1989) and made this topic the center of attention in my talks with faculty, staff, and administrators. The second visit was directed toward curricular transformation to include more information from women's studies and ethnic studies germane to science courses. The public presentation for this visit was "Female Friendly Science: Curricular Transformation" (Rosser, 1993b), which also served as the basis for meetings with faculty, staff, and administrators. During the third visit, a major aim centered on ensuring that the campus took ownership of the project so that pedagogical and curricular efforts would be institutionalized after my departure and at the end of the project. Typically, members of the faculty heavily involved with the project were invited to serve on a panel or as members of a roundtable to explain what they were doing currently or planned to do in their classes to incorporate the information learned through this project. Usually, I moderated the panel or roundtable and gave some version of the presentation "Diversity Among Scientists—Inclusive Curriculum—Improved Science: An Upward Spiral" (Rosser, 1993a) as opening or closing remarks.

A SAMPLE LOG OF CAMPUS VISITS

To provide the flavor of the project as it progressed during one semester on one campus, I include the log of my three visits to the campus. This particular campus is one of the undergraduate (4-year) campuses in the UW System.

First Visit: Assessing the Climate. I arrived at the campus at about 2:30 p.m. on October 6 for my first visit to the campus. At 3:00 p.m. I met with the Dean of the School of Science and Technology, who served as the primary contact for the grant on the campus. For about an hour we discussed the curriculum and faculty strengths and weaknesses, including his vision for changes in the general education courses and introductory courses that he hopes my visits will facilitate.

At 4:00 p.m. I gave a public presentation entitled "Teaching All Students." About 36 people, approximately half faculty and half students, attended the talk. In the lively and informative discussion that ensued, several faculty and one student asked questions. Given the nature of the questions and the fact that some faculty lingered until almost 6:00 p.m., I believe that the ideas were received quite well.

My first appointment on October 7 was with a professor from the biology department who is an old acquaintance of mine; he was a graduate student of a professor with whom I was a post-doc. He teaches a human biology course that is cross-listed with women's studies. He also serves as director of ethnic studies for the campus. He sought my input on the course and asked me to lecture to the class during my next visit to the campus. We also discussed the problems of attracting more minority students to science and hiring and retaining minority faculty, and effective solutions to those problems.

At 9:30 a.m. I met with the current chair of the biology department. We were joined almost immediately by two female and three male faculty in biology who teach the introductory courses. The discussion focused on teaching strategies effective for attracting and retaining women in science. Since most of these individuals had attended my lecture the previous day, they had specific questions. People were especially interested in group work and how to make that successful. I also had a lengthy discussion with a new faculty member who was experiencing some difficulty with the group work and the journal writing that he was using in his environmental science course. This set of meetings lasted until 11:45.

The dean and I had a quick lunch in the Union. Our conversation centered on planning the next visit, in which structured conversations would be held primarily with the chemistry faculty. We also discussed the difficult and isolated situation for women faculty and male minority faculty in the sciences on this particular campus. The biology faculty includes only one female who is African American and on tenure track; other females in the department are in lecturer/academic staff positions. The chemistry faculty has one tenured and one untenured female member; mathematics has one tenured female faculty member. Physics, geology, and computer sciences have no female faculty. Upcoming retirements provide future potential for increasing the number of women and minority faculty on the campus.

At 12:15 p.m. I met with the Integrated General Science Planning Group (consisting of one faculty member from geology, one from chemistry, one from physics, and the dean) who were planning an integrated general science course to be offered for general education credit. This group had been meeting for 2 years and planned to offer a pilot version of the course the next year. After a substantial discussion of group work, we considered the pedagogical and practical virtues of different models for the course format. Since students enrolled in teacher certification and nonscience majors would be the primary course enrollees, we discussed ways to make the course particularly appealing to women.

After a brief closure talk with the dean about some details for my next visit, I met with the director of women's studies. She shared some information about the history and current status of women's studies at the campus. We then turned to a more general discussion of the climate for women faculty at the campus and the particular isolation of the small number of women faculty in the sciences. We considered strategies for involving the women in academic staff/lecture positions in the formal course planning meetings during my future visits.

From 3:00 to 5:00 p.m. I attended the preconference meeting of the UW Women's Studies Consortium Administrators. During the meeting, I gave a report on the progress of my visits under the Women and Science Project.

Second Visit: Women's Studies and Ethnic Studies. I arrived at the campus on Monday evening, October 25. My first appointment on Tuesday morning was with the Dean of the School of Science and Technology, who told me that the reaction to my previous visit had been quite positive; we discussed the schedule and strategies for this visit. Whereas last time I worked mostly with the biology department, this time the bulk of my interactions were with chemistry and physics. The dean's goal was to have me interact with as many faculty as possible within his college.

At noon I met with the Integrated General Science Planning Group. Having met with this group during my prior visit, I was familiar with the four male faculty who compose the group. The group still had fears that this course would not be successful, based on experiences with similar courses. We considered strategies to help them get immediate feedback from students, which might correct problems early in the course, and appropriate pedagogical techniques to match the interdisciplinary curricular content.

After lunch, I met with the Interim Vice Chancellor. In addition to a general discussion of the aims and goals of this NSF project for the UW System, we focused on the particular goals for this campus. I encouraged him to facilitate recruitment and retention of more women faculty in the sciences at the campus, where most departments have one tenure-track woman faculty member. The institutionalization of the curricular and pedagogical objectives of this project will be facilitated by having more women faculty in tenure-track positions.

At 3:00 p.m. I met with a faculty member from chemistry who is a UTIC (University Teaching Improving Center) Teaching Fellow. He was revising the introductory chemistry course to make it more friendly to all students, including females. At 3:30 we were joined by a first-year, tenure-track woman faculty member in chemistry. Since she also teaches an introductory course, the three of us contemplated teaching strategies to retain students, particularly those having difficulty with the mathematics components in the course. The UTIC Teaching Fellow left about 4:15, and the faculty member and I continued our conversation for another half hour. I spent some time with her discussing ways to fit in as the sole woman currently present in the department, since the other woman in the department is away for 2 years.

At 6:45 p.m. I went to the dean's house for drinks. Then I accepted the kind invitation to join him and his family for dinner at a local restaurant.

At 8:00 a.m. on October 27, I met with the chair of the chemistry department. He briefed me on the department, where two of the seven faculty are women; one is tenured. At 8:30 we were joined by two faculty from the department, one female and one male. We discussed teaching strategies and the lesson that might be learned from women's colleges about retaining women in science.

At 10:30 I met with the chair of the physics department, who briefed me on that department. We discussed strategies and his strong desire to attract a woman faculty member, since the department was at that time all male. At 11:00 we were joined by four other members of the department. Much of the discussion centered on how to convince some of the highly talented women who take their introductory courses to continue and declare majors in physics. Considerable dismay also was expressed over the poor image and status of scientists in general and physicists in particular.

At noon I presented a seminar on "Transforming Curricula." Approximately 20 faculty from the sciences and two from women's studies attended. The presentation appeared to be well received; it generated a lively discussion and pertinent questions.

After a quick lunch, during which the dean and I finalized plans for my final visit on November 22 and 23, I met again with the professor from biology. We briefly discussed the topic for the presentation I would give for his human biology course during my final visit. We decided that "Gender Bias in Clinical Research and the Difference It Makes for Women's Health" (Rosser, 1993c) would be the topic. In his role as director of ethnic studies, he then asked my opinion about individuals who are not of the minority or oppressed group under consideration teaching about that group. We discussed this thorny and recurring question, which has plagued both women's studies and ethnic studies for some time.

At 2:00 I met with the director of women's studies. We continued the discussion of this thorny question and the particular form in which it was being played out on this campus. We also discussed plans for my final visit to campus and the composition of faculty to serve on the panel for the roundtable presentation. This panel was crucial, since the future work that the campus would undertake to continue efforts begun by this project depends substantially on their taking ownership of the initiative.

Third Visit: Institutionalization. On Monday, November 22, I drove from Madison, arriving at the campus about 9:15 a.m., which allowed me to check in at the dean's office and get settled before the class I was to present at 10:00 a.m.

At 10:00 I gave the presentation to the human biology course. This course, cross-listed with women's studies, had received some criticism that semester from students in women's studies because of the lack of emphasis on women's health issues. The students in the class, particularly the female students, responded very enthusiastically to the presentation. Perhaps this helped, in some small way, to alleviate the problem that had arisen in the course.

At 11:00 a.m. I met with a member of the biology faculty who is also chair of the committee responsible for general education requirements. We discussed issues surrounding how language in science may distort or inhibit students' understanding of certain concepts. For example, many students have difficulty grasping that dominant traits in genetics are not necessarily always positive. We also discussed criteria that might be used to evaluate syllabi for general education courses to ensure that they include gender and multicultural concerns.

At noon I participated in a roundtable on "Thoughts and Updates on Courses." About 13 faculty, including participants, were present for the roundtable. I had asked the dean to arrange an occasion where the faculty might talk about what they were doing or planned to do in light of this project. A male faculty member initiated the discussion with some information about the planned integrated science course. A female faculty member from biology and the director of women's studies, a sociologist, also made some appropriate comments; I made some summative statements at the end. Although not quite what I had envisioned, the event did spark some discussion among faculty about curricula and courses.

At 1:15 p.m., the vice chancellor held a luncheon that included the dean, the department chairs, and the members of the Integrated General Science Planning Group. The discussion focused on general strategies and issues surrounding the retention of women in science. There was also some talk about institutional supports necessary to facilitate efforts in curricular and pedagogical change.

At 2:30 p.m. I met briefly with the director of women's studies. We talked a bit about the 1994 UW Women's Studies Consortium Conference, which would focus on women and science.

I was supposed to meet with the faculty from computer science at 3:15. Apparently some miscommunication resulted in their not being able to attend at that time.

From 4:00 to 5:00 p.m. I met with the geology faculty. We had an interesting discussion about changes that might be made in the introductory geology course to make it more attractive to students, particularly females. I had just received a chapter for a book I was editing from three women geologists on exactly this topic, and that chapter provided many useful ideas for our discussion.

In the evening I had dinner with an old friend who had been a technician in the Primate Center when I was a graduate student there; she now lives in Milwaukee. Quite active in Women in Science in Southeastern Wisconsin, she filled me in on details of that group, as we reminisced about old times.

At 9:00 the next morning I met with the woman who heads the newly formed teaching center on the campus. Since she is in the College of Liberal Arts, she is especially interested in methods to attract science faculty to workshops she gives on good teaching.

At 11:30 I met with the woman who serves as an academic staff person in biology and has responsibility for health science advising, as well as teaching some introductory laboratories. She is very interested in issues that affect teaching. She expressed some problems that she has observed since policies no longer permit academic staff to teach the lecture portion of courses.

At noon I had lunch with the academic staff person and a retired female faculty member from biology. We discussed the situation for academic staff on campus. We also considered various organizations such as AWIS (Association for Women in Science) and GWIS (Graduate Women in Science) in Wisconsin.

From 1:00 to 2:30 p.m. I met with the Integrated General Science Planning Group. This time only three group members were able to attend. They expressed considerable anxiety over the fact that their request to hire an academic staff person to teach the labs for the course had not been approved. They feared that developing and teaching labs without sufficient released time would result in less than optimal, piecemeal exercises. I also expressed concern that the topics most appealing to women and minorities are concentrated almost exclusively in the second half of this two-semester course.

At 2:30 I met with the dean for a debriefing session on this visit in particular and all three visits in general. We concluded that the visits had been particularly helpful for the Integrated General Science course, which constituted the focus of the proposal from the campus to this project. The visits also raised general consciousness about good teaching techniques and those most useful in attracting and retaining women.

SPINOFF BENEFITS

The primary objective of the project included faculty development to revise teaching techniques and curricular content to make them more inclusive of women. This objective was directed toward the ultimate goal of attracting and retaining more women students in science, mathematics, and engineering in the UW System. During the course of my work with faculty on the different campuses throughout the semester, other opportunities arose that were related to, but not anticipated by, the original objectives of the project. These were talks at other institutions and the development of biology of women courses.

As I traveled throughout the UW System, faculty and administrators from other institutions became aware that I was in the area and asked me to give talks or workshops. Although these were not formally a part of my work with the project and were arranged separately, they were in some senses, a spinoff from the project, which benefited a broader spectrum of the community and individuals.

In the mid-1970s, I had been asked by the UW–Madison campus to develop a course on women's health. This course, Women's Studies 103: Women and Their Bodies in Health and Disease, has continued to be offered every semester since then; it typically has very large enrollments. Since many faculty throughout the UW System are aware of my involvement with the course and the publications and national work I have done in this area, I was asked by individuals on a couple of campuses to explore with appropriate faculty the possibilities for such a course on their campus.

On two campuses, I met with faculty to explore the feasibility and desirability of offering this course; on another campus, I met with the women's studies director and the individual teaching the course that semester to aid in ironing out some particular problems that had arisen during that semester in this long-established course. Although not directly related to the grant, such work may have an impact on the grant, since typically this course is cross-listed between women's studies and biology or another science-related department. Some women who do not intend to major in biology or another science first become attracted to science through this course. Thus, it may serve as a tool to recruit women to science.

STRENGTHS AND WEAKNESSES

As with all projects, the UW System-wide Women and Science Project has its particular strengths and weaknesses. To the extent that the strengths have been built on and the weaknesses have been minimized or eliminated, this project and its effects have been enhanced. The strengths of the project include its comprehensive, system-wide nature, its strong external funding combined with reliance on internal resources, and its linkage with extant institutional structures.

Since the project was initiated by the UW Women's Studies Consortium, it has the potential to affect every campus in the system. As the University of Wisconsin is one of the largest statewide university systems, and Wisconsin contains no state-funded institutions outside the system, the project has the potential to affect all public institutions of higher education, except for technical colleges, in the state. Few NSF projects can hope to have such a broad impact on an entire state, because most states lack such an inclusive, comprehensive system.

The Women and Science Project received substantial funding from the NSF in its initial grant, which was extended through an additional grant plus a grant for evaluation. This infusion of funds from outside sources permitted the project to be initiated by hiring some outside personnel, which avoided placing undue burdens on currently busy UW faculty and administrators. However, the structuring of the project so that individual campuses submitted proposals for faculty development and Visiting Professors ensured that changes were more likely to remain and become institutionalized. Most Visiting Professors came from the UW System (visiting from one campus to another), thereby decreasing the likelihood that innovations would leave concurrently with personnel from the outside.

The use of the UW Women's Studies Consortium to initiate the grant and the use of faculty from within the system as Visiting Professors meant that the grant meshed with existing programs and individuals within the system. The women's studies directors and the executive committee of the Consortium, who were already knowledgeable about the Consortium and its workings and could be particularly aware of the impact this project might have on their individual campus, could supplement the role of the Advisory Committee (composed primarily of scientists) to the Project and serve as informal advisors.

Weaknesses of the project included administrative chaos, the absence from the initial proposal of a comprehensive evaluation plan, and the low number of tenured or tenure-track faculty women in science in the UW System. Since these weaknesses are not unique to this project, I detail them to suggest how they might be avoided in similar efforts.

The Women and Science Project suffered from chaos in its central administration. A high turnover in personnel, including project directors and clerical staff, coupled with individuals in key positions who lacked appropriate credentials, rank, and/or experience in science, academia in general, and the UW System in particular, severely undercut aspects of the project, particularly in its early phases. Much of this chaos could have been avoided by providing released time for a tenured woman scientist from one of the campuses to serve as project director. Since the principal investigator of this project was not a scientist, engineer, or mathematician, the project director had to be one. A tenured woman scientist, preferably a full professor, from one of the campuses who had experience with women's studies and women in science issues, as well as rank and experience with colleagues and workings of the UW System, would have known how to prevent many of the frictions and miscommunications that arose in the project. Current graduate students and/or individuals who recently received a Ph.D. or other equivalent professional credential are unlikely to possess the experience with the academic hierarchy, curriculum, and scientific colleagues to serve as competent project directors. Science faculty who have earned rank and tenure are more likely to have the skills and credibility with colleagues to ensure greater impact and institutionalization of the project.

The initial proposal for this project included only an outline for an evaluation plan. The more comprehensive plan was developed later and eventually received substantial funding. This sequence of events meant that faculty and administrators who submitted proposals for early rounds of Visiting Professorships were given little or no information about the way that evaluation would occur or the type of data they needed to collect for project evaluation. Aside from questions that might be raised regarding the validity and reliability of evaluation data collected in such circumstances, this procedure made the primary contacts feel that they had had a new, unanticipated administrative burden placed on them while the project was in process.

As I traveled among the nine campuses with which I was working, I found a dearth of women in tenure and tenure-track positions on science, mathematics, engineering, and agriculture faculties. Many departments have no women in such positions; often a department has one woman in her first, second, or third year of a tenure-track position. Several entire colleges have no women or only one in such a position. In contrast, most departments hire women in academic staff positions; these individuals carry a large portion of the undergraduate teaching load, particularly at the introductory level.

As I visited campus after campus with low numbers of women faculty in the sciences, I recognized this had direct implications for the ultimate success of the project. Female role models constitute a significant factor for retaining female students, and the presence of female faculty is important to aid in the institutionalization of curricular changes and pedagogical techniques. To address this issue, I began to discuss with department chairs, deans, and vice chancellors their plans for recruiting and retaining more women in tenure-track positions in the near future.

Since many campuses will face retirements of large numbers of white male faculty in the sciences (in some cases more than one-third of departments will retire within the next 5 years), opportunities will exist to recruit women faculty without creating new positions. I encouraged administrators to persuade faculty to write job descriptions as broadly as possible to attract a larger pool of candidates. I suggested that they develop 5-year plans for hiring, in which overall departmental needs, including gender/race diversity, might be taken into account, rather than replacing each individual in piecemeal fashion. More women and minority male science faculty will be needed if institutionalization of curricular and pedagogical initiatives begun by this and other projects is to be attained.

UNIVERSITY OF SOUTH CAROLINA SYSTEM MODEL PROJECT: TEACHING TO REACH WOMEN

"Transformation of Science and Math Teaching to Reach Women in Varied Campus Settings" was a 2-year program to design, implement, evaluate, and disseminate a model for helping teachers better to reach women in the classroom and retain them in science and technological careers. The project required collaboration among nine campuses that serve diverse populations throughout South Carolina. The 25 participating science and math faculty came from five 2-year campuses, three 4-year campuses, and one large graduate research institution.

The University of South Carolina (USC) System Model Project for the Transformation of Science and Math Teaching to Reach Women in Varied Campus Settings funded by the National Science Foundation established four overall goals and objectives to be met by the program and its participants.

1. To actively encourage more women to enter science and math courses and to pursue science/technology careers. Success toward this goal helped to meet a national need and improve women's access to more lucrative, rewarding livelihoods.

2. To introduce science and math faculty to the body of research findings in women's studies that can apply to the teaching of science, mathematics, and engineering. As a result of enlarging teachers' knowledge about barriers to women's involvement in these fields and methods of dismantling those barriers, participants were better equipped to evaluate their own teaching methods and better able to understand the needs of their women students. Success toward this goal produced pedagogical and curricular transformations.

3. To establish a cooperative and mutually supportive network of faculty from the different campuses who share a commitment to increase the number of women entering and staying in math and science. A network of faculty from diverse settings encouraged cooperation, sharing of knowledge, and development of teaching strategies tailored to each campus population.

4. To focus on faculty and student diversity as a strength. Success toward this goal fostered an understanding of the positive correlation of diverse per-

spectives and intellectual achievement. Diversifying the pool of those who study science should lead to better science.

In order to activate the participants' awareness and knowledge of gender differences in learning and teaching, I chose five strategies to use in achieving the project goals. Of primary importance was increasing the knowledge of faculty participants in the project regarding women and science. Participants then evaluated their teaching strategies in light of this knowledge and considered improvements in these strategies. Each participant tailored the teaching strategies to her or his particular campus and student population. Exchange of useful and new curricular content and strategies was facilitated through the establishment of a cooperative network among faculty from the nine campuses.

Three plenary conferences formed the backbone of the project. During these 2-day meetings, participants received substantial information and interacted with each other and the project's facilitators. The first of these, held in May 1992, introduced concepts about climate issues for women in the classroom, including pedagogical methods and curricular content that provide more female friendly courses in science and mathematics. The second plenary conference, held in January 1993, focused more directly on transforming science and mathematics courses to be more inclusive of men of color as well as of all women. Some attention also was given to other diversity issues and to successes and problems participants were having as they attempted to incorporate new methods and materials in their courses. The final conference, held in January 1994, centered on evaluation and dissemination. Participants presented their experience with the project and discussed with their colleagues the long-term impact that they felt the project would have on their teaching.

Between plenary conferences, site visits were made to each participant on each campus. The purpose of the visits was to help participants incorporate in their courses the new information they had learned from the plenary conferences and recommended readings. These visits, plus correspondence with me, in my capacity as project director, and with research assistant Bonnie Kelly during interim periods, helped to individualize the design and implementation of the teaching model. Each campus also participated in the design and testing of the teaching model, so that it would be suitable for adaptation to various types of institutions. The objective was to reach women where they are most likely to be found and then retain them so they may be recruited to graduate research programs.

CAMPUS VISITS

To provide an example of the site visits, I include the log of two visits made to a campus, with a focus on a meeting with an individual faculty member from each visit. For comparability with the Wisconsin project, I chose one of the 4-year campuses.

First Visit: Organic Chemistry. On November 23, 1992, Bonnie and I went for our first visit with faculty participants from a 4-year campus. The dean of sciences there has been most supportive of this project. She attended the first plenary conference in its entirety and arranged for these visits to be held in her conference room.

Our first meeting was with a chemistry professor. During fall 1992, she had two lecture sections, two recitations, and two labs for this course. Unfortunately, not all of the same students were involved in each aspect; some students had other instructors for lab or recitation. She felt that she had a better connection with students that she taught in recitation and lab, as well as in lecture sessions.

She worked on implementing some of the strategies suggested in handouts from the first plenary session. Given the size and shape of the room, she found it difficult to maintain eye contact with all students. In recitation, she divided the students into groups of three. After an icebreaker on the first day, she used the groups for problem solving. She felt that this was successful, particularly in the portion of the course dealing with dimensional analysis. This participant developed her own questionnaire to assess the effectiveness of this project. One of her goals was to encourage more women to enter the field of chemistry. Organic chemistry seemed to be a particular hurdle for many women. One of the female students indicated that this course influenced her decision to go into pharmacy.

Second Visit: Physics. Our meeting was with a physics professor who was using group work in both algebra- and trig-based and calculus-based physics courses during fall 1992. In the lecture portion of the course, he emphasized the contributions of women. He also made a concerted effort to ensure that women were included in the statement of problems. He chose a text that showed little gender bias.

Although he did not teach all labs, in the labs he did teach, he arranged students in male-only, female-only, and mixed-sex groups. He then gave a lab-skills test at the end of the semester. He found that the male-only groups performed less well on this test. He planned to examine this observation.

This participant said he was successful in retaining females in his section; in the lab section taught by a part-timer, 6 out of 7 students who dropped were female. This left only 6 females out of the remaining 14 students. In contrast, in his section, no one dropped; he had 7 female students out of 14 total students in his section.

STRENGTHS AND WEAKNESSES

The USC System Model Project for Transformation of Science and Math Teaching to Reach Women in Varied Campus Settings had several of the same strengths as the UW System-wide Women and Science Project. The USC project also was system-wide and involved faculty from all campuses within its system. As was the case with the UW System, this project had the potential to have a significant impact on science, mathematics, and engineering teaching throughout the system. A difference existed between the two projects in impact on individual campuses compared with the state as a whole. Whereas the USC project involved faculty from all nine campuses within the system over a 2-year period, the Wisconsin project did not directly involve faculty from every campus. The Wisconsin System is much larger, including 28 campuses and virtually all public higher education with the exception of the technical colleges within the state. In South Carolina, many other institutions—including Clemson University, South Carolina State University, Charleston University, Winthrop, Lander, and Medical University of South Carolina—are public 4-year colleges and universities. Thus, the potential for impact of the project on science and math teaching in public higher education throughout the state is not as great in South Carolina.

Like the UW project, the USC project had substantial funding from the National Science Foundation, which lent credibility as well as support. The USC project relied more directly on internal personnel and on faculty working with their own campuses rather than the Visiting Professors used so extensively in the UW project. The UW model may have enhanced exposure to external ideas, although the outside speakers at the plenary conferences at USC permitted this to a certain extent; the USC model may have enhanced institutionalization at individual campuses.

The fact that the principal investigator of the USC project was a scientist, a tenured full professor on the research campus, and the director of women's studies for the system, eased some of the administrative problems that arose in the UW project. Since the principal investigator worked with the faculty as a colleague on a variety of levels (administrative, teaching, and research), she knew them and ways to approach them with the project that would be likely to obtain their support. Evaluation also was included as a major component of the initial grant.

The USC system also suffers from a dearth of women in tenure and tenure-track positions in the sciences, engineering, and mathematics, although perhaps not quite as severely as UW on its 2- and 4-year campuses. Increased numbers of women would be likely to facilitate institutionalization of this and similar projects.

The USC project worked intensively with 25 faculty over a 2-year period. The project had the most impact on the 25 faculty participants and their students, although faculty were encouraged to share project results and what they were learning with their colleagues. The UW project involved intense interaction with faculty fellows on participating campuses; this UW faculty fellow component was roughly equivalent to the USC faculty participant component. The public presentations by the Visiting Professors, and the fact that one Visiting Professor devoted herself entirely to faculty development with considerable numbers of faculty on nine campuses, broadened the impact of the UW project to increased numbers of faculty. Failure to build in a dimension of the project to reach a broader spectrum of faculty might be seen as a weakness of the USC project.

HOW COMPLETE A TRANSFORMATION?

As suggested in writings about curriculum transformation effected by individuals in the humanities and social sciences (McIntosh, 1984; Schuster & Van Dyne, 1985; Tetreault, 1985) and by me regarding the science, engineering, and mathematics curriculum (Rosser, 1990, 1993b, 1995), transformation occurs in several stages. The transformation from a curriculum and pedagogical practices in which the absence of women is not noted (stage 1) to a final, truly inclusive stage (stage 6) is a difficult process that can take a long period of time for an individual; as I suggest in this book, departments or entire institutions typically cannot progress beyond the stages that most individuals in them have reached.

To assess the final stage reached by individuals, departments, or curricula developed through the USC and UW projects, immediately after the formal project and its funding have ended, would be premature. Principal investigators and project directors hope that long after its formal termination, participants will continue to read, to develop ideas, and to reform their curricular content and teaching techniques based on some aspect of the project.

Experience with many other projects, as well as the UW and USC projects, however, provides indicative answers to some of the questions raised at the beginning of this chapter. As demonstrated through the logs included here, science, engineering, and mathematics faculty appear much more willing to change their pedagogical approaches than their syllabi and curricular content. Even though the primary focus of both projects was curricular reform, with a clear emphasis on curricular content, faculty in both projects initially displayed much more comfort with attempting different teaching techniques; this trend continued throughout the projects for the majority of faculty. In part, this may stem from the dearth of information on men of color and women available for integration in science, engineering, and mathematics courses. In part, it originates from the idea repeatedly articulated by faculty that science is objective and therefore "gender-free." Faculty who continue to state these ideas after participation in a project such as the UW or USC project clearly have failed to progress beyond stage 1 (absence of women not noted). Many faculty who intellectually progress beyond phase I in their own thinking and reading continue to have difficulty in changing their syllabi to reflect those changes; in contrast, they embrace and incorporate pedagogical changes with much greater facility.

Evaluation and research based on projects such as this provide considerable evidence (Rosser & Kelly, 1994c) that the projects improve teaching and retention of students (also see Chapter 7). This includes all students—both male and female. The UW and USC projects reinforce previous research (AAUW, 1992; Baker, 1986; Grayson & Martin, 1990) from projects with a gender focus that revealed that although the rates and areas of improvement sometimes differed for males and females, performance of all students improved. In many ways, this is not surprising because such projects provide faculty with support, opportunity, and credibility to focus on their teaching. In large public university systems that include a major research campus (such as UW and USC), rewards and attention often have been focused on research, particularly for faculty in SEM. Any major effort that involves substantial grant funding, commitment from the upper administration and faculty, and other rewards to permit faculty to consciously focus on their teaching, is likely to improve teaching and student retention.

CHAPTER 2

Consequences of Ignoring Gender and Race in Group Work

Peter Adams is beginning his third year as an assistant professor in the physics department at GIT *(Generic Institute of Technology). He has decided that improving his teaching is a high priority for this academic year. Receiving a grant, although cut by two-thirds from his requested support, means that he can devote less than 100% of his time to thinking about research, at least temporarily.*

He had better give some attention to his teaching, since his teaching evaluations have been less than outstanding. His department chair emphasized the importance of teaching in his annual review last year and suggested fairly pointedly that Peter had "room for improvement in that area." Word has been getting around that under the new president, undergraduate teaching is being reaffirmed as a major focus of the institution. Rumor has it that the decision for early promotion and tenure of the best researcher in his department was held up because that person had received poor student and peer evaluations for his teaching. Given the horrendous job market in physics, Peter certainly wanted to hold on to this job.

Peter has decided to focus on improving the instruction in the calculus-based course in introductory physics that he is teaching in the fall term. The course attracts bright students who have indicated their desire to major in physics. Although the department chair always keeps a close watch on that course since it is the feeder course for majors, this year he will monitor it especially carefully because four Howard Hughes Project students—two Hispanics, one male and one female, and two African Americans, one male and one female— have been placed in the course.

In some ways Peter welcomed the pressure that would force him to devote more time to his teaching. The summer had slipped away before he had a chance to study the literature on teaching science, as he intended. But he had ordered and scanned a couple of articles from the massive bibliography that his graduate assistant had gathered on the topic. He also had attended about a third of a half-day symposium at a professional meeting on "Teaching Techniques to At-

tract Diverse Students in Science." Although not very certain of how they worked, he had picked up the idea that study groups and group projects were what the experts seemed to be talking about as successful ways to attract students, particularly women and minorities, to science. He wished that he had delved more deeply into the literature or had a colleague who was an expert on this with whom he could discuss exactly how to implement these techniques in the classroom, but how difficult could it be anyway? Surely someone who is a nuclear physicist could figure it out. In addition, Peter believed that women and minorities could and should be physicists. Surely that belief and his conviction that he always treats all students the same way, regardless of their gender, will carry him through. After all, aren't being fair and treating all students equally the bottom line in good teaching?

When Peter received his final student roster the first day of class, he was quite pleased. All the students seemed attentive and indeed had the prerequisites required for the course. In addition to 10 white males and six Asian American males (usually representing the extent of diversity in his classes), the class contained two Asian American women, two white women, and the four Howard Hughes students. This diversity was ideal for the new teaching techniques he had decided to try. He divided the students into six study groups for informal support and study outside of class. Each group included one female, one Asian American male, and at least one white male. Four groups had two white males. He placed the African American male in a group with a white woman, and the Hispanic male in a group with an Asian woman.

In the laboratory, he assigned partners to ensure gender and racial equity. The Howard Hughes males were paired with the white females. The four women of color were paired with white males; the six Asian American men were paired with the remaining six white men. Peter used the same laboratory pairs for the "problem competitions" that he introduced during the last 20 minutes of every Friday class. Each week, half of the laboratory pairs went to the blackboard. Peter gave them a problem to solve, which was related to, but different from, the type of problem they had been solving that week. The laboratory partners within a pair competed against each other, in front of the other half of the class, to see who could solve the problem correctly first. The winner of each pair received a piece of candy; the winner for the half of the class received a minor prize, such as a computer disk or a ticket to a basketball game.

During the third week of class, Peter assigned the four groups for the major project, a cooperative effort on which 50% of the course grade depended. Peter announced that all members of a group would receive the same grade on the project. In each group, the leader was to ensure equal participation of all members and smooth functioning of the group. Group one included two white males, two Asian males, a white female, and the Hispanic female as group leader. Group two included three white males, one Asian male, one Asian female, and

*the black male as leader. Group three included two white males, one as leader,
two Asian males, the Hispanic male, and a white female. Group four included
three white males, the black female, an Asian female, and one Asian male as
leader. Peter was proud to note that he had chosen group leaders to reflect gender and racial equity.*

*By midterm, when Peter evaluated the effects of his pedagogical changes
and group work, he was . . . (Please complete the scenario with your predictions
of what happened based upon the situation he has created.)*

BACKGROUND: IGNORANCE IS NOT BLISS

Group work has become popular in disciplines ranging from the humanities
through the social sciences to the sciences. Faculty in classrooms at levels from
preschool through adult education now integrate group work into their teaching. For some, the group work represents an unusual or isolated experience,
which they attempt during one class period or for one project or assignment
outside of class. For others, group work has become the focal point of the
course and has caused them to rethink entirely their curricular content, syllabus
organization, problems, laboratory exercises, and methods of teaching.

Although few faculty may be as inexperienced as Peter Adams and create
quite the complicated mess likely to result from the scenario depicted above,
most faculty have not explored in depth the research surrounding group work.
They are relatively unknowledgeable about the actual studies that have examined the circumstances surrounding the general effectiveness of group work—
parameters for participant selection, appropriate assignments, grading, and
congruence with objectives for the course. Very few have delved into the literature surrounding the significance of gender and race dynamics within groups.

In contrast, a recent study (Brown, 1995) revealed that students, particularly minority women students, understand the significance of group work.
Their most highly ranked piece of advice to other women minority students
seeking graduate degrees in science, engineering, and mathematics was to become a member of a study group. Many of these minority women revealed that
they had been excluded from study groups, which they felt had deterred their
success in graduate school.

The lack of attention to the research about group work on the part of science faculty teaching at the college level should not surprise anyone familiar
with the world of academic scientists. The considerable demands of research,
supervising a laboratory, keeping up with cutting-edge research in their spe-
cialty and in any more general areas in which they must teach, coupled with
committee assignments within the department and institution as well as those

within their broader professional community, leave faculty little time to browse in the literature devoted to pedagogy. Since science faculty holding Ph.D. degrees within a science discipline were trained to do research and probably received little or no formal training in science education or methods of teaching science, most have little acquaintance with the journals publishing research in science education. Although committed to their teaching and desirous of using the most effective methods possible to convey curricular content, few science faculty at the college level are aware of the many parameters that enhance or detract from group work in general or the particular role that gender and race may play in group dynamics.

The purpose of this chapter is to focus on the attention that needs to be paid to gender and race in the group work portion of science teaching. If the dynamics of race and gender are understood and this information is used effectively, group work may enhance learning for all students, especially women and men of color. If these dynamics are ignored or misunderstood, group work actually may inhibit or detract from learning. This chapter will explore parameters such as group size and selection, roles and leadership, assignments and grading, student resistance, and the particular interaction of gender and race with each parameter in group dynamics.

SETTING UP GROUPS

Faculty inexperienced with group work may assume that dividing the class into groups requires little forethought on their part and little explanation to the students. Particularly at the college level, where considerable student autonomy and maturity are assumed and where faculty may have no information about prior achievement or other indicators about students who sign up for their classes, faculty may assume that self-selection and random assignment represent the reasonable alternatives for dividing the class into groups. Simply asking the class to form itself into groups with four members each or to count off by fours often results in situations that inhibit, or fail to enhance, learning for the more vulnerable students. Studies have documented that when students choose their own teams, they tend to choose others whom they know and who are like themselves (Slavin, 1990). Study groups formed outside of class on an informal basis, or lack of supervision by faculty to ensure that all students are included in a group, often leads to exclusion of women and minority students. A graduate student in engineering recounted her difficulties in completing group projects by herself (Brown, 1995) because she found she was excluded from groups formed by white women, as well as by men of color or white men.

ONE SIZE DOES NOT FIT ALL

Ideal group size varies, depending partly on class size and, more important, on the nature of the task or project that the group will carry out. Most research (Johnson & Johnson, 1994) documents that teams should include between three and six members; one tested cooperative learning method for mathematics is called "Groups of Four" (Burns, 1981). Although many faculty report that groups larger than four may encounter problems with smooth functioning, meeting times, and substandard participation by one or more group members, for some tasks larger groups may be useful. Given the current trend toward large cooperative teams for scientific research, some experience with relatively large groups may be appropriate in upper-division undergraduate or graduate level courses.

As with all parameters surrounding group work, the size of the group should be established in light of its objectives or tasks and the reason a team approach best solves this particular problem. For example, for a laboratory experiment in an introductory course that depends on each member of the team having access to the same equipment during a limited period of time, having more than three individuals on the team could be prohibitive. In contrast, for a design project carried out at the senior level over several weeks, where each individual completes a substantial portion of the project alone and then the team synthesizes the results of all team members for a final product or theoretical conclusion (the so-called "jigsaw puzzle" approach), teams composed of five or six members may be needed to complete the function. Setting the group size keeping clearly in mind the objectives of what should be learned from the task and the ideal way to complete it, is more likely to lead to the selection of teams of appropriate size.

SELECTION OF GROUP MEMBERS

Faculty selection of groups, as opposed to random or self-selection, permits the faculty member to take race, gender, abilities, and experience into account in determining group membership. An alternative, which is particularly useful in upper-division undergraduate and graduate courses, is to explain the characteristics that need to be considered in group formation to the students and then ask them to use those characteristics to form their own groups. This alternative approach informs the students about the importance of group dynamics and allows them to take some responsibility for forming functional groups. Since learning how to work as a team is one of the objectives of a course in which group work is used, group dynamics and the importance of appropriate group selection are part of the material that the students need to learn, even if the faculty member does the actual group selection.

SCIENCE ABILITIES

What are the significant characteristics that should be taken into account by faculty or students in group selection? A characteristic emphasized in the cooperative learning literature (Oakes, Ormseth, & Camp, 1990) for the K–12 classroom is the importance of forming groups composed of individuals with mixed abilities. In the public schools, where mainstreaming can result in wide variance in student ability within one class and standardized testing requires that all students reach a certain level of proficiency, mixed-ability grouping helps to minimize discrepancies in group progress.

At the college level, the necessity for, or significance of, mixed-ability grouping becomes less evident. Most faculty are forced to assume that students in a particular class have roughly the same abilities. Since most science, engineering, and mathematics courses are lock-step, the fact that students have passed the prerequisite courses diminishes some of the variance based on student ability.

Even in introductory courses, the selective admissions policies of many institutions of higher education ensure relative homogeneity of ability compared with the K–12 mainstreamed classroom. For those institutions with relatively open admissions policies, placement testing for mathematics and science courses for first-year students provides some reduction in variance. Even when considerable variance can be assumed, aside from placement test scores, most college faculty have few indicators of the abilities of their students at the beginning of a course. Because of these factors, the research surrounding the results of mixed-ability grouping generally has little relevance for the college science, engineering, and mathematics classroom. For initial group assignment, most college faculty find it practical not to make ability a major consideration in grouping. After the first examination, project, or other major assessment measure, performance ability might become one of the bases for reassignment of groups (along with other factors such as dysfunctional personality combinations), if it appears that the performance among groups is widely disparate.

GENDER AND RACE: REPRESENTATION VS. ISOLATION

In contrast to abilities, race and gender should be considered in initial groupings. Much of the K–12 literature advocates having each group statistically reflect the overall racial/gender mix of the class as a whole (Oakes, Ormseth, & Camp, 1994; Slavin, 1990). This literature supports the notion that having minority perspectives represented in each group will help the majority to understand alternative approaches and ideas contributed by people from diverse backgrounds. For example, a class of 25 students, five African American and 20 white, and approximately equal numbers of males and females, might be divided into five groups, each containing four white students and one African American student.

Although this apparently "equitable" distribution may be helpful in exposing the majority to minority perspectives, it may in fact be harmful to the minority students. Particularly when the area is a nontraditional major or career choice for the minority, distributing (or isolating) the minority within a majority grouping may lead to the minority dropping out of the group, the course, or the major. The work of Treisman (1992) demonstrated this for African American students at the University of California–Berkeley in mathematics and for Hispanic students at the University of Texas–Austin.

A similar phenomenon may haunt women pursuing nontraditional majors such as science, engineering, and mathematics. Four females and 16 males would not be an uncommon gender distribution in an introductory calculus-based college physics class. Four groups of five individuals each, with one female in each group, appears to represent an equitable (or at least representative) division along gender lines. From the research on study groups at Harvard (Light, 1990) and other work, evidence suggests that women are more likely to drop out of the group if they are the only female, particularly if the subject is a nontraditional one for women, such as science, engineering, or mathematics.

In the college science classroom, where, in contrast to K–12, dropping out or switching majors is a viable option, the research does not support having each group reflect the overall statistical profile of the class with regard to gender and race. Developing individual groups that contain a critical mass (Etzkowitz, Kemelgor, Neuschatz, Uzzi, & Alonzo, 1994), or at least more than one individual of the minority gender or race, leads to less isolation or "spotlighting" of women or men of color. The calculus-based physics class in the example above still might be divided into four groups, with two groups containing two women. Although such groupings result in some groups with only males, the few women in the class are less likely to experience isolation and drop out.

The intersection of race and gender further complicates group selection. While assigning an African American woman to a group whose other members consist only of white men clearly constitutes isolation, questions arise about whether the African American woman is still isolated when another woman (not African American) or an African American male is assigned to the group along with the white males.

RACE RECONSIDERED

Somewhat different, but overlapping, issues surface over definitions of racial minorities for scientific purposes. The National Science Foundation (1994c) has defined Asian Americans, because of their relative overrepresentation in science compared with their percentages in the overall population, as not a minority or protected class in science, engineering, and mathematics. Although Asian American men are not a minority, Asian American women are underrepresented. Their gender places Asian American women in a status of underrepresentation similar to that of white women because of their gender. Although the status of Asian American women in science may be similar to that of white women, the differential treatment of Asian American women compared with white women in the overall society means that they will bring a different set of experiences and expectations to the group work.

Defining Asian Americans as not a racially underrepresented group also overlooks diversity among Asian Americans. Although some groups of Asian Americans, such as Chinese Americans and Japanese Americans, may be relatively overrepresented in the SEM workforce, other groups, such as the Hmong, are clearly underrepresented. A growing body of literature (Middlecamp, 1995) has begun to air the misconceptions surrounding the designation of "model minority" or Asian prowess in science, engineering, and mathematics, particularly for some Asian American women, for Asian Americans from particular ethnic backgrounds (such as the Hmong), and for some Asian American men. Considering all Asian Americans as a monolith obscures not only differences in country of origin and language, but also issues such as immigrant or nonimmigrant status and class, which may have more impact on science, engineering, and mathematics representation and performance than does race or gender.

For some groups, race may be a more significant factor than gender for underrepresentation in the sciences. For example, repeated studies (Clewell & Anderson, 1991; Clewell & Ginorio, 1996; Malcom, Hall, & Brown, 1976) have documented that minority women find both racism and sexism to be significant barriers, with many women ranking racism as more problematic, particularly at the undergraduate level. One study suggested that sexism may be more problematic than racism at the graduate level (Matyas & Malcom, 1991). A complicating factor for minority women that may shed some light on their differential responses was uncovered in the Brown (1995) study. Her study revealed that women pursuing graduate studies in science, engineering, and mathematics who were easily identifiable as nonwhite reported more difficulties with racism; those, such as some Cuban and American Indian women, who stated that others appeared to perceive them as white reported more problems with sexism.

LEADERSHIP AND OTHER ROLES

Viewing women or all members of a designated racial group as a monolith obscures diversity within groups. Individual differences become especially prominent in the choice of group leaders and assignment of other roles. Assigning a Hispanic woman the role of group leader, assuming that the other group members include a Hispanic male and a white male and female, places her in a role counter to the stereotypes of dominance for her race and gender. Although many individual Hispanic women do not fit the stereotype and feel comfortable with assuming leadership positions, this initial leadership assignment may be difficult for some Hispanic women, perhaps especially in an introductory course when students do not know each other or the faculty member.

For the first group task or project, encouraging students to select their own leader and make their own assignment of roles typically results in group members choosing roles or portions of the task with which they feel most comfortable. This works particularly well when the faculty member has chosen a project where each member has a clearly defined task and where the responsibilities of each role have been delineated. The self-selection of roles within a group facilitates group comfort and functioning, and may mitigate against the loss of autonomy felt due to faculty designation of group membership.

Although initial self-selection of roles may facilitate comfort with group work, roles must be rotated throughout the course, with monitoring to ensure that each student fills each different role for a variety of tasks. Reports from the engineering industry reveal problems when such rotations fail to occur. If students are permitted to stay with the same group all semester, filling essentially the same role to complete several projects or smaller tasks associated with a semester-long project (not an uncommon phenomenon in a senior engineering course), the overall group project may be excellent. All group members may receive an A, because each did her or his part well, particularly since members were permitted to work in their area of strength and the group functioned well as a whole.

Because they were not forced to assume roles with which they had less comfort and for which they held less expertise, however, members may have missed some skills and perspectives developed by the project as a whole, but not available to each member unless rotation of roles occurred. In the industrial setting, where the role available in the work group for the new employee is not the one that she or he assumed in the senior group project, the new employee finds her- or himself at a severe disadvantage.

Gender may be a factor in role preference or comfort. Sometimes a woman prefers or is assigned the role of group manager. Previous socialization as a female in our society may have provided her with better skills in social organization than those of most males. She may be better at interacting with other members of the group to ensure that the group functions smoothly to complete the task on time; her overview of the process as a manager and her writing skills may enhance her abilities to produce the final report on behalf of the entire group. In contrast, a man may have more experience with computers and seem to prefer to interact more with the hardware than with the other people in the group. He may develop superior computer programs to solve design problems encountered by the group and enhance the written portion of the final report with outstanding computer graphics.

As new employees in the industrial setting, both the woman and the man described in the paragraph above may lose their jobs. It is unlikely that the role each assumed repeatedly in the class group will be the only role required for satisfactory performance on the job. Because their group work did not force them to rotate roles, each holds deficiencies in the tasks that each did not have opportunities to develop during the group projects. The man has not learned the social skills and management strategies useful for handling group dynamics; the woman has insufficient experience with hardware and software.

Faculty members must do more than delineate clearly the group roles required for a particular task in order for the group to function smoothly. Monitoring the role assumed by each student during each project permits rotation of roles, while ensuring that individuals will not avoid roles that require new skill development or run counter to gender role expectations.

GROUP PROJECTS, ASSESSMENT, AND CONSIDERATIONS OF GENDER AND RACE

Group size, selection, and roles may influence gender and race dynamics within groups and overall group functioning in ways not envisioned by Peter Adams and other faculty who have not read the literature or had experience with group work in the science classroom. In a similar fashion, inexperienced faculty may fail to consider the changes in types of assignments, projects, or methods of assessment necessitated by group work, or how best to mesh group work with overall course objectives.

GROUP-APPROPRIATE ASSIGNMENTS

An error made by some faculty attempting group work in the science, engineering, or mathematics classroom is to make no change in the assignments traditionally used in the course; they simply expect the students to do the same assignments in groups. If the problems, experiments, or projects traditionally used in the course have been designed for individual work, they are unlikely to be particularly appropriate for group work. Students rapidly perceive that this is a task they could complete on their own, perhaps even more quickly, and resent the group work as an unnecessary bother that complicates their schedule, especially if the group work is expected to take place outside of class.

In the work world, teams or groups are used to solve problems where the perspective, skills, and knowledge of one individual are inadequate or where the complexity and/or amount of time required to solve the project are excessive for one person. Individuals actively depend on the other members of the group because they understand that they cannot complete the project alone. They cooperate with the group because their self-interest is dependent on successful completion of the team project.

Problems or projects assigned to groups in the science, engineering, or mathematics classroom also need to reflect complexity, time pressures, and a variety of skills to reveal that team work is critical to their solution. For the faculty member who previously has taught the course using traditional, individual assignments, the transition to groups involves substantial rethinking and work. Contrary to an expectation held by some faculty that group work will lighten their class preparation, it involves considerably more time and preparation, especially the first few times the course is taught using groups.

Development of guided design problems, complex projects, and multifaceted experiments with appropriate and clearly defined roles (Brown & Campione, 1994) usually requires considerable upfront time for faculty. It may take more time than conceptualizing a new course or redesigning the content of a previously taught course while retaining the traditional teaching methods. A faculty member who has never worked in a setting where teams are used or taken a course where group work figured extensively will be rethinking his or her own ingrained patterns of teaching and problem solving, while trying to develop assignments appropriate for group work.

Problems and projects developed need to draw on and reflect experiences and issues significant for both males and females and individuals of all races. Overall course objectives and tailoring of problems for the team structure serve as the primary principles guiding this development. However, gender or race may influence the perception of the faculty member if she or he has selected to undertake group work because of the research suggesting that women and men of color may respond particularly well to cooperative learning and practical applications. When that becomes a major motivation driving group work, the faculty member may come to wonder whether it is really worth all the extra work to redesign the course, especially if the students demonstrate an initial response to group work that is less than enthusiastic.

One source of student resistance may result from having assignments that are inappropriate for group work. Because until recently most students have experienced more passive forms of content delivery, such as lectures, in science, engineering, and mathematics courses, they do not expect the more active form of learning required by group work. This expectation for passive learning leads most students to resist group work initially, especially because it requires more work for them.

Some of the most resistant students often are high-ability, high-achieving minority women. When many faculty using group work reported this to me (Rosser & Kelly, 1994a), I explored some of the reasons for the resistance. Although no statistical data were collected about this, the belief of the faculty, based on conversations with these students, was that the resistance stemmed from the fact that the students had worked very long and hard to develop skills that helped them to do well in science, engineering, and mathematics. Many of them also had significant outside responsibilities such as families and full-time employment. They viewed group work as a situation in which they again would be asked to be responsible for someone else (i.e., they would have to teach the other students and bring them along) and/or as an additional complication to an already difficult schedule. After the initial resistance, almost all students, including these high-achieving minority females, reported high satisfaction with group work as an experience that aided their learning, if assignments were appropriate for team efforts.

METHODS OF ASSESSMENT

Concerns over methods by which group work will be assessed and reflected in the final individual course grade often contribute to student resistance. Many faculty also express discomfort with assessment of group work. Studies (Champagne & Newell, 1992) reveal a range of approaches from not assessing or counting group work at all to making the common group grade count as the individual final grade for each student. Faculty also vary in the extent to which they take complete responsibility for grade assignment or consider student assessments of individual contributions to the group effort.

The sample peer evaluation form reproduced in Figure 2.1 provides one example of how a faculty member using team projects in a large course assesses the group work.

In this example, the faculty member assigns an overall project grade and adjusts the individual student grades based on students' assessment of their own work and that of the other team members. This assessment conveys to students that the group work is important (i.e., it counts as part of the course grade), that the group product as a whole will be assessed (i.e., the faculty member will grade the product, possibly in relationship to other group products or against a standard of what is a correct answer or good outcome), and that the perceptions of the teammates as to who is doing the work also count.

In cases where students undertake group work, but the grade assigned is based on a laboratory write-up done individually by each student, a different message is conveyed. Students will recognize the significance of individual performance. Group work and cooperative learning do not count, except insofar as they enhance the individual laboratory report.

In contrast, making the group work count for 100% of the course grade and having the group grade be the same for all individuals in the group relay a very different message. This assessment implies that group work counts for everything and that individuals will do well only when the group functions to

FIGURE 2.1. Peer Evaluation Form

Objective: I will assign a score to each team project and then adjust each member's individual score by his or her evaluation from peers. These evaluations provide you with protection against team members who wish to receive a good grade without doing the work.

Procedure: You are to assign 100 points among yourself and the other members of the group. If, say, there are four members in your group and all made equal contributions, then each member, including yourself, would receive 25 points. If, however, three members did most of the work and the fourth person malingered, your point assignment might be 27 points to each of the three workers and only 19 points to the malingerer. (Note: Each team member must submit a PE form on April 23 when project is due.)

Print or clearly write names of all group members in the spaces provided:
How would you characterize the amount of *time and effort* spent and the *overall* contribution of each group member?

Member 1 (yourself)_____points_____
Member 2 _____points_____
Member 3 _____points_____
Member 4 _____points_____
Member 5 _____points_____
                                            TOTAL _____

In the following space and on the back of the page, explain why you have given a team member (or members) fewer points than you have given yourself. *Note:* All team members will receive equal credit unless a written explanation is provided. Your explanation will be held in confidence. I will share the explanation with the person receiving the reduced grade but I will *not* identify you by name.

produce an excellent product, which in turn will benefit the grade of each group member.

This last example may seem to give extreme emphasis to group work and penalize individuals in groups with one or more nonfunctioning members; in certain instances, this may be an appropriate assessment. In a senior-level engineering course, after which most students will take jobs in industry, a major course objective may be to teach students to function well in teams. In industry, all members of a team may experience small salary increases or lose their jobs, if they fail repeatedly to function well and produce. Perhaps the best method to prepare students to grasp the importance of group functioning in the work world is to have all members of a team receive the same individual grade.

This last example stresses the important principles that should underpin all assessments of group work: The assessment should be appropriate for the significance accorded group work and consonant with the course objectives for the use of group work. Students receive conflicting messages when teaching students to work in teams is listed as a major course objective, but group work does not count toward the final grade. It appears equally inappropriate to base the entire final grade of each student on the group project grade, while not including group work as a primary objective of the course.

Issues of race and gender may enter into assessment of group work, particularly during the stage of evaluation of the contributions of individuals to the group. Research on gender roles in group dynamics documents differences in the ways individuals are perceived and treated, based on their gender. Studies in formal groups containing both men and women have demonstrated that men talk more than women and exert more control over the topic of conversation (Kramarae, 1980; Tannen, 1990). White men also interrupt women much more frequently than women interrupt men, and their interruptions more often introduce trivial comments or statements that end or change the focus of the women's discussion (Zimmerman & West, 1975). Further, the more frequent use by women of "tag" questions ("This is true, don't you think?"), excessive use of qualifiers, and excessively polite and deferential speech forms may make women's comments more easily ignored or seem to carry less weight in a group. Another form of ignoring women's contributions occurs when an idea or suggestion initially made by a woman is attributed later by another group member to a male in the group, who then receives credit by having his name attached to the idea.

In peer evaluations of individual group members by themselves and others in the group, the contributions of women may be undervalued because of this gender bias that operates against females in group interactions. In science, engineering, and mathematics groups, the contributions of females may be further underrated if they have played the role of group manager or facilitator. Particularly if they have done an excellent job of making all members feel that they are part of the group and of facilitating smooth group functioning, much of their work may have been "behind the scenes" or barely perceptible to other group members. In the sciences, where experimental data, ability to work with hardware or equipment, and theorizing may be highly valued, individuals in those roles may be perceived as particularly valuable or hardworking, which may be reflected in the peer evaluations they receive from others and themselves. In contrast, the role of group manager or facilitator may be devalued and receive lower peer evaluations, particularly when that role is consonant with the stereotypical expectations for women.

CONCLUSIONS

Most faculty who undertake group work in the science classroom assume that it represents a positive force for retaining women and men of color, if they

consider the impact of group work on those students at all. Aware that cooperative learning and reduction of competition may attract women and men from
some ethnic/cultural backgrounds, faculty assume that use of a group format
will facilitate learning for individuals traditionally underrepresented in science,
engineering, and mathematics. Without some knowledge of the role that gender and race dynamics may play in group interactions, groups may be set up to
function in ways that deter men of color and women. In contrast, when faculty
give attention to gender and race in determining group size and composition,
selection of leaders and other roles for individuals within the group, and particular assignments and grading, they may enhance the learning for all students,
especially men of color and women.

CHAPTER 3

Fruitful Dialogues: What Single-Sex and Coeducational Institutions Can Tell Each Other About Women and Science

Recently the tensions surrounding single-gender education versus coeducation have erupted again. Much of the popular press (Associated Press, 1995a, 1995b, 1995c) has focused attention on the attempts of women to gain access to Virginia Military Institute and the Citadel, the last two state-supported military colleges to admit males only. Students at Texas Woman's University protested when men were permitted to enter the only remaining state-supported women's college. These particular incidents have brought more general arguments regarding the pros and cons of single-sex education to the fore. In some instances, the intersection of single-sex education with other hot topics in education provided new perspectives from which to examine problems. Science education for women serves as an example of such an intersection. In this chapter, I explore two rather different aspects of the single-sex situation: Translation of the female-only classroom to the coeducational environment, and coping mechanisms for women's college graduates in the male-dominated world of the science graduate school and workplace.

Virtually every scientific professional society, governmental agency, or foundation that funds science research or training (Matyas & Malcom, 1991; NRC Committee on Science, Engineering, and Public Policy, 1995; NSF, 1988, 1990), as well as several independent groups (American Women in Science, 1993; Astin & Astin, 1993; Seymour & Hewitt, 1994; Vetter, 1988; 1992), has conducted studies that document the dearth of women in science. Most suggest possible causes; fewer present potential solutions to attract and retain girls and women in science and mathematics.

In the early 1990s, mainstream scientists and educators, influenced by more than 2 decades of research and substantial numbers of statistical studies, began to recognize the numerous subtle and not-so-subtle factors that discourage females from science. The series of studies and publications produced by the American Association of University Women (1990, 1992; Orenstein, 1994), es-

pecially How Schools Shortchange Girls, *has proved instrumental in drawing public attention to daily discouragement provided by public schools for the career advancement of females in general, and for careers in science, mathematics, and engineering in particular.*

Simultaneous with the numerous studies documenting the gender inequity in schools and the insufficient numbers of females in science, during the past 2 decades a parallel series of studies and research concerning the problems with science and mathematics as they are currently taught in the United States also has emerged (described in the Introduction). These studies have generated considerable attention at professional meetings and in the general media.

Because of the publicity focused on science education and women's education, both the professional and public communities seek change in the way science is taught. They would like to attract a more diverse pool of individuals, including women, to science. Although many studies have explored the dimensions and depth of the problem, fewer have focused on concrete solutions that might be implemented in the classroom. The success of female-only institutions in attracting and retaining women in the sciences suggests strategies or aspects of the single-sex situation that might be transferred successfully to a coeducational environment.

SUCCESS OF THE SINGLE-SEX ENVIRONMENT

WHAT WOMEN'S COLLEGES DO RIGHT

Women's colleges serve as a major source for successful strategies because they have an excellent track record in attracting women to science. Data from the Women's College Coalition (Sebrechts, 1995; Sharpe, 1995) document that women attending women's colleges are one-and-one-half times more likely to earn baccalaureate degrees in the life and physical sciences or mathematics than women at coeducational institutions (Tidball, 1986). Small, private liberal arts colleges produce more science majors per capita than larger public institutions (PKAL, 1991). In a study examining the baccalaureate-origin institutions of women (1976–1986) who earned doctorates in the physical sciences through 1991, Sharpe and Fuller found that "one-half of the top-producing institutions of women doctorates in all fields—and approximately two-thirds of them in physical science—are liberal arts colleges" (Sharpe, 1995, p. 13). They also found that formerly men's institutions (FMIs) and historically women's institutions (HWIs) were significantly overrepresented, with 61% of FMIs and 42% of HWIs in the upper quartile (Sharpe, 1995). They further uncovered substantial variation by field, with HWIs having the highest concentration of women doctorates in chemistry. Mount Holyoke and Bryn Mawr ranked in the top 5% of institutions graduating the highest number of women who earned doctorates in all three fields—chemistry, math/computer science (CS), and physics/environmental sciences (ES)—in the physical sciences. In addition to the general environment of a small liberal arts college, which produces higher percentages of science majors, women's colleges appear to provide an environment that fosters women in science.

Based on the strength of these data from female-only institutions, some coeducational, public institutions have begun to experiment with female-only classes in mathematics and science. For example, 90 girls at Anacapa Middle School in Ventura, California signed up for an elective math class that allows only girls to enroll. "In addition to teaching the regular curriculum, the class explores gender issues in education, opportunities, and expectations" (Belitski, 1995, p. 3).

Basic information about the particular factors that contribute to the attraction and retention of women in science at single-sex institutions has been sought to undergird such experiments. A considerable literature focused on these factors has been painstakingly accumulated (AAUW, 1992). The less competitive, more cooperative classroom atmosphere of the single-sex environment, coupled with an awareness of gender issues (Belitski, 1995), permits females to develop problem-solving skills, become divergent thinkers, and increase their math competency and confidence.

In the single-sex institution, a variety of factors—the female-only living situation, female-only study groups, female alumnae to serve as role models, a larger percentage of female faculty and administrators, women holding all leadership positions in student government, as well as faculty who have learned to gear their teaching toward women—support the attraction and retention of women in science. For example, in single-sex institutions, all study groups are composed only of women. Arranging study groups so that women do not drop out of a science study group because of feeling isolated among a group of men (Light, 1990) is not an issue at a single-sex institution. Similarly, avoidance of certain majors because they are nontraditional for a particular sex does not occur at a women's college; by definition, all majors are selected only by women.

A PLACE FOR FEMALES IN COEDUCATIONAL SETTINGS

With the current attacks on affirmative action (Wheeler, 1995) and increased use of Title IX legislation by white males, the legality of female-only classes in a coeducational public school environment may be questionable. One of the many negative aspects of these Title IX and affirmative action questions is that they may prevent significant research on which aspects of the single-sex situation may be translated successfully to the coeducational environment to retain women in science.

In the absence of the additional supporting factors of a single-sex institution, the female-only science/mathematics classroom in a coeducational environment still has features thought to be important for retaining women in science. First, the absence of males in the classroom means that faculty may concentrate on females. Studies on both the K–12 (AAUW, 1992; Sadker & Sadker, 1994) and the college level (Erhardt & Sandler, 1990; Hall & Sandler, 1982) have documented that instructors focus considerably more attention on males in a variety of subtle and overt ways. Research has documented teachers making more eye contact with males, calling on them more often, asking them more questions, and other pedagogical biases.

Second, a growing body of evidence also documents a bias toward curricular content (such as physics examples and problems) based on experiences more common in men's lives than women's lives. The female-only environment encourages faculty to develop curricular content and teaching techniques that are particularly appealing to and successful with women. Third, the absence of male peers changes the dynamics among the students themselves. Studies have demonstrated that men tend to dominate classroom discussions, interrupt women more frequently, dominate laboratory equipment and computers, and squeeze out women from viewing demonstrations (Hall & Sandler, 1982). The female-only environment gives women an equal chance. Although some women like competition, many prefer collaboration. Cooperative techniques such as group work, guided design problems, and ensuring that everyone understands the concepts, have proved particularly successful in all-female environments. Since these techniques overlap considerably with techniques identified as reforms indicative of improved science, engineering, and mathematics teaching, the all-female classroom permits implementation of the techniques without males who may resist the absence of competitive approaches.

The female-only science, engineering, and mathematics classroom in a coeducational institution functions without the supports of a surrounding single-sex environment. In addition, the female-only classes face attacks on their credibility. For example, a *New York Times* article ("To Help Girls," 1993) reported a concern voiced by a few teachers but no female students at Marin Academy in San Rafael, California, "that the girls move too slowly, ask too many questions and discuss things endlessly" (p. B10).

Without several years of research on the single-sex classroom in the coeducational environment, we will not know the following: (1) Which techniques, if any, are particularly successful? (2) Is there an age, developmental stage, or point in a course sequence at which it is especially useful to pursue a single-sex alternative? (3) What strategies are helpful and at what stage is it useful to ease the transition back to the coeducational environment?

A fundamental question has received less attention, but must be explored if the experimental classes are to be successful: How can some of the factors known to be especially effective for retaining females in science be replicated in the coeducational environment without obtaining a negative or inferior stigma? The differing approaches, absence of competition, and commitment to mastery of the material by every student may be viewed by other faculty and students as inferior rather than different. Putting aside Title IX difficulties surrounding the possible illegality of creating sex-segregated classes in publicly funded schools, another issue emerges from the classes for females: Will separate female-only classes really be viewed as equal in a coeducational environment? Or will separate be viewed as inferior, baby math, femme-chem, or touchy-feely science? Although many teachers involved in single-sex classrooms feel that these classes allow girls to blossom, not all teachers agree. For example, "Cinda Beem, a teacher at Anacapa, said her boys were five lessons ahead of her girls, boosted to greater accomplishment by their competitive natures. She worried that the meeker girls would not complete the year's work" ("To Help Girls," 1993, B10).

TRANSITION TO THE COEDUCATIONAL ENVIRONMENT

The issue of transition raises a different, but related, situation in which the translation between the single-sex institution and the coeducational environment may be explored. As someone who has contributed a good bit to the debate on successful strategies to attract and retain women in science, I have become accustomed to discussing the ramifications of the single-sex issue with faculty and students from coeducational institutions and with the public. Often I have extolled the benefits of single-sex education for women, pointing out that I obtained most of my ideas for *Female Friendly Science* (Rosser, 1990) during the 10 years I spent teaching at a women's college. The atmosphere, teaching techniques, and curricular content there contrasted sharply with my own previous educational and subsequent teaching experiences at large public coeducational institutions. Since only 3% of women graduate from women's colleges (Sebrechts, 1995), most faculty and students have not attended single-sex schools. They are eager to discuss the topic because of the data documenting success for women in science. Recently, at a lecture I gave at a women's college on female friendly science, I was surprised when a former colleague turned the question around. She asked me what advice I would have for faculty teaching in women's colleges to increase student success and retention in science, particularly as they make the transition to graduate school and careers in science. At first I was somewhat taken aback. Having taught the past 9 years at a large public coeducational institution and having spent considerable time conducting faculty development workshops all over the country to encourage faculty to make the science classroom more inclusive for women and minority men, I had forgotten that science students from women's colleges might face a different set of problems.

As I stood in front of the audience, thinking how to answer the question, the first memory that popped into my mind was the amount of time I had spent, while teaching at a women's college, convincing very bright students that they could do well in graduate school. Many of them feared that their separate education was not equal; because they had not been forced to compete with men in the undergraduate science classroom, they lacked confidence in their ability to do so.

The next thoughts that came to mind were the statistics regarding persistence of graduates of women's colleges in science. The Great Lakes College Association found that between 1970 and 1982, only 4.3% of women received their baccalaureate degrees from women's colleges, but these graduates were 7.2% of all women with doctorates in math and physical sciences and 6.6% with doctorates in the life sciences (Sebrechts, 1995). In 1986, Tidball reported that women's college graduates were two to three times more likely to go to medical school than women from coeducational institutions. Sharpe (1995) reports data from their baccalaureate-origin study that show that "the proportion of women doctorates for each institutional gender group is highest for both FMIs and HWIs (15.5% and 15%, respectively)" (p. 12) compared with the historically co-educational institutions (HCIs). The HWIs have the highest concentration of women doctorates in chemistry. Of the eight institutions that fall in the top 5% for production of women doctorates in all three physical science fields (chemistry, math/CS, physics/ES), two (Mount Holyoke and Bryn Mawr) are women's colleges (Sharpe, 1995).

More recent statistics emerging from Wellesley regarding science students 6 months after graduation seem more disturbing (Rayman & Brett, 1993, 1995). Although Wellesley boasted a higher percentage of students with majors in science and mathematics than most women's colleges, in a study of 369 women, 6 months after graduation, who graduated between 1983 and 1991 with majors in science and mathematics (astronomy, biology, biochemistry, chemistry, computer science, geology, mathematics, physics, and psychobiology), 103 (27.9%) returning questionnaires had left science. Another 41 (11.1%) left sometime between their graduate school and early career years (Rayman & Brett, 1995). In short, close to 40% of science majors left the field within a relatively short time.

As I made some suggestions about internships and summer jobs that would provide the students with "real-world" experiences with the culture of science, including male scientists, I realized that I had given the question posed by my former colleague virtually no thought in recent years. Since leaving my faculty position at a women's college some 8 years before, I had become so focused on how to translate the benefits of the women's college experience for the 97% of women attending coeducational institutions that I had forgotten that the women's college experience might pose a different set of problems for women in science.

A CLASH OF CULTURES

Faced with an audience composed primarily of faculty teaching at a women's college, I confessed my lack of attention to this question and solicited their observations and ideas. Their insightful comments suggested that for women in science who attend women's colleges, major problems with retention might surface further along the pipeline. Some, whom the faculty judged as capable and interested in further education in science, feared they would not be able to compete in graduate school. Others entered graduate school with enthusiasm, but dropped out after a semester or a year or two, sometimes after completing a master's degree. Usually, their reason for leaving graduate school centered on not liking the atmosphere or not finding what they expected, rather than poor academic performance or a dislike of the subject. Could this be viewed as a later surfacing of the trend for women undergraduates, noted in recent studies (Astin & Astin, 1993; Seymour & Hewitt, 1994), who leave science because they perceive it to be "uncaring" and "uninteresting"? Perhaps the nurturing environment of the women's college mitigates this loss until its alumnae find themselves in an atmosphere more typical of the world of science.

Many continued their graduate education in other fields; some switched to a science-related field such as technical writing, science education, or business, with the intention of combining their love of science with a field in which they found the atmosphere to be more tolerable. Of the considerable number who continued their graduate science education, some reported relatively few problems aside from those typically mentioned by most students, both male and female, about adjusting to graduate school. A few articulated quite clearly the problems they encountered in moving from the relatively nurturing and supportive environment of the women's college, where cooperation and open discussion about their topics of interest and experiments were fostered in both the classroom and laboratory, to the comparatively competitive environment of graduate school where both male peers and faculty often encouraged rivalry and cut-throat competition.

Not wanting to allow this question to supersede discussion of matters others might want to pursue, I solicited questions on other topics. Later that day and in subsequent encounters with faculty and students from women's colleges, I returned to the subject. I also sought information from graduate science faculty who had taught a considerable number of students with undergraduate degrees from women's colleges as well as from coeducational institutions. I sought more information about the reactions of science majors from women's colleges to graduate school and job experiences, to determine the answer to my colleague's question: What could women's colleges do better to prepare their science majors to survive and thrive in the culture of science they encounter in the real world?

The picture that emerged from these sources regarding the graduates of women's colleges proved interesting and useful. First, some faculty, particularly women who teach graduate students at research universities, knew exactly what I meant when I posed the question. "Oh, the women's college phenomenon," replied one female faculty member, "I see it all the time. They're absolutely shocked when they first encounter the harsh realities of the competitive scientific world. Most of them arrive from that nurturing, supportive environment of the women's college pretty unprepared for the way they'll be treated here by both their male peers and the faculty. A number never make the adjustment; it's pretty clear that they don't want to have much to do with a science which involves cut-throat competition. Most develop coping strategies fairly quickly that allow them to adapt to the new environment. I'm really not sure in the final analysis that we lose more women who come from women's colleges than we do those who come from coed institutions. Graduate school is hard on most women in science; there's no doubt about that."

Coping in Graduate School

At least two aspects of what the woman faculty member recounted, warranted further investigation. First, I wanted to know what coping mechanisms the women developed to adjust to graduate school. Knowledge of these might be used to inform faculty at the women's colleges, who could initiate measures to aid their students in developing these mechanisms while still in undergraduate school. Second, the graduate school dropout rate of women's college graduates compared with women graduates from coeducational institutions needed to be verified.

Although I know of no existing studies that compare the number of women graduates of women's colleges with those of coeducational institutions who leave science, engineering, and mathematics graduate school, some recent data reveal related information. Seymour (1995), in a study of undergraduate science, math, and engineering majors, found that 38% of undergraduates leave engineering; 51% each leave biology, physics, and chemistry; and 63% leave mathematics. These data, while including both males and females and pre-graduation rates, provide some perspective for the almost 40% of graduates from one women's college (Rayman & Brett, 1995) who left the field within a few years after graduation. Several recent studies have documented a particularly bad job market for Ph.D.s. A report by the Stanford University Institute for Higher Education Research and the Rand Corporation found that the

United States currently trains 25% more Ph.D.s in science and engineering than the job market can accommodate (Massey & Goldman, 1995). The Committee on Science, Engineering, and Public Policy (COSEPUP) of the National Research Council (1995) quotes an American Chemical Society finding that 16% of all 1993 chemistry Ph.D.s were looking for work the summer after graduation; an American Institute of Physics statistic that 14% of new physics Ph.D.s did not have job offers at graduation in 1993; and an American Mathematical Society statistic that 14% of math Ph.D.s were searching for employment the summer after their 1994 graduations. These studies may be relevant to the findings by Rayman and Brett (1995) that external economic factors may influence career choices to leave or remain in science, engineering, and mathematics.

Cooperators Face Competitors

Consulting with faculty involved with the Duke–University of North Carolina project (O'Barr & Wyer, 1992) provided some insights about problems encountered by women's college graduates and therefore what sorts of coping strategies the students needed to develop. A major problem, as predicted earlier, involved the competitive atmosphere. Many laboratory heads or major professors encouraged competition among their students to see who could get results on assigned projects first, who did better in courses, and who kept up with the latest literature. Although none of the faculty condoned cheating, the students stated that they personally knew of cases where data had been fabricated for lab reports, computer programs stolen, and problem solutions copied. The students felt that the highly competitive environment fostered this sort of behavior, which they perceived as contrasting with the cooperative atmosphere in a women's college. In addition to establishing some sort of honor code that requires students to take responsibility for other students who cheat, many women's colleges have downplayed competition and encouraged cooperation. The untimed tests, collaborative learning groups, and guided design problems and projects appear to be particularly favorable for women who tend to prefer situations where everyone wins.

Valued Classroom Interactions

Another set of problems seemed to revolve around what might be called "valued interactions" in the classroom. One mathematics graduate student recounted that in her undergraduate classes in her major at a women's college, students had been encouraged to ask questions and reveal parts of the problem that they did not understand. Such revelations were perceived by both the faculty and other students as useful and as an important way to initiate problem solving. Active participation in class discussion contributed positively toward the course grade. In contrast, when the young woman continued this active discussion approach in graduate school, she felt that both her peers and the faculty viewed it as a sign of weakness and lack of understanding. The ethos of the class included students taking notes and responding to questions only when they knew the answers. When she attempted to ask questions that revealed only partial understanding of a problem, the woman perceived that the other students viewed her as less competent (or, at least, foolish); she also believed that the instructor had graded her down because of her questions.

An additional part of this problem centered on what might be described as depth vs. breadth of coverage. Several graduates of women's colleges suggested that their undergraduate major courses had emphasized exploring a topic in depth over moving through vast amounts of material. Their perception of coeducational classes suggested that breadth of coverage took precedence over depth of coverage. It might be argued that this depth vs. breadth perception simply reflects the difference between undergraduate and graduate courses; at the graduate level, instructors might expect students to have the capacity to explore problems in depth on their own outside of class. However, some of the women who noted this rather subtle distinction between women's colleges and coeducational classes remarked specifically that they had observed the phenomenon as undergraduates when they transferred to or took courses at a coeducational institution. This depth vs. breadth phenomenon also is suggested by anecdotal reports from the single-sex section of mathematics for girls being tried in coeducational middle and high schools. "Another Anacapa teacher, Pam Belitski, said her girls had kept pace with the boys by working fewer problems for each lesson once they understand the concept. And the boys, she said, often barrel forward regardless of whether they all understand" ("To Help Girls," 1993, p. B10).

MALE-FEMALE INTERACTIONS

A third set of problems revolved around gender dynamics in the classroom and laboratory. Many of the graduates of women's colleges encountered the panoply of problems now commonly known to be responsible for the "chilly climate in the classroom" for women (Hall & Sandler, 1982): Male students dominating the discussion; males taking over the computer hardware or equipment, thereby preventing female students from having equal access to "hands-on experiences"; males unintentionally squeezing out females from seeing laboratory demonstrations because of their average larger physical size; faculty giving more eye contact to male students; faculty calling on male students more frequently, asking them higher-order questions, and waiting longer for them to respond; faculty assigning higher value to the responses given by male students.

Even faculty who keep abreast of the debates surrounding teaching science and mathematics often fail to give adequate attention to the effects of gender when trying new pedagogical techniques in the classroom. As suggested in Chapter 2, although many science faculty attempt group work in their undergraduate classes, often they fail to consider the relevance of the research on gender dynamics in group interaction.

Often unaware of the literature on gender dynamics in the science classroom or inept at adapting the relatively extensive research on pedagogy to their own undergraduate coeducational classrooms, faculty find themselves especially ill-equipped to handle gender dynamics with female graduate students. As Sheila Widnall (1988) pointed out in her AAAS Presidential Address, gender aside, little research has highlighted the dynamics of a successful graduate student major–professor relationship in science. Given the dearth of information about how to educate someone to be a successful researcher, it is not surprising that women graduate students have an especially difficult time.

CRITICAL JUNCTURE

The first year of graduate school appears to be a crucial time for many women in science. Some combination of attrition and stopping with a master's degree creates a major loss from the pipeline for women (Alper, 1993). Although unresearched, it has been suggested (Widnall, 1988) that the following may be responsible for some of this loss: differential treatment of females on some relatively subtle factors such as holding informal lab discussions in the locker room after a game of squash or over beer at 5:00 p.m. on Fridays (which may make it difficult for women who have small children to attend), more damaging actions such as assigning less interesting or significant topics for research, or overt sexual harassment.

Some recent evidence (Astin & Sax, 1996) indicates that faculty who have made considerable efforts to "warm up" the chilly climate for women in science on the undergraduate level have not translated these efforts successfully to women graduate and postdoctoral students. Women who enter graduate school with the express purpose of obtaining only a master's degree, may make the attrition of women from the Ph.D. pipeline appear more severe than it really is. However, the loss of larger numbers of women (although substantial numbers of male graduate students leave without a Ph.D.) and of women who earn better grades than the men who persist, suggests that women who have the ability to do science leave because of factors unrelated to talent and interest in science on the graduate level, just as they do on the undergraduate level (Astin & Sax, 1996; Seymour & Hewitt, 1994).

In the wake of the failure to fund the Superconducting Supercollider and the scarcity of grant funds, jobs in science have become relatively tight (Watanabe, 1995). Rather than using this as an excuse to decrease efforts to attract men of color and women to science (Watanabe, 1995), why not continue the efforts, thereby increasing quality in the pool of scientists? Since the women who leave tend to have grades that are as good or better than those of the men who persist, changing the gender ratio should improve the quality of the pool of scientists. An improvement in quality, in turn, should help both women and science.

LESSONS FROM THE SINGLE-SEX EXPERIENCE

To return to the question posed by the faculty member, What can faculty at women's colleges do better to prepare their students to persist when they face the realities of coeducational science? Consideration of the research and anecdotal information about the persistence of women's college alumnae in graduate school suggests several measures that might be useful for retention. These fall into the following three broad categories: (1) necessity for additional research data, (2) suggestions applicable to graduate school years, and (3) suggestions for the undergraduate years at women's colleges.

THE NEED FOR ADDITIONAL RESEARCH DATA

When searching for data to refute or confirm the perceptions and anecdotal information regarding persistence of graduates of women's colleges in graduate school, I learned that the data on this topic are being updated. In addition to the Tidball (1986) study, the new data from Sharpe (1995) and Rayman and Brett (1993, 1995) provide recent information on the rates at which women's college alumnae are receiving degrees from graduate and professional schools.

For a more complete understanding of the current picture, the following data should be collected:

1. The percentage of SEM graduates of women's colleges who enter graduate and/or professional school within 5 years following graduation.
2. The percentage of female SEM graduates of coeducational institutions, separated by private and public, as well as size, who enter graduate and/ or professional school (medical or dental) in SEM within 5 years following graduation.
3. The percentage of 1. and 2. that complete the terminal graduate or professional degree.
4. The percentage of 1. and 2. that leave graduate/professional school with no degree.

5. The percentage of 1. and 2. that leave school with a degree (e.g., master's), but entered postbaccalaureate education hoping for a more advanced degree.
6. The percentage of 1. and 2. who only sought and received a degree such as a master's.

These quantitative data, combined with some qualitative information on the reasons women in categories 4. and 5. leave, should provide insights into differential persistence rates, if they exist, and possible reasons for the differences.

REMEDIES AT THE GRADUATE LEVEL

Graduate schools might simulate various aspects of the women's college environment demonstrated to promote successful retention of women in science. Although the graduate schools should take the initiative in developing such supports, alumnae of women's colleges themselves may need to seek support and develop mechanisms to help them succeed. As an example of such supports, women graduate students might form a women in science group, based in the department or college (depending on the size and number of women), that meets regularly (weekly, monthly). Although the group will probably wish to have speakers and discussions on scientific topics, mechanisms and time should be built in to encourage informal discussion about who and what *helps* women in SEM and who and what *hurts* women in SEM in the department/college/institution.

Women students also might discuss among themselves and gather statistics on the gender ratios of students who enter graduate school in the department/college compared with those who receive degrees. They might consider the following questions: Does the percentage of women receiving master's and Ph.D. degrees differ relative to their matriculation rates compared with the percentage of men? Does it take one sex longer than the other to receive a particular degree? Are there differences by sex in the type and amount of financial aid given? Do some professors have a particularly good (or bad) track record regarding the number of women who receive degrees when they are the major professor and whose laboratories are rumored to be particularly supportive (unsupportive) of women.

Finally, women students can affiliate with the women's studies program, the women's center, and/or other programs and groups on campus with missions that support women and women's education. These programs and centers may provide valuable resources and experience for the women in dealing with chilly climate issues experienced in graduate school. Although some of these issues may present themselves differently or in a new fashion for women in science, often they represent "old issues" that women's studies and women's center staff have found in most departments on campus in one form or another. Attending presentations and events sponsored by these programs and centers also may help to alleviate some of the isolation felt by women's college graduates when they find themselves as the only woman or one of very few women in a mostly male SEM department in graduate school. Women may find that the support from women in departments outside of science helps them cope with a hostile laboratory or class environment in their home department.

REMEDIES AT THE UNDERGRADUATE LEVEL

To increase graduate school persistence of their alumnae, women's colleges should expose their students to some aspects of coeducational classroom and real-world work experiences while still in undergraduate school. Ideally, the duration and intensity of such exposures would increase as students approach graduation. If students have some exposure to the competitive male world of science and the influence of gender roles in group dynamics while still in the supportive environment of a women's college, they will have less adjustment to make on that score while they are adapting to other new aspects of graduate school. Summer or semester-long internships, the cooperative work experience where semesters of work are interspersed with semesters at college, and semester or year-long exchanges at coeducational institutions all provide opportunities for women's college students to interact in a coeducational scientific environment for an extended period of time. These opportunities, when coupled with summer or school-year, SEM-related jobs or occasional selected courses in the major taken at nearby coeducational institutions, may help to ease the transition to the competitive coeducational graduate school environment.

Faculty should openly discuss issues surrounding the chilly climate in the SEM classroom and laboratory for women in the coeducational environment. Students should be asked, and helped, to consider the aspects of classroom, laboratory, and informal environmental interactions at a women's college that have helped them to persist in science, and should be made overtly aware of how these dynamics change when male students become part of the interaction. Faculty might invite alumnae in SEM who represent achievement of success at different points along the pipeline (a current graduate student who has just received a master's degree; a student about to receive her Ph.D.; a post-doc; someone in her first academic or industrial job; a woman who has received tenure or achieved a middle management position in industry; a senior scientist; a laboratory or department head; a major professional award winner and/or dean or industry CEO) to discuss the factors that helped them persist, especially when they encountered a chilly climate.

Finally, students should be exposed to as much science, engineering, and mathematics as possible, with particular emphasis on work with equipment, computer hardware, and/or field experience. Studies (NSF, 1994c) reveal that girls and women have less experience with equipment used in SEM and express less desire and comfort with handling equipment. The relatively small size of most women's colleges, coupled with their focus on undergraduate education, means that these institutions may provide their students with comparatively more diverse and extensive opportunities to conduct hands-on research. Increased time spent on more kinds of equipment, solving a variety of problems in different contexts, together with strong theoretical training, will provide the young women with a depth and breadth of knowledge and experience in science unavailable to most graduates of coeducational institutions. This superior foundation will help give them the confidence to persist when they encounter the chilly atmosphere of coeducational science.

CONCLUSIONS

The success of single-sex institutions in attracting and retaining women in science provides challenges and questions for coeducational institutions in their attempts to increase their percentages of women. Since SEM classes in single-sex institutions exist in a surrounding supportive environment, substantial research is needed to reveal which factors of the single-sex classroom translate successfully to the coeducational environment.

Substantial research also might reveal contrasting aspects of the single-sex vs. coeducational environment issue at the graduate level. The first year in graduate school represents a time when a significant number of women leave SEM despite their superior grades and scores compared with their male counterparts. The particular success of women's colleges in producing a larger percentage of SEM graduates than do coeducational institutions may postpone the exodus of their alumnae until they reach the coeducational world of graduate school or work. This may be responsible for findings of a recent study (Rayman & Brett, 1993, 1995) and anecdotal information suggesting that a relatively high percentage of these alumnae from women's colleges leave SEM within 6 months after graduation.

More data are needed to determine whether this exodus does occur and, if so, its causes. A long-term solution to reverse this loss revolves around creating a female friendly environment that reflects the women's college environment in coeducational worlds of graduate school and work. In addition to retaining increased numbers of women's college graduates, this more hospitable environment should help in retaining all women in SEM. In the short run, women's colleges may encourage their students to have more interactions with the coeducational science world. In addition to bridging the transition for women's college graduates, these interactions may help to advance the long-term goal.

CHAPTER 4

Gender Equity in the School-to-Work Movement: Reinforcement of Race, Class, and Gender Stereotypes

with Charlotte Hogsett

When the School-to-Work Opportunities Act was crafted in the early days of the Clinton Administration, its creators envisioned a mechanism to revitalize technical curricula and solve problems surfacing for working-class students receiving inadequate and inappropriate training to prepare them for the labor force. They responded to industry's comments that students lacked basic mathematics and technical skills needed to assume entry level positions upon high school graduation and to invidious comparisons with the technical training given to students in Germany, Japan, and other international competitors in the global economy. The Act focuses on a class issue—higher wages for working people. This issue, however, cannot be addressed adequately without attention to another matter inherent in it but often ignored—the status of women. An impact on the status of women in the workplace can have important consequences both for individual women and for society itself.

Women constitute 45% of the workforce; 74% of all women between the ages of 25 and 54 work. However, they are clustered in only 20 of the more than 400 job categories (Kerka, 1993). Two out of three people who are earning minimum wage are women. Sixty percent of women in the labor force work out of economic need; they are single, divorced, widowed, or with spouses who earn less than $15,000 a year. Sixteen percent of all families are maintained solely by women (Fear-Fenn & Kapostasy, 1992). Women's status in the labor market seems indeed to be the family issue of the nineties (Spalter-Roth & Hartman, 1991). Therefore, education, the key to better jobs, becomes a crucial issue.

Fifteen percent of young men but 31% of young women receiving high school diplomas in 1992 were unemployed. Among high school dropouts, 35% of young men and 44% of young women did not participate in the workforce. Even of those girls who pursue vocational education, 70% are preparing for low-wage jobs (Kerka, 1993). Most young women going directly into the labor force after high school graduation go into administrative support (30%) and sales (22%) positions that pay an average wage of $338 every 2 weeks. In contrast, their male peers cluster in industry as operators, fabricators, and laborers (39%) or trade occupations (20%) with an average pay of $448 for the same time period (Milgram & Watkins, 1994). The pay differential of more than $220 per month between males and females provides substantial evidence to explain why many women, particularly those who must support children and pay for child care, end up on welfare or as the working poor.

Unfortunately, not only vocational education as it is practiced today but also some important current initiatives aimed at improving it are failing adequately to address the issue of breaking the cycle of poverty by preparing girls for better jobs. In this chapter, after a brief overview of some major problems for girls in vocational education, we examine one government initiative, the School-to-Work movement, to show why the needs of girls and women are not likely to be met more effectively as it takes effect. We also suggest, both in general and as exemplified by a few programs already in place, what kinds of efforts toward gender equity in vocational education for girls might have a better chance of success. If feminist educators, legislators, administrators, and policy makers wish to work for gender equity in vocational education, what must we do? What can we learn about how the School-to-Work movement is another example of how gender and race have been overlooked again in reforms in science/technology?

The path from legislation to social change is tortuous, its outcome, uncertain. From the time an idea is conceived and expressed, to the final writing of a bill, a number of people with different interests intervene. Compromises are negotiated continually, making it impossible to trace the entire process through written records. The effect of the bill also depends on how the call for grants is written, what priorities are established, and how points to be awarded for the various areas are allocated. Our account is an incomplete and schematized version of a complex reality, but certain themes emerge insistently and, we think, instructively.

GENDER INEQUITIES IN VOCATIONAL EDUCATION TODAY

Vocational education has tended to perpetuate the wage differential between men and women rather than to eradicate it. The areas in which one finds a greater concentration of girls in high school have channeled them, like their mothers before them, into low-prestige, low-skill, low-wage jobs. Young men and women receive different training for different jobs. Most male high school students concentrate in trade and industry; most females concentrate in clerical skills courses (National Center for Education Statistics, 1990). For example, females account for only 6.5% of all apprentices, with 90% clustered in cosmetology. Only 0.5% of apprentices in car repair are female (General Accounting Office, 1992).

Girls in vocational education not only find themselves in different courses; they also confront different treatment than the boys. In an observation of 10,213 interactions in 182 secondary vocational classes, it was found that males received more teacher interactions than did females, even from female teachers (Smith, 1991). A study of experiences of girls in middle school technology courses indicated that "(1) girls appeared to enjoy technology education and to have confidence in their abilities, but emerging sexism among peers began to affect participation on the basis of gender; (2) girls were discouraged from taking more technology education in high school due to stereotypes about appropriate careers and (3) girls who took technology education in high school were willing to challenge stereotypes but had less confidence in their abilities" (Silverman & Pritchard, 1993). Not only the subjects studied but the treatment received contribute to the continuation of low-wage patterns for girls and women.

THE SCHOOL-TO-WORK OPPORTUNITIES ACT OF 1994

The School-to-Work Opportunities Act (STOWA) was introduced in early 1993. During the Presidential campaign of the previous year, Bill Clinton had spoken extensively about his plan for a national youth apprentice system. He presented his idea for study by the Departments of Education and Labor, which expanded it to include several models in addition to apprenticeships—Tech Prep, cooperative education, career academies, and school-based enterprises—and gave the redefined and expanded initiative its new name, School to Work (Career Pathways Report, 1993).

ATTEMPTS AT GENDER INCLUSION

Neither Clinton's original plan nor those that began to be developed in early 1993 had gender as their central focus or even contained elements concerning gender equity. However, groups interested in the improvement of women's labor market status soon set to work on the task of including specific language concerning girls at various critical stages of advancement. They based this recommendation on the kinds of observations suggested by two previous initiatives in the area, of which the first was the Nontraditional Employment for Women (NEW) Act of 1991. This Act requires Private Industry Councils and States to set goals for training in nontraditional jobs through the Job Training Partnership

Act (JTPA). In their plan to set and meet goals, the Private Industry Councils and States must collect and regularly report data by sex, race, age, and occupation. Wider Opportunities for Women (Milgram & Watkins, 1994) reports that within 2 years after the passage of that law, they observed extensive proactive efforts by the JTPA system to train women for nontraditional jobs.

Second, Wider Opportunities for Women (WOW) made a survey of the sex-segregated data collected on 15 School-to-Work transition demonstration sites overseen by the U.S. Department of Labor and Jobs for the Future. They saw these data as a crucial indicator of the impact of the School-to-Work Opportunities program on women for the following reason: "It was WOW's understanding that the Administration's School-to-Work bill would build upon and advance existing youth apprenticeship and School-to-Work programs, so we wanted to examine how some of the Department's demonstration sites were serving young women" (Milgram & Watkins, 1994, p. 3).

The 14 regular demonstration sites had fewer women (236) than men (337) (Milgram & Watkins, 1994, Table 2, p. 4). Of 14 regular demonstration sites, three had no young women and three had only one or two young women. Over 90% of the young women clustered in five demonstration sites where the occupational areas were traditional for their gender—allied health careers, teaching and education, graphic arts, and office technology. Even when a fifteenth, non-traditional site (Manufacturing Technology Partnership in Flint, Michigan) was included in the data, only 16% (41 women) were in nontraditional skills training; almost half (20) of them were in the single nontraditional site.

These two initiatives indicated that a focus on women, such as that made by the NEW Act, does have a significant impact, whereas early efforts under the School-to-Work transition, without a focus on women, tended to neglect them. Thus women's groups dedicated to the improvement of the status of women in the workforce set to work. Central to the effort was the Coalition on Women and Job Training, consisting of 27 organizations working on issues of employment and training for girls and women (Milgram, Testimony, October 14, 1993). As early as June 1993, a draft overview of the School to Work initiative, announcing implementation grants to be available to states, called on them to include "the State's plan for ensuring that young women and minorities will have opportunity to participate in school to work programs that will lead to employment in nontraditional occupations" (Career Pathways Report, 1994, p. 50).

On October 14, 1993, Donna Milgram of Wider Opportunities for Women testified before the Employment and Productivity Subcommittee of the Senate Labor and Human Resources Committee on behalf of the Coalition. Having spoken about the wage differential between men and women and explained that the Department of Labor School to Work transition demonstration sites were not working toward the goal of breaking traditional employment patterns, she listed the elements of program content and administration that the Coalition believed would be more effective in reaching that goal.

Milgram's testimony evidently was successful in persuading the Senate to include gender-specific language. Less than a month after this meeting, both the House and the Senate issued reports on School-to-Work. The House, in defining what was meant by stating that the Act must address the needs of "all students," did not include a reference to gender; the Senate, however, before whom the Coalition representative had spoken, reflected at least some of her suggestions. It referred to ideas the Coalition had introduced (Career Pathways Report, 1993) and, while sometimes eliding females as included in "all students" (p. 70), echoed the call, already included in the June 1993 draft, for female employment in nontraditional occupations. Young women were mentioned still another time. Further, the document contains the following strong language:

> Ensuring that all young women have the same opportunities, encouragement and options as young men is an integral component of this Act. The Departments should maintain a statistical breakdown of girls trained in nontraditional occupations. The breakdown should include the occupation and wage-at-placement figures. In addition, the Departments should assess whether proactive measures have been taken by School-to-Work Opportunities programs to recruit, train, place, and retain young women in nontraditional occupational skill areas. (p. 77)

Next, in January 1994, a memorandum concerning the School-to-Work initiative was issued by a joint task force of the Departments of Labor and of Education. Its intention was to "inform the administration and the members of the education community of the structure, timetable, and goals of the new program" (Career Pathways Report, 1994). The Departments had decided to jump-start School-to-Work by offering grant monies through the Job Training Partnership Act and the Carl D. Perkins Vocational and Applied Technology and Education Act. This announcement is a brief two pages. Perhaps it is not surprising that the gender element is not mentioned, but it was unfortunate, since this introductory statement inevitably formed the basic expectations of those who were to participate.

Indeed, in the February 3, 1994 and March 9, 1994 issues of the *Federal Register* (1994), regulations for the State Implementation Grants Program were published. The former, apparently reflecting comments made on initial priority statements, contains more specific language about ensuring opportunities for young women. Comments on these regulations include a request for child-care provisions, which in fact were to be included in the bill itself.

The process of working toward inclusion of women and women's issues was clearly difficult and not always successful. Although both documents call for "awareness and outreach" to young women, gender is not mentioned as one of the categories under "all students" in either of the two places "all students" are mentioned—and they are crucial places: definition and criteria for evaluation. Thus, both regulations statements mirror the less inclusive House version of the bill rather than the more responsive Senate version.

Perhaps in recognition of the precarious status of gender in the School-to-Work Opportunities Act, Wider Opportunities for Women, one of the groups represented in the Coalition, issued a working paper in March 1994, written by Donna Milgram and Kristin Watkins. This paper reproduces Milgram's testimony before the Senate subcommittee and adds a detailed list of inclusive language, urging that in the final version of the bill this language be retained. Further, they request language preventing waivers of the Nontraditional Employment for Women Act and the sex equity provisions of the Carl D. Perkins Vocational Education and Applied Technology Act.

The following is some of the language stressed by the representatives of Wider Opportunities for Women:

- One of the purposes of the Act is to "increase opportunities for minorities and women by enabling individuals to prepare for careers which are not traditional for their race or gender."
- The definition of "all students" means "male and female students from a broad range of backgrounds and circumstances."
- A School-to-Work Opportunities program shall "provide all students with equal access to the full range of . . . program components . . . and to recruitment, enrollment, and placement activities."
- The school-based learning component of a School-to-Work Opportunities program shall include "career awareness and career exploration . . . in order to help students who may be interested to identify, and select or reconsider their interests, goals, and career majors, including those options that may not be traditional for their gender, race, or ethnicity."
- The connecting activities component of a School-to-Work Opportunities program shall include "collecting information regarding post-program outcomes of participants in the School-to-Work Opportunities program and analyzing such information, to the extent practicable, on the basis of socioeconomic status, race, gender, ethnicity, disability, limited English proficiency, school dropouts, and academically talented students."

The bill was passed by both houses of Congress in April 1994. The text was published in the *Federal Register* on April 19. In many ways, it represents a victory for all those who worked so hard to include gender-specific language. In fact, a comparison of the requests made in the Milgram and Watkins paper with the final version of the bill reveals that in almost every instance, the language that they sought was retained. The Act also contains a section concerning guidance toward career options and encouraging careers in nontraditional employment.

A BACKSEAT FOR WOMEN

In two crucial ways, however, what Milgram and Watkins requested was not granted. First, quoting the Senate version, they had included the following language in their list of items to be retained: "Ensuring that all young women have the same opportunities, encouragement, and options as young men is an integral component of this Act." This language was, unlike the rest, not retained. Under "Purpose," the framers of the Act specify 14 aims. This is the thirteenth: "to increase opportunities for minorities, women, and individuals with disabilities, by enabling individuals to prepare for careers that are not traditional for their race, gender, or disability." Lower wages for women do not appear as one of the major "Findings" with which the Act opens. Thus, gender concerns are marginalized and are not an "integral component."

Second, the two acts that Milgram and Watkins specified did not appear under the sections concerning "Waivers Not Authorized." This means that the central place women occupy in the Nontraditional Employment for Women Act is not reflected in the School-to-Work Opportunities Act of 1994, and that the sex equity provisions of Carl D. Perkins, most crucially the participation of the sex equity coordinator mandated by that act, could be bypassed.

It is also important to note that in neither of the two events arranged by the White House for the signing and celebrating of this Act did the President mention opportunities for women. For the President, from the time he brought his youth apprentice system into the public debate, the issue was centrally one of class and, insofar as minority status sometimes leads to lower class status, race. It was also, both for him and for the executors and legislators who worked on the bill, an issue of U.S. competitiveness in the world market. Clinton stated, "In today's global economy, a nation's greatest resource—indeed, the ultimate source of its wealth—is its people. To compete and win, our work force must be well-educated, well-trained, and highly skilled" (Career Pathways Report, 1994, p. 139).

The argument here is not that effective international economic performance is unimportant and certainly not that class and race issues are trivial. It is rather that neither the interests of a strong workforce nor those of any socioeconomic or racial group are well-served if half of the people who constitute or might constitute it are underserved. Race and class intersect with gender; failing to take into full account any one of these factors undercuts any initiative. The making of the School-to-Work Opportunities Act of 1994 was marked by the determined efforts of women's groups to ensure attention to young women; it is marked as well by the mixed success of those efforts. In the end, the message the Act sent to the states concerning the place that opportunities for young women should occupy in their plans was a weak one. Gender was included, but it did not occupy a central and integral place, nor were sufficient safeguards for inclusion established. Moreover, the President, whose prestige can set the tone for a movement, privileged matters other than gender.

SCHOOL-TO-WORK AT THE STATE LEVEL: FOLLOWING THE FEDERAL LEAD

At the same time as the federal School-to-Work Opportunities Act was being hammered out, many states were working on their own versions of the initiative. It is not surprising that, following the cue of actions taken and not taken at the federal level, the states have tended to drop gender as a major consideration of their efforts, or to ignore it entirely.

Washington State, for example, classifies itself as "a leader in planning for education improvement" (Billings, 1994, p. 1). Indeed, Governor Booth Gardner of Washington, along with Bill Clinton of Arkansas, Richard Riley of South Carolina, and Madeleine Kunin of Vermont, led the National Governors' Association in its education summit and in the adoption of six national education goals in 1991. When Clinton became President, he appointed Riley and Kunin as Secretary and Deputy Secretary of Education, respectively; they proposed the "Goals 2000: Educate America Act," which was enacted by Congress in 1994 and formally adopted the national education goals and provided grants for state and local school improvement planning (Billings, 1994).

Washington State accepted federal support for its educational improvement efforts, including the development of its School-to-Work Opportunities System (Lowry, 1995); in November 1993, Washington successfully applied for a federal grant to support its planning of a school-to-work transition system. In 1994, Washington students in 45 school districts participated in model programs in which the state invested $2.55 million (Dinsmore, 1994). "Federal and regional experts have recognized Washington as the only state which has invested substantial state dollars to develop school-to-work initiatives" (Dinsmore, 1994, p. 8).

Because the state perceives itself, and is recognized by others, as a leader in School-to-Work initiatives, the absence of a focus on gender in its materials bodes poorly for other states that may use its materials as a model. Although the *Final Report to the Governor* (Dinsmore, 1994) constantly repeats that School-to-Work is for ALL (their capitals) students, gender is referred to only once in the entire document. In the Template for School-to-Work Best Practice, an item concerning the consistency of local program design with the state

School-to-Work plan, the following statement appears: "Integration of school and workplace begins in early grades; non-traditional options [are] presented for boys and girls alike and for persons with disabilities" (Dinsmore, 1994, p. 1).

One of the 13 "agreements" in the document was to "address the special needs of special populations" (Dinsmore, 1994), which is described as follows: "School To Work is an effort to enrich the educational opportunities for all students, but it can be especially important for populations that have been less well served by the current educational system." Later in the document, specialized marketing to "target audiences (cultural and racial groups, persons with disabilities, limited English speakers; youth, parents, educators, business, labor, urban and rural communities)" is recommended. Another agreement is to "provide diverse populations, including special and targeted populations, equitable opportunities to all educational programs, and services," and still another is to "integrate programs and services available through private industry councils with other education and training services targeted for disadvantaged youth." The document does not state that women and/or girls are a special or targeted population, although it also does not state that they are excluded as special or targeted populations. With the exception of the statement under Best Practices quoted above, gender remains entirely absent from the document. In summary, the *Final Report to the Governor* on School-to-Work in Washington State reflects the lack of focus on women and girls in the federal Act.

PROGRAMS THAT WORK: SUCCESS STORIES FROM THE WORKPLACE

The School-to-Work movement seems to have been ineffectual in terms of addressing the "family issue of the 90s." Like vocational education in general, it will succeed only in enabling and even encouraging a continuation of the employment patterns that have led to low wages for women and therefore poverty for many families in the United States. Schools will persist in guiding young women not necessarily toward those careers in which they might be most interested, for which they may be best fitted, and that it would be in their best economic interests to pursue, but rather toward those considered appropriate for them in this society.

Sufficient evidence exists about how to break those patterns. For example, in their study of the 15 School-to-Work transition demonstration sites, Wider Opportunities for Women identified one site that, unlike the others, was successful in attracting young women to nontraditional work. Nothing in the site itself would make it clear that it would be particularly attractive to females. The Manufacturing Technology Partnership (MTP) aimed initially at enabling students to perform well on the General Motors–United Auto Workers Apprenticeship Test. Later it integrated academic subjects like algebra and physics with skilled trade training. The structure of the program was similar to many others—a combination of academic work and on-the-job training during the school year and work experience in the summer.

WOW discovered the major difference between this and other model sites. The MTP site specifically focuses on training young women for nontraditional careers. This focus is emphasized in its recruitment efforts, which include the use of female role models. Sexual harassment prevention workshops, access to female mentors, emphasis on incentives for employers to recruit women for nontraditional careers, and training for counselors, principals, teachers, and parents also serve as critical elements for retaining the women, once they have been recruited.

Just as in the JTPA study, a specific focus on training young women for nontraditional careers yields success. Of the 122 applicants to the MTP program for the 1993–94 school year, 59 were female; 25 of the 58 students accepted were young women (Milgram & Watkins, 1994). In contrast, the metalworking/ manufacturing technology portion of the Illinois Youth Apprenticeship Program accepted 28 men and no women; the Pennsylvania Youth Apprenticeship Program in metalworking had 91 men and nine women; the Seminole County School District and Siements Stromber–Carlson (Florida) site in telecommunications and electronics had 20 young men and two women.

Although open to both male and female students, with statements in their recruitment materials explicitly indicating that they welcome female students, most high-tech or skilled trade demonstration sites fail to attract women students, without proactive recruitment, expanded career counseling, and female role models in these nontraditional fields.

> WOW asked an administrator of one of the nontraditional programs that had no young women what efforts were made to recruit them, and he said, "Since this work is associated with being dirty, girls generally aren't interested." . . . WOW thinks it is unlikely that getting dirty is a barrier to skills training for most young women; at least 13 women in the sites are doing nursing externships where they are required to change bedpans and bathe patients, certainly very dirty work. (Milgram & Watkins, 1994, p. 5)

If the elements of successful programs have been identified at least in part, the remaining challenge is to set in motion the kinds of structures that will elicit and nurture their development. Efforts toward that have been and are being made. We have already followed the work of the Coalition on Women and Job Training as it endeavored to bring women into the School-to-Work initiative. More recently, the Department of Education, in inviting applications for new awards for 1995 under the Women's Educational Equity Act (WEEA) Programs, states one of the targeted areas as follows: "School-to-work transition programs, guidance and counseling activities, and other programs to increase opportunities for women and girls to enter a technologically demanding workplace and, in particular, to enter highly skilled, high-paying careers in which women and girls have been underrepresented" (U.S. Department of Education, 1995).

While STWOA seems to be faltering in its gender-related activities, the WEEA effort is not yet underway. How successful it will be is open to question. Whereas STWOA was centrally concerned with work and peripherally concerned with gender, WEEA focuses on gender, with work as a secondary concern.

In contrast, the NEW Act requires Private Industry Councils and states to set goals for training women in nontraditional jobs, according to WOW (Milgram & Watkins, 1994). WOW comments:

> Since the passage of the law, WOW has seen extensive proactive efforts by the JTPA systems to train women for nontraditional jobs. Workshops on nontraditional training are now a regular part of national and state job training conferences. Our network members in most of our states report that the JTPA system now regard their community-based organizations as a resource for training women for nontraditional jobs. (Milgram & Watkins, 1994, p. 7)

NEW, then, focuses centrally on both gender and work. This would appear to be the approach most likely to lead to change for women in the workplace.

CONCLUSIONS

Lessons both strategic and theoretical are inherent in this narrative of recent initiatives concerning women and the workplace. As STWOA got underway, gender was not a concern at all. The struggle to include gender, although in many ways successful, met with a resistance that is nearly palpable as one watches inclusive language appear and disappear in successive documents. As in a nightmare where one fights through thick molasses to arrive at a goal, the Coalition moved deliberately but slowly, encountering resistance at every step. Clearly, advocates of women here were not encountering a mere innocent oversight.

Where does this resistance come from? Did some nameless legislator or lobbying group decide that women should not be included and fight behind the scenes just as doggedly as the Coalition? Or, is it rather that U.S. society, particularly at this moment in history, is a wall so thoroughly cemented with sexism that no specific decision making is required to keep it in place, while monumental efforts must be made even to make a small opening through which a few women may pass?

Some patterns, at any rate, emerge. The first is that what is not central not only is marginalized, but probably will remain so. Efforts to add gender to a plan that has already been put in place without that consideration tend to be met with unsatisfactory results.

The second is well illustrated by a story told by a state sex equity coordinator. As her state prepared its own School-to-Work Opportunities Act, she noted that the definition of "all students" did not include gender-specific language. When she asked a legislator about the omission, he told her that of course it was understood that both males and females were included. She argued that it was important actually to state that in the bill itself. She knew, but was not able to convince the legislator, that what is taken for granted or understood will not surface as a real factor. Gender must be named.

Finally, the fact that well-meaning people, concerned as they should be about socioeconomic issues, failed to address gender in launching this important national movement, suggests that before gender will be included effectively, feminists working from several different theoretical perspectives will need to bring their insights and their work to bear on the problem. A radical feminist who studies the story we have told here might well want to point out that it exemplifies the basic tenet of her theoretical position: Oppression based on sex is the most fundamental of all oppressions; it exists within all other oppressions, dominant or muted. She would argue that this narrative indicates that society can more readily imagine and accept a workplace open to persons of socioeconomic groups currently underrepresented than entertain the possibility of the enormous social changes that would result from a gender-balanced workforce. Such a position can provide solid theoretical underpinnings for an insistence on making gender central and integral to any project.

The voice of the socialist feminist, with her emphasis on the necessity of economic justice and search for new social paradigms that might make it possible, needs to be heard in this debate as well. African American feminists and feminists representing all ethnicities must keep the focus on the women of their groups, for just as one can state that without explicit attention to gender, gender will be ignored, so also race issues, when merely assumed as a concern, will be neglected. The work of liberal feminists, with their belief in the efficacy of government initiatives to bring about social change and their ability and willingness to work with government on such initiatives, will continue to be crucial. These feminist theories will be examined in greater detail in Chapter 5.

Stubborn resistance to social change is evident even in the few threads of the story of one program that we have attempted to follow here. It is perhaps not an entirely uplifting story, but it is one among many that very much need to be told. Since April 1994, when this legislation passed Congress, a major political change occurred with the November 1994 elections. One of the many consequences of the dramatic swing to the right has been the attack on affirmative action. At the time of this writing, it is still unclear as to what the outcome of the attack will be. At worst, legislation may be passed removing federal mandates for equitable treatment of white women and minorities. In the case of STWOA, this would result in many of the safeguards to recruit women being removed from the Act. For example, the states' goals and methods no longer would have to include opportunities for young women to participate.

Even without the official repeal of the federal affirmative action legislation, the debates and polls surrounding the topic have sent people of color and white women a chilling message. Although it is almost impossible to measure the direct impact of the negative verbiage about affirmative action on School-to-Work programs, it is not likely to aid in the recruitment and retention of women. Such debates provide license for less proactive recruitment and hiring of women and minorities, less incentive for women to enter a nontraditional field where they might fear being perceived as an affirmative action hire, and increased subjection to harassment on the job.

At the same time as Congress wages its attack against affirmative action, it also attacks school lunches and welfare for single mothers. School-to-work provides an excellent mechanism to remove from unemployment the 44% of women without a high school diploma and the 31% of those who graduated. It also should aid in closing the 25% salary differential between young women and their male counterparts. Training for high-wage and technical areas is one of the best ways to ensure self-support for young women and their children. Ignoring gender and the importance of affirmative action will only maintain the status quo of low pay, limited job flexibility, and high unemployment for women in our society.

CHAPTER 5

Feminist Critiques of Science as Usual

Demographic predictions indicate that men of color and women will constitute between 80 and 90% of workforce growth by the twenty-first century. The workforce in the year 2000 is predicted to differ significantly from that of today.

> There will be a larger segment of minorities and women: 23% more Blacks, 70% more Asians and other races (American Indians, Alaska natives and Pacific Islanders), 74% more Hispanics and 25% more women, adding 3.6 million, 2.4 million, 6.0 million and 13.0 million more workers respectively. Altogether, the minorities and women will make up 90% of the work force growth and 23% of the new employees will be immigrants. (Thomas, 1989, p. 30)

Despite the relatively low percentages of women in most areas of science and engineering, until recently very few educational programs have directly targeted females. The results of a 1991 study by Matyas and Malcom that surveyed presidents/chancellors of 276 colleges and universities and the directors of nearly 400 recruitment/retention programs revealed that less than 10% of the programs included in the study were focused specifically on the recruitment and retention of women in science or engineering. This study reconfirmed similar findings from previous studies that virtually no programs directly target female students or faculty (Matyas & Malcom, 1991).

Until recently, very little contact occurred between the feminist and scientific communities. A handful of scientists has worked in women's studies since the beginning of the second wave of feminism in the late 1960s, developing feminist critiques of science, pointing out gender bias in basic and clinical research, and evolving curricular and pedagogical techniques to attract and retain women in science. The mainstream community of scientists has remained unaware or, in some cases, has actively ignored or challenged this feminist scholarship produced by their scientific colleagues.

The demographic predictions, coupled with national educational goals and other factors, have led to increased interest in and attention to efforts to attract and retain women in science and engineering. Funds from federal and founda-

81

tion sources have enabled faculty at colleges and universities to develop or en-hance existing projects and specifically target them toward attracting and re-taining females in science. Typically, the faculty who develop these projects come from the sciences, mathematics, and engineering. They tend to have lim-ited knowledge of women's studies and feminist theory.

A few projects (Rosser & Kelly, 1994a) explicitly apply approaches and cur-ricular content gleaned from women's studies. These projects, as well as the bulk of the projects that make no direct applications of, or references to, wom-en's studies or feminist theories, state goals and objectives that might described as liberal feminist: They seek to remove overt and covert barriers and discrimi-nation so that females will have the same access to education and careers in science and mathematics as that now enjoyed by their male counterparts.

Although the stated goals and objectives of many projects appear to have what might be described at best as a liberal feminist theoretical underpinning, elements common to many projects reflect a variety of feminist theoretical per-spectives ranging from essentialist through African American to radical. An ex-amination of various feminist theories reveals that useful information may result from their applications to projects to retain women in science, despite the lack of knowledge about the theory on the part of the individuals designing and implementing the projects.

Individuals unfamiliar with feminism or women's studies often assume that feminist theory provides a singular and unified framework for analysis. In one sense this is correct; all feminist theory posits gender as a significant characteris-tic that interacts with other characteristics, such as race and class, to structure relationships between individuals, within groups, and within society as a whole. However, the lens of gender is used in many ways, resulting in such diverse approaches as liberal feminism, Marxist feminism, socialist feminism, African American feminism, lesbian separatist feminism, conservative or essentialist feminism, existentialist feminism, psychoanalytic feminism, radical feminism, and postmodern feminism. Taken together, these varied and complex feminist theories provide a framework through which to explore interesting issues raised in projects designed to attract women to science.

LIBERAL FEMINISM

Since the eighteenth century, political scientists, philosophers, and feminists (Friedan, 1974; Jaggar, 1983; H. T. Mill, 1970; J. S. Mill, 1970; Wollstonecraft, 1975) have described the parameters of liberal feminism. The differences be-tween nineteenth-century and twentieth-century liberal feminists have varied from libertarian to egalitarian, and numerous complexities exist among defini-tions of liberal feminists today. However, a general definition of liberal feminism is the belief that women are suppressed in contemporary society because they suffer unjust discrimination (Jaggar, 1983). Liberal feminists seek no special privileges for women and simply demand that everyone receive equal consideration without discrimination on the basis of sex.

Most scientists would assume that the implications of liberal feminism for the sciences revolve solely around removal of documented overt and covert barriers (Matyas & Malcom, 1991; NSF, 1992; Rosser, 1990; Rossiter, 1984; Vetter, 1988, 1996) that have prevented women from entering and succeeding in science. Most projects to attract women have this as an explicitly stated goal, with accompanying criteria documenting the barriers and their particular strategies to overcome them. Most scientists, including those who initiate and implement such projects and even those who are brave enough to call themselves feminists, assume that the implications of liberal feminism extend only to employment, access, and discrimination issues.

In fact, the implications of liberal feminism extend beyond this. Liberal feminism shares two fundamental assumptions with the foundations of the traditional method for scientific discovery: (1) both assume that human beings are highly individualistic and obtain knowledge in a rational manner that may be separated from their social conditions; and (2) both accept positivism as the theory of knowledge. Positivism implies that "all knowledge is constructed by inference from immediate sensory experiences" (Jaggar, 1983, pp. 355–356).

These two assumptions lead to the belief in the possibilities of obtaining knowledge that is both objective and value-free, concepts that form the cornerstones of the scientific method. Objectivity is contingent on value neutrality or freedom from values, interests, and emotions associated with a particular class, race, or sex. Although each scientist strives to be as objective and value-free as possible, most scientists, feminists, and philosophers of science recognize that no individual can be neutral or value-free. Instead, "objectivity is defined to mean independence from the value judgments of any particular individual" (Jaggar, 1983, p. 357). Liberal feminism and projects with liberal feminist goals imply that once barriers are removed and women in science receive equal consideration without discrimination on the basis of sex, women will constitute 45% of scientists, since that is their proportion in the overall workforce population. Liberal feminism also implies that this proportional representation will be achieved without changes in science itself, except for the removal of barriers, and that women scientists, just as their male counterparts, will perceive the sensations and experiences on which their empirical observations are based separately and individually, while controlling their own values, interests, and emotions.

In the past 2 decades, feminist historians and philosophers of science (Fee, 1982; Haraway, 1990; Harding, 1986) and feminist scientists (Birke, 1986; Bleier, 1984, 1986; Fausto-Sterling, 1992; Hubbard, 1990; Keller, 1983, 1985;

Rosser, 1988; Spanier, 1982) have pointed out a source of bias and absence of value neutrality in science, particularly biology. Because they exclude females as experimental subjects, focus on problems of primary interest to males, have faulty experimental designs, and contain interpretations of data based in language or ideas constricted by patriarchal parameters, experimental results in several areas in biology have been demonstrated to be biased or flawed.

For example, much of the early work in primatology suffered from problems of selective use of species, anthropomorphic and vague language, and universalizing and extrapolating beyond the limits warranted by the data. Yerkes (1943) stated clearly in his early work that he had chosen particular primate species, such as the baboon and chimpanzee, because their social organization, in his eyes, resembled that of human primates. Subsequent researchers tended to forget the "obvious" limitations imposed by such selection of species and proceeded to generalize the data to universal behavior patterns for all primates. It was not until a significant number of women entered primatology that the concepts of the universality and male leadership of dominance hierarchies among primates (Lancaster, 1975; Leavitt, 1975; Leibowitz, 1975; Rowell, 1974) were questioned and shown to be inaccurate for many species.

In addition to the problems of selective use of species, anthropomorphic and vague language, and universalizing and extrapolating beyond limits of the data, feminist scientists revealed another obvious flaw in much animal behavior research: failure to study females. When females were studied, it usually was only in their interaction (usually reaction) to males or infants. Presumably, the fact that until recently most animal behavior researchers were male resulted in an androcentric bias in the conceptualization of design for observation of animal behavior. Because male researchers had *experienced* only male–male and male–female interactions themselves, their male world view prohibited them from realizing that female–female interaction might be *observed* in their own and other species. By focusing on female–female interactions, female primatologists (Fossey, 1983; Goodall, 1971) and sociobiologists (Hrdy, 1977, 1979, 1981, 1984, 1986) revealed new information that led to the overthrow of previously held theories regarding dominance hierarchies, mate selection (Hrdy, 1984), and female–female competition (Hrdy & Williams, 1983).

These and other examples of flawed research revealed by the critiques of feminists have raised fundamental questions regarding gender and good science: Do these examples simply represent "bad science"? Is good science really gender-free or does the scientific method, when properly used, permit research that is objective and unbiased?

Liberal feminism suggests that now that the bias of gender has been revealed by feminist critiques, scientists can take this into account and correct for this value or bias that previously was not uncovered. It implies that good scientific research is not conducted differently by men and women and that in principle men can be just as good feminists as women can and that women can be just as good scientists as men can. Now that feminist critiques have revealed flaws in research due to gender bias, both men and women will use this revelation to design experiments, gather and interpret data, and draw conclusions and theories that are more objective and free from bias, including gender bias (Biology and Gender Study Group, 1989). Once aware of the bias, men and women scientists might design and direct projects equally well to attract women to science and to illustrate the gender-free nature of science.

Liberal feminism also does not question the integrity of the scientific method itself or of its supporting corollaries of objectivity and value neutrality. Liberal feminism reaffirms the idea that it is possible to find a perspective from which to observe that is truly impartial, rational, and detached. Lack of objectivity and presence of bias occur because of human failure to properly follow the scientific method and avoid bias due to situation or condition. Liberal feminists argue that it was through attempts to become more value-neutral that the androcentrism in previous scientific research was revealed. Projects to attract more women to science are important since more women scientists should help to prevent the flaw introduced in the absence of substantial numbers of women scientists, through objectivity becoming congruent with male bias.

It is not surprising that most projects to attract women to science present goals that might be defined in liberal feminist terms. Liberal feminism supports the elimination of bias by adding women scientists as a corrective measure to make the scientific method function better. Liberal feminism shares beliefs in objectivity, value neutrality, logical positivism, and individualism, which constitute fundamental assumptions underlying the scientific method.

In contrast to liberal feminism, all other feminist theories call into question the fundamental assumptions underlying the scientific method, its corollaries of objectivity and value neutrality, or its implications. They reject individualism for a social constructivist view of knowledge, and question positivism and the possibility of objectivity obtained by value neutrality. Many also imply that men and women may conduct scientific research differently, although each theory posits a different cause for the gender distinction.

SOCIALIST FEMINISM

Socialist feminism serves as the clearest example of a feminist theory that contrasts with liberal feminism in its rejection of individualism and positivism as approaches to knowledge. Marxist critiques of science form the historical precursors and foundations for socialist feminist critiques. Marxism views all knowledge as socially constructed and emerging from practical human involvement in production that takes a definite historical form. According to Marxism, knowledge, including scientific knowledge, cannot be solely individualistic. Since knowing is a productive activity of human beings, it cannot be objective and value-free because the basic categories of knowledge are shaped by human purposes and values. Marxism proposes that the form of knowledge is determined by the prevailing mode of production. In the twentieth-century United States, according to Marxism, scientific knowledge would be determined by capitalism and reflect the interests of the dominant class. Current scientific projects such as the billions of dollars spent on defense-related scientific research and the Human Genome Initiative would be interpreted by Marxists as reflecting the interests of the dominant class. Relatively small amounts of money going into AIDS research and pollution prevention also coincide with interests of the dominant class.

In strict Marxist feminism, where class is emphasized over gender, only bourgeois (liberal) feminism or proletarian feminism can exist. A bourgeois woman scientist would be expected to produce scientific knowledge that would be similar to that produced by a bourgeois man scientist, but that would be different from that produced by a proletarian woman scientist. Some of the data (Holloway, 1993) demonstrating that many other countries, including many less developed countries, produce a higher percentage of women scientists than the United States, might be explained using a Marxist feminist analysis. In many of these countries, such as the Philippines, Brazil, Turkey, India, Portugal, and Thailand, class may be a more significant factor than gender for distinguishing who goes into science (Barinaga, 1994).

Socialist feminism places class and gender on equal ground as factors that determine the position and perspective of a particular individual in society. Socialist feminism asserts that the special position of women within (or as) a class gives them a specific standpoint that provides them with a particular world view. This world view from the standpoint of women is supposed to be more reliable and less distorted than that of men from the same class.

Implicit in the acceptance of the social construction of knowledge is the rejection of the liberal feminist standpoint of the neutral, disinterested observer. Because the prevailing knowledge and science reflect the interests and values of the dominant class and gender, members of that group have an interest in concealing, and may in fact not recognize, the way they dominate. Women oppressed by both class and gender have an advantageous and more comprehensive view of reality. Because of their oppression, they have an interest in perceiving problems with the status quo and with the science and knowledge produced by the dominant class and gender. Simultaneously, their position requires them to understand the science and condition of the dominant group in order to survive. Thus, the standpoint of the oppressed comprehends and includes that of the dominant group, so it is more accurate.

An example that might be cast as socialist feminism is the current work of the National Breast Cancer Coalition. Dissatisfied with the research direction and solutions provided by the modern medical establishment, which was seen as reflecting the interests of the dominant gender and the upper class, the National Breast Cancer Coalition, made up of over 250 organizations nationwide, on October 18, 1993 presented the President and First Lady with petitions containing 2.6 million signatures demanding a comprehensive strategy plan to end the breast cancer epidemic (Women's Community Cancer Project, 1994). In 1992, the Women's Community Cancer Project presented *A Woman's Cancer Agenda: The Demands* to the National Cancer Institute and the federal government asking for alternative treatments and research into environmental causes for the breast cancer epidemic (WCCP, 1992).

Socialist feminism provides a theoretical framework that might be used to explain several issues that continue to be problematic for women in science. Repeated studies have demonstrated that women pursuing graduate training in scientific fields receive less financial aid or different types of financial aid (Vetter, 1996) compared with their male counterparts. For example, the National Science Foundation (1992) documented that women graduate students were more likely to receive teaching assistantships, while male graduate students received research assistantships. Although women often enjoy teaching and are considered to be good teachers, the data, work with equipment, and laboratory procedures developed in research assistantships are more directly applicable to completing research for a Ph.D. dissertation.

Teaching assistantships may prolong the number of years it takes women to complete their graduate work in the sciences. Extension of the time in graduate school becomes especially difficult for women who may receive smaller amounts of financial aid from their institutions, are less likely to obtain federal support, and are more likely than men to have to support themselves during graduate study (Vetter, 1996). Socialist feminism would suggest that the differential treatment of women in financial aid situations provides an example of gender intersecting with class, since higher education in general is available only to those who have adequate resources or can defer paid employment to further their education beyond high school. The time commitment for science and engineering education in particular makes it especially difficult for individuals who must work extensively outside of academia to finance their education.

Women scientists on the average earn less than their male counterparts; the overall salary gap between men and women doctoral scientists in 1991 was about $12,000 per year, with some variation by field (Vetter, 1996). Women scientists and engineers also encounter two to five times the amount of unemployment or underemployment (Vetter, 1996) experienced by their male peers. Despite their relatively lower earnings and higher unemployment compared with men scientists, women scientists fare better than women professionals with comparable training in female-dominated fields. Since science and engineering continue to be male-dominated occupations, women who become scientists and engineers benefit somewhat from the higher wages associated with traditionally male fields, compared with women who enter traditionally female-dominated occupations or fields where women with 4 or more years of college in 1990 earned average salaries ($28,017) that were only slightly above the average salary ($26,653) of men with only a high school diploma and well below the salary of men with a bachelor's degree ($39,238) (Bureau of the Census, 1992). Socialist feminism suggests that the labor market, including the scientific labor market, is gender-stratified as well as class-divided.

Mathematics often becomes the gatekeeping course that determines whether students will be able to pursue courses in science and engineering. To a student without the full complement of 4 years of high school mathematics, 75% of college majors are closed (Sells, 1975). These tend to be the majors in scientific and technical fields, which lead to higher-paying professions with considerable stability.

More girls than boys drop out of high school mathematics (Office of Technology Assessment, 1987) before they have completed the 4-year sequence. Studies have shown that girls who drop out of mathematics in high school and women who switch from mathematics or science majors in college do not do so because of poor grades (Arnold, 1987; Gardner, 1986). The grades of the females leaving are as good as or better than those of the males persisting in the science and mathematics courses. Whatever they studied, the women earned consistently higher grade point averages in college than the men, and the differences were greatest in the traditionally male-dominated fields of engineering, science, and business (Vetter, 1996). A variety of factors, such as differential responses of guidance counselors, parents (Keynes, 1989), and peers to the desire and discussion surrounding decisions to drop out of mathematics or science, may be responsible for the differential persistence rates of males compared with females. For example, parents tend to praise their daughters' hard work in attaining good grades, while attributing their sons' success to talent (Keynes, 1989). As a group, parents have lower educational aspirations for their sons than for their daughters (Adelman, 1991).

A socialist feminist analysis of the gender-differentiated dropout rates for mathematics despite the superior grades of a female, might focus on an analysis of so-called gatekeeping courses in our educational system. In addition to "weeding out" individuals with less skill in a particular area, gatekeeping courses may remove other individuals by differential encouragement (Davis, 1993; Keynes, 1989). Some individuals are removed from the pipeline due to lack of ability and/or performance (which may be related to class, given the structure of public schools in the United States). For females, differential encouragement to continue in mathematics, particularly when difficulties arise, may provide an additional filter.

Studies have documented that when computer camps are relatively inexpensive (less than $100), approximately one-third of the enrollees are girls; when the cost exceeds $1,000, female enrollment drops to one-sixth (Sanders, 1995). This study, coupled with ones (Martinez & Mead, 1988; Sanders, 1985) documenting that families buy computers more often for their sons than for their daughters, suggests that families may provide different amounts of money and emphasis on mathematics, differentiating by gender and possible career goals for their children.

Some projects to attract and retain girls and women in science demonstrate knowledge of the intersection of class with gender as a particular problem. Most projects directed toward K–12 girls have a component designed to encourage females to stay in mathematics. Staying in mathematics in college provides a direct path to more lucrative livelihoods for women, since women achieve near pay equity in some occupations (accounting, management, and engineers) as a correlate of the amount of mathematics they studied in college (Adelman, 1991).

A few programs, such as Operation SMART, run by Girls Incorporated (Wahl, 1993), target girls from the inner city and lower socioeconomic strata. Their emphases on science, hands-on activities, and building teamwork through sports, represent deliberate attempts to provide girls from urban and lower-income families with experiences often available only to boys or to girls from higher-income families to develop skills useful for persisting in science and other male-dominated professions. In their recognition of the role that the intersection of class and gender plays as a barrier for these girls, such programs might be interpreted as adopting a socialist feminist perspective.

AFRICAN AMERICAN/WOMANIST AND RACIAL/ETHNIC FEMINISM

Like socialist feminism, African American/womanist or racial/ethnic feminism also rejects individualism and positivism for social construction as an approach to knowledge. It is based on the African American critique of a Eurocentric approach to knowledge. In addition to the rejection of objectivity and value neutrality associated with the positivist approach accepted by liberal feminism, African American approaches critique dichotomization of knowledge, or at least the identification of science with the first half, and African American with the latter half, of the following dichotomies: culture/nature; rational/emotional; objective/subjective; quantitative/qualitative; active/passive; focused/diffuse; independent/dependent; mind/body; self/others; knowing/being. African American critiques also question methods that distance the observer from the object of study, thereby denying a facet of the social construction of knowledge.

Whereas Marxism posits class as the organizing principle around which the struggle for power exists, African American critiques maintain that race is the primary oppression. African Americans critical of the scientific enterprise may view it as a function of white Eurocentric interests. The facts that African Americans are underrepresented in the population of scientists while Caucasians are overrepresented, relative to their respective percentages in the population as a whole (NSF, 1994c), makes it particularly likely that in its choice of problems for study, methods, and theories and conclusions drawn from the data, the scientific enterprise does represent and function to further white Eurocentric interests.

A strict, traditional interpretation of African American critiques would suggest that scientific knowledge produced by African American women would more closely resemble scientific knowledge produced by African American men than that produced by white women. In contrast, African American feminist critiques (Giddings, 1984; Hooks, 1981, 1983, 1990; Lorde, 1984) assert that in contemporary society, women suffer oppression due to their gender as well as race. For African American women, racism and sexism become intertwining oppressions that provide them with a different perspective and standpoint from that of either white women or African American men.

In addition to the underrepresentation of African Americans in science, other evidence suggests that science and science education may represent white Eurocentric interests. Despite much more limited funding and other resources, historically black colleges and universities have produced a much higher percentage of African American scientists (Matyas & Malcom, 1991) than have integrated institutions of higher education. Although such integrated institutions enroll larger numbers of African American students than do historically black colleges and universities, some combination of black role models as faculty, encouragement, and lack of identification of certain majors with a particular race at the historically black colleges and universities yields more African American scientists.

The work of Treisman (1992) suggests that isolation or separation of students from their racial peers may have a negative impact on their persistence in mathematics and science. Treisman (1992) demonstrated that African American and Hispanic students were more likely to drop out of mathematics when they were not in study groups or when they were the only person from their race in a study group. Persistence in mathematics was facilitated when two or more students of the same race were in the same study group.

Because of the importance of community and the ethos within the African American community that those who are successful have an obligation to return something to their communities, some careers in science may present conflicts for some African Americans. In some well-documented cases, science and scientific research have been used to produce information that may help white Eurocentric interests while clearly harming the African American community. Such was the case with the Tuskegee Syphilis Experiment (Jones, 1981). African American students majoring in science may be more eager to pursue careers such as medicine, where they can provide positive services that clearly aid and keep them connected with their home communities, rather than moving thousands of miles away to work on a nuclear accelerator that may be of questionable benefit to their own community. An African American analysis provides a perspective on the question of why many projects, such as the Howard Hughes grants, targeted toward minority students have succeeded in attracting them in large numbers to careers in medicine but not to basic science research.

As an African American feminist analysis would suggest, African American women suffer the effects of racism, not an obstacle for their white sisters, and sexism, not experienced by their black brothers. In their survey of programs for women, minorities, and the disabled in science, Matyas and Malcom (1991) found that most of the programs directed toward minorities had no particular component for women; most of the programs directed toward women failed to attract women of color. Treisman's (1992) work, while thoroughly exploring the effects of race on group work in mathematics, fails to address the effects of gender in group dynamics. Similarly, much of the work on gender dynamics in group interactions (Kramarae & Treichler, 1986; Lakoff, 1975; Tannen, 1990) fails to explore the effect of race.

An African American feminist analysis suggests why African American women have fallen through the cracks in research and programs to attract and retain in science. Such an analysis also explains why a historically black women's college such as Spelman has produced a disproportionately large number of successful women scientists (Falconer, 1989). With African American women role models on the faculty at Spelman and teaching approaches geared toward students, African American young women receive the focus and attention missing from other programs to attract and retain them in science.

ESSENTIALIST FEMINISM

Essentialist feminist theory focuses on differences between women and men due to biology, specifically secondary sex characteristics and reproductive systems. Frequently, essentialist feminism may encompass gender differences in visuo-spatial and verbal ability, aggression and other behavior, and other physical and mental traits based on prenatal or pubertal hormone exposure. Nineteenth-century essentialist feminists (Blackwell, 1875/1976; Calkins, 1896; Tanner, 1896) often accepted the ideas of male essentialist scientists, such as Freud (1924) (anatomy is destiny) or Darwin as interpreted by the social Darwinists, that there are innate differences between men and women. These nineteenth-century essentialist feminists proposed that the biologically based gender differences meant that women were inferior to men in some physical (Blackwell, 1895/1976; Smith-Rosenberg, 1975) and mental (Hollingsworth, 1914; Tanner, 1896) traits, but that they were superior in others. Biological essentialism formed the basis for the supposed moral superiority of women that nineteenth-century suffragettes (DuBois, Kelly, Kennedy, Korsmeyer, & Robinson, 1985; Hartmann & Banner, 1974) used as a persuasive argument for giving women the vote.

In the earlier phases of the second wave of feminism, most feminist scientists (Bleier, 1979; Fausto-Sterling, 1992; Hubbard, 1979; Rosser, 1982) fought against some sociobiological research, such as that by Wilson (1975), Trivers (1972), and Dawkins (1976), and some hormone and brain lateralization research (Buffery & Gray, 1972; Gorski, Harlan, Jacobson, Shryne, & Southam, 1980; Goy & Phoenix, 1971; Sperry, 1974) that seemed to provide biological evidence for differences in mental and behavioral characteristics between males and females. Essentialism was seen as a tool for conservatives who wished to keep women in the home and out of the workplace. More recently, feminists have re-examined essentialism from perspectives ranging from conservative to radical (Corea, 1985; Dworkin, 1983; MacKinnon, 1982, 1987; O'Brien, 1981; Rich, 1976), with a recognition that biologically based differences between the sexes might imply superiority and power for women in some arenas.

Many of the earlier projects to attract and retain women in science might be seen as underpinned by an essentialist theoretical perspective. Programs to improve the visuo-spatial ability of females (Wheeler & Harris, 1979), increase problem-solving ability, or provide assertiveness training might be interpreted as essentialist feminist, if biological differences such as X-linked genes for visuo-spatial ability (Benbow & Stanley, 1980) and hormonal differences causing differential aggression patterns between males and females serve as the rationale for such programs.

Some interpretations of research such as that by Belenky and colleagues (1986) on *Women's Ways of Knowing* and by Gilligan (1982; Gilligan, Ward, & Taylor, 1988) on women's moral and ethical decision making, may spring from an essentialist feminist perspective. Programs that develop methods of teaching science and mathematics more in tune with preferred ways of learning for the majority of females, apply such research. If the individuals developing and implementing these programs believe and convey to the students that they may learn science more easily because these techniques were developed to account for the inherent biological factors that make males and females learn differently, such programs might be said to use an essentialist feminist perspective.

EXISTENTIALIST FEMINISM

In contrast to essentialist feminists, many individuals who develop and implement exactly the same types of programs as described above do so from an existentialist perspective. Existentialist feminism, first elaborated by Simone de Beauvoir (1974), suggests that women's "otherness" and the social construction of gender rest on society's interpretation of biological differences, rather than the actual biological differences themselves.

> The enslavement of the female to the species and the limitations of her various powers are extremely important facts; the body of woman is one of the essential elements in her situation in the world. But that body is not enough to define her as woman; there is no true living reality except as manifested by the conscious individual through activities and in the bosom of a society. Biology is not enough to give an answer to the question that is before us: why is woman the other? (de Beauvoir, 1974, p. 51)

In other words, it is the value that society assigns to biological differences between males and females that has led woman to play the role of the Other (Tong, 1989); it is not the biological differences themselves. Existentialist feminism would suggest that visuo-spatial differences between males and females and disparate preferential learning styles between the two sexes might be the result of the differential treatment and reactions that males and females in our society receive based on their biology.

For example, studies demonstrating that parents and other adults present more visual objects or toys to baby boys and talk and interact verbally more with girls to comfort and quiet them when they are upset might partially explain the differing visuo-spatial ability of boys and verbal ability of girls. These studies and others documenting differential treatment of girls and boys from birth onward (Sadker & Sadker, 1994), when coupled with sex-role stereotyping enforced by toys and extracurricular activities, indicate reasons why males and females in our society may develop different learning styles and skills. Playing video games, building model airplanes, and working with chemistry and erector sets provide boys with practice in visuo-spatial skills in play activities. In contrast, playing with dolls, talking on the telephone, and playing school stimulate verbal and interactional skills in girls.

Superficially, programs to address the enhancement of girls' visuo-spatial abilities, to provide them practice in using circuit boards, or to teach them to approach topics in a more relational fashion (Belenky et al., 1986) that are developed using an existentialist theoretical framework would resemble in content and approaches, and might be exactly the same as, those that are undergirded by an essentialist feminist perspective. The difference would lie in the rationale for the programs, which might or might not be expressed to the participants. For essentialist feminists, inherent biological differences become the rationale for such programs. In contrast, the differential treatment, activities, and social experiences that boys and girls in our society have because of their underlying biological differences, would constitute the rationale for such programs evolved from an existentialist perspective.

PSYCHOANALYTIC FEMINISM

In many ways, psychoanalytic feminism takes a stance similar to that of existentialist feminism. Derived from Freudian theory, psychoanalysis posits that girls and boys develop contrasting gender roles because they experience their sexuality differently and deal differently with the stages of psychosexual development. Based on the Freudian prejudice that anatomy is destiny, psychoanalytic theory assumes that biological sex will lead to different ways for boys and girls to resolve the Oedipus and castration complexes that arise during the phallic stage of normal sexual development. As was the situation with existentialism, psychoanalysis recognizes that gender construction is not biologically essential; in "normal" gender construction, the biological sex of the child–caretaker interaction differs depending on the sex of the child (and possibly that of the primary caretaker; in some cases it is same sex, in others opposite). However, psychoanalytic theory is not strictly biologically deterministic, since cases of "abnormal" sexuality may result when gender construction is opposite to or not congruent with biological sex.

In recent years, a number of feminists have become interested again in Freud's theories, after a period of attacking Freudian and successor analytic theories (Firestone, 1970; Friedan, 1974; Millett, 1970). Rejecting the biological determinism in Freud, Dinnerstein (1977) and Chodorow (1978) in particular have used an aspect of psychoanalytic theory known as object relations theory to examine the construction of gender and sexuality. Chodorow and Dinnerstein examine the Oedipal stage of psychosexual development to determine why the construction of gender and sexuality in this stage usually results in male dominance. They conclude that the gender differences resulting in male dominance can be traced to the fact that in our society, women are the primary caretakers for most infants and children.

Accepting most Freudian ideas about the Oedipus complex, Chodorow and Dinnerstein conclude that boys are pushed to be independent, distant, and autonomous from their female caretakers, while girls are permitted to be more dependent, intimate, and less individuated from their mothers or female caretakers. Building on the work of Chodorow and Dinnerstein, feminists (Harding, 1986; Hein, 1981; Keller, 1982) have explored how the gender identity proposed by object relations theory with women as caretakers, might lead to more men choosing careers in science.

Keller (1982, 1985) in particular applied the work of Chodorow and Dinnerstein to suggest how science has become a masculine province that excludes women and causes women to exclude themselves from it. Science is a masculine province not only in the fact that it is populated mostly by men but also in the choice of experimental topics, use of male subjects for experimentation, interpretation and theorizing from data, as well as the practice and applications of science undertaken by the scientists. Keller (1982, 1985) suggests that since the scientific method stresses objectivity, rationality, distance, and autonomy of the observer from the object of study (i.e., the positivist neutral observer), individuals who feel comfortable with independence, autonomy, and distance will be most likely to become scientists. Because most caretakers during the Oedipal phase are female, most individuals in our culture who will be comfortable as scientists will be male. The type of science they create will, in turn, reflect those same characteristics of independence, distance, and autonomy. It is on this basis that feminists have suggested that the objectivity and rationality of science are synonymous with a male approach to the physical, natural world.

Although some adaptations of science teaching to accommodate the ways women learn more easily, as suggested by the research of Belenky and colleagues (1986), may evolve from individuals who hold essentialist or existentialist feminist theoretical perspectives, many people proposing such adaptations are likely to align themselves with a psychoanalytic perspective. The particular interest of females in the social applications of science (Hynes, 1989, 1995; Rosser, 1990), in the connection of science to human beings (Harding, 1985; Lie & Bryhni, 1983; Rosser, 1990), and in feelings for the organism under study (Goodfield, 1981; Keller, 1983) seems understandable in light of the differences encouraged in males and females by the primary caretaker, as suggested by psychoanalytic feminism.

Mentoring of female students by women scientists (Association for Women in Science, 1993) may be particularly crucial for attracting and retaining women in science because women are socialized to value connection. Psychoanalytic feminism also would suggest that female students might feel more comfortable having a closer degree of dependence on and connection with a female mentor than they would with a male mentor. The notion of a critical mass of female students in a class, the success women's colleges have in retaining women in science (Sebrechts, 1992; Tidball, 1986), and the significance of women in science dormitories or other living arrangements where connection among female students is supported, might be explained partially by the socialization of women for close interaction and interdependence with other females.

Part of the success of programs such as EQUALS (Steinmark, Thompson, & Cossey, 1986) may be attributed to a component in which parents are included explicitly as one of the factors that must be targeted for the successful recruitment of females to science. Although parents serve as a critical determinant in the career choice of both males and females, psychoanalytic feminism would suggest that because females are encouraged to be less separate, parents, especially the mother, may be particularly important in the career decision of females. Women who choose engineering as a career are particularly likely to have no brothers (Vetter, 1996).

Other programs to encourage women in science also might be explained as attempts to compensate for the lack of autonomy, separation, and independence that girls might have experienced during resolution of the psychoanalytic crisis with female primary caretakers. Programs to teach females to be risk-takers; strategies that foster competition, rather than cooperation and connection among peers (including female–female peers); and assertiveness training might be viewed as attempts to correct the "deficit" in female socialization and to equip women to enter the world of scientists in which competition, objectivity, and separation are fostered.

Research demonstrating that male mentors provide significant, but different, information and support for female students compared with that provided by female mentors (Yentsch & Sindermann, 1992) suggests that male mentors play a crucial role that may come from their socialization as more separate, distant, and autonomous individuals whose personalities may be more congruent with the culture of science (Haraway, 1989; Keller, 1985). Similarly, the studies documenting the importance of both parents (Hennig & Jardim, 1977; O'Connell & Russo, 1983), including the father and professional mothers, in encouraging daughters who become scientists, would suggest that they may compensate for dependence and other characteristics that may be engendered by traditional female primary caretakers.

Psychoanalytic feminism implies that if both males and females become involved as primary caretakers of infants and if both male and female scientists serve as mentors for students of both genders, gender roles will be less polarized. Science itself might then become gender-free and less reflective of its current masculine perspective. Equal numbers of men and women would be attracted to the study of science, and the science produced by male and female scientists would be indistinguishable since it would be freer of gender constraints.

RADICAL FEMINISM

Radical feminism, in contrast to psychoanalytic feminism and liberal feminism, rejects the possibility of a gender-free science or a science developed from a neutral, objective perspective. Radical feminism maintains that women's oppression is the first, most widespread, and deepest oppression (Jaggar & Rothenberg, 1992). Since men dominate and control most institutions, politics, and knowledge in our society, they reflect a male perspective and are effective in oppressing women. Scientific institutions, practice, and knowledge are particularly male-dominated and have been documented by many feminists (Bleier, 1984; Fee, 1982; Griffin, 1978; Haraway, 1978, 1989; Hubbard, 1990; Keller, 1985; Merchant, 1979; Rosser, 1990) to be especially effective patriarchal tools to control and harm women. Radical feminism rejects most scientific theories, data, and experiments precisely because they not only exclude women but also are not women-centered.

The theory that radical feminism proposes is evolving (Tong, 1989) and is not as well developed as some of the other feminist theories for reasons springing fairly directly from the nature of radical feminism itself. First, it is radical. That means that it rejects most of currently accepted ideas about scientific epistemology—what kinds of things can be known, who can be a knower, and how beliefs are legitimated as knowledge—and methodology, that is, the general structure of how theory finds its application in particular scientific disciplines. Second, unlike the feminisms previously discussed, radical feminism does not have its basis in a theory such as Marxism, positivism, psychoanalysis, or existentialism, already developed for decades by men. Since radical feminism is based in women's experience, it rejects feminisms rooted in theories developed by men based on their experience and world view. Third, the theory of radical feminism must be developed by women and based in women's experience (MacKinnon, 1987). Because radical feminism maintains that the oppression of women is the deepest, most widespread, and historically first oppression, women have had few opportunities to come together, understand their experiences collectively, and develop theories based on those experiences.

Radical feminism deviates considerably from other feminisms in its view of how beliefs are legitimated as knowledge. A successful strategy that women use to obtain reliable knowledge and to correct distortions of patriarchal ideology, is the consciousness raising group (Jaggar, 1983). Using their personal experiences as a basis, women meet together in communal, nonhierarchical groups to examine their experiences in order to determine what counts as knowledge (MacKinnon, 1987).

Research by Tidball (1986) and Sebrechts (1992) has documented the disproportionate number of female scientists who received their undergraduate education at women's colleges. A variety of factors present in women's colleges, such as collective living with other females, a relatively large number of female faculty to serve as role models, teaching strategies geared to a female-only audience, and the absence of gender role prescriptions for use of equipment or major selection, may account for the success of women's colleges in attracting and retaining women scientists. Radical feminism would suggest that the presence of an environment that permits female-only classes and discussions would serve the role of a consciousness-raising group to influence women in their decision to become scientists.

Several strategies, such as women in science groups, summer science camps for girls, or after-school programs to encourage girls in computers or science, attempt to provide a female-only experience within the overall context of a coeducational environment. In the female-only environment, concepts can be introduced at the appropriate developmental stage for females. Teaching techniques more in tune with female styles, which emphasize interrelationships and connection, and cooperative approaches, rather than competition for equipment with males, may be attempted. These programs seek to duplicate some of the benefits of the single-sex environment for females found naturally at a women's college.

LESBIAN SEPARATIST FEMINISM

Lesbian separatism, often seen as an offshoot of radical feminism, would suggest that in a patriarchal society separation from men is necessary for females to understand their experiences and explore the possibility of becoming scientists. Lesbian separatist theory would provide an explanation for the success of women's colleges in producing a much higher proportion of female scientists than comparable private liberal arts colleges that are coeducational. The absence of male classmates, designation of certain majors as predominately for one sex, and coeducational science-related activities, coupled with increased numbers of female science faculty, living with females only, and strong alumnae role models, create a mini-female-only environment within a larger patriarchal society. To the extent that interactions among the women students simulate a consciousness-raising group that permits them to explore their ideas, attitudes, and beliefs about science and becoming a scientist in the absence of a hierarchical structure, these environments simulate the methods of radical feminism.

POSTMODERN FEMINISM

In the discussion of liberal feminism earlier in this chapter, I emphasized its fundamental assumptions of individualism and positivism and the extent to which the traditional method for scientific discovery also shares these two assumptions. Based on liberal humanism (Rothfield, 1990), which suggests that the self is an individual, autonomous, self-constitutive human being, liberal feminists (Grimshaw, 1986; Lloyd, 1984; Tapper, 1986) critique liberal humanism for its implicit assumption that the abstract individual is male or congruent with man. While criticizing liberal humanists for inappropriately universalizing to all individuals, both male and female, what are really characteristics of men, liberal feminists do not reject or critique other aspects of liberal humanism, such as equality and freedom of the individual (Rothfield, 1990). Liberal feminism suggests that women have a unified voice and can be addressed universally (Gunew, 1990).

In contrast to liberal humanism, postmodernism problematizes the self in "decentered modes of discourse. The self is no longer regarded as self-constitutive, but rather as a production of, variously, ideology, discourse, the structure of the unconscious, and/or language" (Rothfield, 1990, p. 132). At least some postmodern feminists (Cixous & Clement, 1986; Kristeva, 1984, 1987) suggest further that women, having been marginalized by a dominant male discourse, may be in a privileged position, that of outsider to the discourse that otherwise might threaten to rigidify all thought along previously established lines. Perhaps women can find the holes in what appeared solid, sure, and unified. In short, postmodernism dissolves the universal subject, and postmodern feminism dissolves the possibility that women may speak in a unified voice or that they may be addressed universally. Race, class, nationality, sexual orientation, and other factors prevent such unity and universality. Although one woman may share certain characteristics and experiences with other women because of her biological sex, a number of factors—her particular race, class, and sexual differences compared with other women, along with the construction of gender that her country and society give to someone living in her historical period—prevent universalizing her experiences to women in general. Insofar as postmodern feminism questions the nature of understanding the subject as defined in the Western world, it also puts the entire edifice of knowledge into question. This questioning may create the cracks or openings through which marginalized women might be able to walk.

As programs for women in science have increased in number and have operated for lengthier periods of time, individuals administering such programs have become wary of suggesting that strategies that work to attract and retain particular groups of girls and women to science might work for all women. It has become increasingly clear that no panacea will be found to make science, mathematics, and engineering attractive to all women and girls.

Some of the more successful programs have begun to target specific groups of girls. Several projects, such as the Model Program to Motivate and Educate Women Minority High School Students for Careers in Science, run as a partnership between Wright State University and the Dayton Board of Education (NSF, 1994c), are aimed at girls from particular racial/ethnic backgrounds. Other projects select participants on the basis of class, geographic location, academic ability, or age. For example, the New Careers in the Sciences for Rural Girls in Nebraska Project (NSF, 1994c) is geared particularly toward girls from rural families. Although many programs to attract girls to science aim at particularly gifted students, some projects (Tobias, 1990) target the "second tier" of girls who tend to receive Bs and have above-average, but not outstanding, scores on achievement tests. The Regional Employer–Education Partnerships to Attract Women into Engineering at the University of Tennessee–Chattanooga (NSF, 1994c) aids nontraditional-age, working-class women returning to school who seek careers in engineering.

Few of the individuals who design and implement such programs specified for particular groups of women are likely to be aware of postmodernism or to think of themselves as operating from a postmodern feminist perspective. However, in their recognition that the standpoint and experiences that impinge on any one girl or woman in her decision to become a scientist are shaped by a multitude of socially constructed factors—including, but not limited to, her race/ethnic background, class, sexual orientation, family dynamics, education, and intellectual abilities, as well as her gender—they are operating from a perspective consistent with postmodern feminist theory.

CONCLUSIONS

As feminism of the latter half of the twentieth century has matured, feminist theory has become increasingly complex. Springing from a growing knowledge that the diversity among women meant that the universalism suggested by liberal feminism was not appropriate to describe the experiences of all women, other feminist theories evolved. Although essentialist and existential feminism might be seen to imply that biological sex and its interpretation in our society provide an overriding similarity to the experiences of all women, other feminist theories suggest that other factors may be equally or more important than sex/gender. Marxist feminism emphasizes the importance of class as well as gender. African American, Chicana, Asian American, and other racial/ethnic theories of feminism underline the significance of both race and gender/sex. Family dynamics and the role of the primary caretaker become powerful determinants in psychoanalytic feminism, while radical feminism questions all categories and knowledge developed in a patriarchal society in which women are oppressed. Postmodern feminism suggests that each woman in each society during a particular historical period may have a differing standpoint from which to view the world, as shaped by her race, class, and numerous other factors, including her gender.

As women in science programs have begun to evolve, partially as a result of feminism, and in some cases with little formal knowledge of feminism or feminist theory, they too have become increasingly complex. Most projects continue to state goals and objectives that might be described as liberal feminist in their attempts to remove overt and covert barriers and discrimination so that females will have the same access as males to careers in science and mathematics. Although few individuals developing such programs have a grasp of the breadth and depth of feminist theories, the programs they develop to attract and retain women in science include elements from feminist theoretical frameworks ranging from Marxist through African American to radical. Larger numbers and increased longevity of projects have led to a recognition that no one universal strategy will reach all females. The evolution of particular strategies in response to the needs and experiences of individual females whose situation is shaped by a variety of factors, may demonstrate a postmodern feminist approach to what works to attract and retain women in science.

CHAPTER 6

Applying Feminist Theories to Women and Science Programs

In 1993, the NSF initiated its Program for Women and Girls to reflect a reorganization and expansion of the gender-focused component of the Career Access Program. The reorganization established Model Projects for Women and Girls, Experimental Projects for Women and Girls, and Information Dissemination Activities.

The overall goal of the Program is to elicit projects that have high potential for effecting both short- and long-term changes in the representation of women in science, engineering and mathematics careers and the overall SEM education of women and girls. Efforts involved in the initiative address education issues from preschool through the graduate level, as well as professional issues (NSF, 1993a).

Model Projects are designed to produce significant and immediate changes through the design and implementation of innovative, short-term, highly focused activities that improve the access to and/or retention of women and girls in SEM education and/or careers. The award amount for Model Projects typically does not exceed $100,000 and the duration is usually 1 to 2 years.

Experimental Projects focus on comprehensive projects to produce long-term infrastructure changes and bring about permanent results. The award amount for Experimental Projects may be up to $300,000 per year for as long as 3 years.

Information Dissemination Activities attempt to accelerate efforts to increase girls' and women's involvement in SEM areas through strategies such as conferences and publications. Not exceeding $75,000, these Information Dissemination Activities and other Special Projects tend to target one-time events or unusual opportunities to attract and retain women in SEM.

I thought it might be useful to apply the feminist theory scheme from liberal through postmodern feminism, described in Chapter 5, to classify or characterize abstracts of 80 projects funded by the National Science Foundation through fiscal year 1994 under the Program for Women and Girls (and including some gender-focused proposals from the older Career Access Program). Using feminist theories as a basis for categorizing women in science projects funded by the Program for Women and Girls produced some interesting results.

First, as suggested in Chapter 5, virtually all projects articulated, either overtly or covertly, liberal feminist goals—an overarching aim of achieving equity or equal access for women in science. Second, none of the projects could be categorized as essentialist (i.e., none of the abstracts suggested that biological differences in hormones, brain anatomy, or other characteristics were responsible for the differences in access, representation, or achievement between men and women in science). This is not surprising, since people who believe that innate biological differences cause lower numbers of women in science are unlikely to propose projects to change the educational or extracurricular environment as a mechanism to attract and retain women in science.

Finally, in reading the abstracts and through hearing principal investigators describe their projects, threads, and sometimes dominance, of theories other than liberal feminism typically emerge. Although most projects include some aspects of more than one feminist theory, often a particular theory characterizes the core around which the project is organized. Of the 80 projects funded, I was able to categorize 67 under a single theory. Only 11 of the projects found their major basis from more than one theory. One was classified under three theories; the other 10 had roots in two theories.

LIBERAL FEMINISM: ATTEMPTS AT EQUITY

Almost all the projects provided a rationale for their existence in terms of some form of liberal feminism, such as increasing the numbers of women scientists to equal the numbers of men scientists. However, only four[1] used language that led me to classify them in the liberal feminist category.

Originally funded under the Career Access Program, the Committee on Women in Science and Engineering series of projects, for which Linda Skidmore (previously Linda Dix) serves as the principal investigator, exemplifies the liberal feminist category. Its abstract reads:

> The continuing Committee on Women in Science and Engineering (CWSE), within the Office of Scientific and Engineering Personnel of the National Research Council, is comprised of expert scientists and engineers who are particularly knowledgeable about the under participation of women in the technological work force of the United States. This project helps to fund activities of the Committee to achieve greater representation of women in science and engineering (S&E) at undergraduate, graduate, postdoctoral, and professional levels in the United States. CWSE is

continuing and expanding the multifaceted program of activities developed during the past three years to address the under representation of women in S&E careers. While recognition of the barriers to participation in science and engineering by women, and of the need for more comprehensive measures to spur the development of female scientists and engineers, have been evident for some time, parity representation of scientists and engineers has not been achieved. CWSE is helping to address this problem by: serving as a resource to collect and disseminate data on the needs of and opportunities for women in science and engineering; exerting its influence on the S&E community, and society as a whole; working toward the removal of barriers to the participation of women in the sciences and engineering; encouraging interactions between concerned groups; and stimulating development of innovative programs to increase the representation of women in scientific and engineering careers. The Committee is setting an example in the S&E community, playing an effective role in revealing the status of and the opportunities for women in the areas in society, as well as making recommendations for policy and program changes that will enhance the participation of women in S&E careers. (Skidmore, 1994)

This abstract typifies a liberal feminist project. Through such approaches as using "expert scientists and engineers" and a goal of "parity representation of scientists and engineers," it seeks equity for women in science without seeking to change the status quo of the way science is taught and practiced. Its emphasis on "removal of barriers to participation" and "enhancing the participation of women in S&E careers," makes no critique of the value-free and objective nature of science or the scientific enterprise or of the positivistic approach to scientific research.

The host institution for this award, the National Academy of Sciences, represents the pinnacle of success and prestige within the scientific community in the United States. In 1994, out of 367,440 employed scientists (excluding engineers), .6% had been elected to the National Academy of Sciences; 95% of the members are men (NRC, 1994). Activities to "collect and disseminate data" and "working toward the removal of barriers" document unjust discrimination against women. These activities use the scientific method itself to challenge the underrepresentation of women as a potential form of bias; equity for women scientists would serve as a corrective to make the scientific method function better, if bias has resulted from too many male scientists.

SOCIALIST FEMINISM: SIGNIFICANCE OF CLASS

Ten of the projects[2] stipulated that low-income or low socioeconomic status women and/or girls served as the target population for project efforts. None of the 10 abstracts used language that overtly stated socialist feminist tenets such as "in a capitalistic society, scientific research and knowledge reflect the interests of the dominant class and gender." This is hardly surprising, since these abstracts came from proposals seeking funding from an agency (NSF) of the U.S. government. The language of the abstracts did indicate a recognition, however, that women in general, and low-income women in particular, have been excluded from careers in science, engineering, and mathematics. Rather than emphasizing the standpoint of low-income women and the potential impact of the absence of individuals from such groups on scientific knowledge, the abstracts imply negative effects of exclusion from science on the women themselves. Careers in science and technology become defined as implicit gateways to increased income and upward mobility for women.

The abstract for the Regional Employer–Educational Partnership to Attract Working Women into Engineering, a project directed by Merl Baker at the University of Tennessee–Chattanooga, typifies a project with the dual focus on gender and class common to socialist feminism.

> This model project sought to encourage established working women to embark on an engineering program and receive degrees. One hundred and thirty-three working women registered after being nominated for the program by twenty-five regional employers. Partnerships were successfully established for planning, designing, and sustaining programs integrating jobs and study. Success was achieved in motivating employers to pay fees and provide some time during the day for students to pursue classes. The University strove to enhance student-friendly schedules and delivery modes.
>
> Solutions to retention problems in the program were pursued. Employers were asked to increase support of those already involved in the network, and also to nominate others for future introductory classes. Techniques for retention included more time for day classes, and credit toward degrees for elements of experiential know-how. Parallel efforts to attract younger working women seem highly promising.
>
> The inadequate backgrounds in mathematics of many students and the time required to complete arranged remedial programs at either UTC or regional community colleges were deterrents. This model provided a significant boost for attracting women into engineering. It could become more effective if recognized retention problems are moderated. However, realizing the full potential for relating jobs and structured study for enrolling and graduating women engineers and scientists requires early planning and initiation of a structured program by student-employees immediately after high school graduation. (Baker, 1994)

Located in an area with a substantial working-class population, this project targeted these "working women" who had completed "high school graduation" or its equivalence. Language such as "motivating employers to pay fees" and "credit toward degrees for elements of experiential know-how," as well as the use of "regional community colleges," underline the significance that economic factors play in deterring these women from taking engineering courses while working full time. This abstract only suggests the gender role constraints imposed by family responsibilities through its discussion of "techniques for retention [that] included more time for day classes" and "efforts to attract younger working women." Many of the other nine projects categorized as socialist feminist address the gender as well as class components explicitly.

AFRICAN AMERICAN OR RACIAL/ETHNIC FEMINISM

Emphasis on the intersection of race and gender as deterrents to careers in science, engineering, and mathematics characterize 12[3] of the projects. Much as in the situation with projects categorized as socialist feminist, projects classified as springing from African American feminist theories do not have abstracts that overtly articulate the notion that science and scientific research in the United States represent Eurocentric approaches to knowledge. Instead, the language of the abstracts emphasizes the exclusion of women of color from science.

The abstract for Girls and Science: Linkages for the Future, a project of the American Association for the Advancement of Science, for which Yolanda George serves as the principal investigator, demonstrates this emphasis.

> Based upon the premise that what happens outside the school setting is critical to fostering girls' interest in math and science, AAAS is adapting the successful *Girls and Science: Linkages for the Future* "pass through" training model to deliver hands-on extracurricular science activities to girls, ages 5–17, from underrepresented minority populations, through a network of community-based organizations (CBOs). It is felt that this population is doubly at risk for falling out of the pipeline leading to careers in science, engineering, and mathematics. In this training model, which has been used for years by some CBOs such as the Girl Scouts, AAAS staff are training local trainers who, in turn, are training leaders in their organization to deliver the science activities to the girls. AAAS is utilizing CBOs that already use pass-through models to help establish the training model where it does not now exist.
>
> The effectiveness of the program is being enhanced by including minority female college students enrolled in science programs as assistants, mentors, and role models. A second enhancement is the rerun of parent workshops designed to encourage parents to raise the expectations they hold for their daughters' educational activities. The effectiveness of these enhancements has been proven in other AAAS equity projects. Materials and publications developed by AAAS for similar projects are being adapted where necessary to better meet the needs of the targeted populations. Some new products are also being developed. (George, 1994)

Phrases such as "doubly at risk" and "minority female college students" reinforce the notions of the difficulties faced by women of color in science. The use of "community-based organizations (CBOs)" and "parent workshops" demonstrates the recognition of the significance of community and family, also underlined in African American feminism.

Five (Cid, Dix, Kerr, Marshall, and Warren) of the 12 projects categorized as ethnic/racial feminist also were categorized as socialist feminist. This represents the largest overlap in classification between two categories. In many ways, this intersection is not surprising, since women of color also have lower average income than white men and women or men of color. Since many projects submitted to the Program for Women and Girls target individuals most at risk for dropping out of the science, engineering, and mathematics pipeline, females of color from low-income families become the focus for several projects.

The Career Access Opportunities for Impoverished Minority Children and their Mothers project at the University of Hartford led by Douglas Dix demonstrates the race, class, gender focus.

> This project sought to improve interest and achievement in science among Hartford area elementary children and their parents. Every 3rd, 4th, and 5th grader in Hartford (93% minority enrollment) and its suburb, Bloomfield (80% minority enrollment), was invited to participate in a morning or afternoon program of 12 two-hour Saturday sessions each fall and spring session. Free bus transportation and babysitting were available, and a small stipend was paid to parents and guardians who completed the program with regular attendance. The only requirement for admission was that each child be accompanied at each session by a parent or guardian. Because the program was held on Saturdays, children would not come if it was not fun, and parents would not come if it was only fun. Thus, attendance was one measure of program quality. The fall 1991 program began with 106 parents and guardians divided between morning and afternoon sessions. Over the next 10 weeks, attendance varied between 68 and 100, with a mean of 80. Fourteen parents had perfect attendance, 18 were absent once, 20 were absent twice, and 28 were absent three or four times. Parents and guardians with four or fewer absences received a stipend of $80.
>
> To estimate the role of the stipend in motivating attendance, stipends were distributed to qualifying participants before the end of the program. Of the 53 participants who received stipends before the 11th session, 41 (77%) returned for the 11th session. Of the 75 participants who received stipends before the 12th session, 53 (71%) returned for the 12th session. In response to questionnaires, parents uniformly found the program to have improved their children's, and their own, interest and achievement in science, and to have stimulated interest in science as a career.
>
> Hartford has 26 public elementary schools. Participants from 22 of these schools began the Fall 1991 program and participants from 18 of these schools completed the program. In addition, participants from 4 Hartford parochial schools

and from each of the four Bloomfield elementary and middle schools completed the program. (Dix, 1994)

The abstract emphasizes the importance of financial concerns through repeated discussions of "stipends" and of parental involvement ("the only requirement for admission was that each child be accompanied at each session by a parent or guardian") for these minority women and their children. A feature evident in the program was the attempt to improve the mothers' interest and achievement in science and science careers while also attracting children to science.

EXISTENTIALIST FEMINISM: SOCIETY INTERPRETS THE BODY

Although none of the projects found its basis in essentialist feminist theory, 22[4] were categorized as having existentialist feminist roots. These projects seek to provide girls and women with experiences that may have an impact on their interest and achievement in science and that tend to be more common in the lives of boys and men in our society.

In the abstract for Designing for Equity: A New Approach for Girls and Engineering, principal investigator Margaret Honey describes activities to provide girls with experiences in designing, manipulating, and imagining technical objects.

This project sought to create a new learning context for girls to support and facilitate their experience of themselves as active shapers and designers of engineered objects. To achieve this goal, the project refined the Imagine software prototype, a computer-based design environment, created a set of curricular activities to accompany the program, and created an interactive curriculum guide (the Imagine Tour) to support teachers in implementing this design-based curriculum. "Designing for Equity" helps engage girls in an engineer's activities: creating, reflecting on, researching, and revising designs, and, when appropriate, accessing information to expand knowledge. The activities, and software itself, were specifically designed and modified to encourage girls to reflect on and enact the process of technological design.

The software and integrated curriculum activities were evaluated in an intensive field trial over the course of the spring school term in a diverse, public middle school in New York City. A total of nine 11–13 year-old girls participated in the field test that was offered as an alternative class at the school. The class met twice a week for 8 weeks (one 45 minute period and one 90 minute period).

The goal of the field test was to investigate the following issues: (1) stimulating girls' technological imaginations; (2) articulating technical relationships; and (3) overcoming fears and obstacles. The fourth issue was to support teachers' understanding of the ways in which the Imagine curriculum could be used with their students. Additional software was created to introduce them to the process of designing engineered objects and using Imagine with their students.

The Imagine Tour draws together a variety of information from the research and development phase of the Designing for Equity projects. Using examples of student work, curriculum activities, and reflections from the research and development team, the Imagine Tour enables teachers to see student examples, explore the curriculum activities that led to the students' design ideas, and learn more about the pedagogical issues that arose in the classroom. (Honey, 1994)

The language of the abstract suggests that a theoretical premise underpinning this project is that boys typically have more experience with technology, engineering-type activities, and computers than do girls in this culture. Therefore, the project creates "a new learning context for girls to support and facilitate their experience of themselves as active shapers and designers of engineered objects." The role of teachers as individuals who can support new, creative experiences for girls or reinforce the status quo of gender role experiences and expectations also is recognized.

PSYCHOANALYTIC FEMINISM:
SIGNIFICANCE OF ROLE MODELS AND MENTORING

From reading abstracts describing the projects considered here, it can be relatively difficult to distinguish the underlying theoretical perspectives. The distinction between existentialist and psychoanalytic theoretical underpinnings may appear particularly blurry. Both suggest gender differences in the experiences, messages, and upbringing that boys and girls receive in our society, based on their biological sex. Existentialist feminists propose that these differences emanate from society's reaction to the biological differences; because of their differing anatomy, males and females have a different set of experiences and socialization processes, (de Beauvoir, 1974), including those surrounding science, mathematics, engineering, and technology (SMET). Psychoanalytic feminists propose that the differences spring from the resolution of conflicts in psychosexual development in a society in which females become the primary caretakers for most infants and young children (Chodorow, 1978; Dinnerstein, 1977); boys, in contrast to girls, are encouraged by their female primary caretakers to become more independent and autonomous, which are characteristics more in keeping with the training of scientists (Keller, 1985).

Since many abstracts describe projects that propose to provide females with SMET experiences comparable to those of males in our society, separating the projects into existentialist or psychoanalytic theoretical categories can be relatively arbitrary. If a project particularly emphasized relationships and mentoring, I categorized it in the psychoanalytic category, since the influence of individual human beings on the development of scientists figured centrally in the project. Twenty-seven[5] of the projects fit into this category.

The project for which Barbara Kerr and Sharon Robinson at Arizona State University served as the co-principal investigators exemplifies this categorization, although it also was categorized under socialist and racial/ethnic feminist theories because of its focus on at-risk girls.

> This project was a research-through-service program developing strategies for the career guidance of science and math talented at-risk girls. Career development interventions designed to encourage young women in math and science often fail because they treat career choices in isolation from relationship decisions; they do not focus on girls' values and needs; they are short-term; and they do not use mentors and hands-on activities effectively. This project created a career development intervention which was relationship-oriented, values-based, long-term, and girl-friendly.
>
> About 100 participants took part in the Talented At Risk Girls: Encouragement and Training for Sophomores (TARGETS) program. The participants were 15 year-old girls with high grades in math or science, who were at risk for not achieving their potential. TARGETS girls were Hispanics, Native Americans from four different tribes, African Americans, and Anglo girls from low SES environments. Girls attended the workshop in groups ranging in size from three to ten.
>
> The staff for the project included doctoral level and masters' level counselors trained in working with this population; volunteers from the American Association for University Women, and the Women in Science and Engineering; and, ASU women science faculty.
>
> The first phase of the intervention was a pre-test session and discussion at the girls' home schools. Girls learned about the nature of the program and were challenged to examine their talents and career goals. The second phase of the project was a two-day, intensive career workshop on the ASU campus. Assessment was a core component of the intervention; therefore, the girls were administered vocational, personality, and values inventories which were state of the art instruments. Each girl received an individual counseling session in which she received precise, comprehensive information about her interests, needs, and values, as well as suggestions and encouragement to pursue her goals. In addition, girls participated in a Perfect Future Day exercise in which they were asked to imagine in detail a working day ten years in the future and an At-Risk Discussion in which girls were asked to identify internal and external barriers to the achievement of their goals. Girls left the workshop with a detailed "Personal Map of the Future." (Kerr and Robinson, 1994)

Follow-up activities included letters from counselors on a set schedule and a posttest and discussion group in the home school 4 to 6 months after the workshop. Preliminary analyses of data show increases in self-esteem, math-science efficacy, and career exploration activities immediately following the workshop. Post-tests at home schools helped to clarify the long-term impact of the program. The language of this abstract underlines the interconnection of human values and relationships with SEM for many young women. The project focused on "relationship-oriented, values-based, long-term, and girl-friendly" interventions. The use of counselors, as well as women scientists and engineers, as staff for this program, assigns a priority to relationships as significant factors in the retention of females in science.

RADICAL FEMINISM: WOMEN-CENTERED ENVIRONMENTS

True radical feminism not only suggests that women's oppression is the most widespread and deepest oppression (Jaggar & Rothenberg, 1984), but it also rejects most currently accepted ideas about scientific epistemology and methodology. Abstracts for projects submitted to the National Science Foundation would be unlikely to articulate goals that would be read as a rejection of the kinds of things that can be known and legitimated as knowledge using the scientific method. However, many of the abstracts overtly acknowledge or recognize through a covert assumption that scientific institutions, practice, and knowledge are male-dominated. Through those acknowledgments and recognitions and through their attempts to use women's experience to attract females to science, they might be categorized as based in radical feminism.

The Kieve Science Camp for Girls directed by Sally Crissman models one of the 14[6] projects categorized as based in radical feminist theory.

> Kieve Science Camp for Girls is a one-week residential experience for 60 fourth, fifth, and sixth graders from three rural and peer Maine communities. Building on research and the expertise of Kieve Science Camp instructors and the Kieve Leadership Decisions Institute, this program is designed to tackle issues known to stifle the confidence and enthusiasm of girls in science. All activities are hands-on. Kieve recognizes the importance of informal education: asking questions, exploring, designing, testing, trying again, and reaching decisions based on direct application and evidence are the "daily bread" at camp. Group problem-solving challenges, requiring collaboration, and risk-taking, often a new skill for girls, is encouraged throughout the program, and on the ropes and adventure course. An important goal is a positive attitudinal shift: girls should think science is fun, important in their lives, and that they can be full participants in the scientific world which they inhabit. The carefully selected female instructors and staff address the importance of role models. The inclusion of two teachers from each home school will sustain the successes of the Kieve experience and further spread the Kieve educational methodology. Project staff are documenting and evaluating this program for the purpose of replication. (Crissman, 1994)

The female-only environment of this project permits the students to experience a consciousness-raising group consistent with the methodology of radical feminism. The camp situation permits the girls to explore science in a situation in which they are relatively free and separated from the influence of patriarchy, a notion that lesbian separatism would purport as necessary for girls to understand their relationship with science in our current society.

POSTMODERN FEMINISM: NO UNIVERSAL SOLUTIONS

Since postmodern feminism dissolves the possibility that women speak in a unified voice or can be addressed universally, its implications for attracting women to science suggest that no one approach or solution will work for attracting all women and girls to science, engineering, and mathematics. The standpoint and experiences that impinge on any one girl or woman in her decision to become a scientist are shaped by a multitude of socially constructed factors in addition to gender, including, but not limited to, her race/ethnic background, class, sexual orientation, family dynamics, education, and intellectual abilities.

Given that most of the projects use a variety of approaches, they might all be categorized as operating from a postmodern feminist theoretical base. Two projects[7] explicitly articulated their multiple approaches as mechanisms necessary for attracting women coming from diverse standpoints. The abstract for the Women in Science Project at Dartmouth College, for which Mary Pavone serves as principal investigator, typifies this approach.

The Women in Science Project (WISP) is an innovative program designed to encourage women who enter college with an interest in science to retain their interest and consider careers in science and engineering. The goals of the project are to increase the number of women choosing scientific and technical careers.

Because the reasons for attrition vary from one individual to another, WISP offers a variety of retention strategies under one interdisciplinary "umbrella." WISP was designed to employ strategies of hands-on research activity; support systems including faculty and student role models; and extra encouragement, orientation, and advising programs in a deliberate, comprehensive way with undergraduate women, with particular emphasis on first-year students. Initiated in 1990, the WISP includes: (1) a program of paid part-time research internships for first-year women, (2) a mentoring program, (3) seminars, panel discussions, and informal opportunities to talk with women scientists and engineers in industry, academia, and government, (4) industrial site visits and field trips, (5) a science study room with women tutors, and (6) an electronically distributed newsletter, published every two weeks.

While the Project targets first-year women for the internship program, all undergraduates and graduate students can participate in other programs offered. The Project has attracted nearly 800 undergraduate and graduate participants to date and voluntary participation of a pool of nearly 130 faculty and researchers who have sponsored students in their labs and participate in other ways, such as program speakers and advisors. Faculty from the undergraduate science division, as well as from Dartmouth's Thayer School of Engineering and Medical School, also participate. Nearby cooperating partners in WISP programs include researchers at the Veteran's Administration Research Center, the Montshire Museum of Science, and the U.S. Army Corps of Engineers' Cold Regions Research Laboratory. Dartmouth's president, administration, and faculty fully support the project, and students have received it with great enthusiasm. More than 50% of the women in each incoming class request to participate in the Project.

The notion of an "interdisciplinary 'umbrella'" and a "variety of retention strategies" suggests recognition of the necessity of an eclectic group of approaches. The six components, which range from internships to "a science study room with women tutors," vary "because the reasons for attrition vary from one individual to another." Postmodern theories imply that women have various and unique experiences and backgrounds that contribute to various (as opposed to a universal) reasons for attrition.

CONCLUSIONS

Although the abstracts for almost all of the 80 projects under the Program for Women and Girls articulated equity (a liberal feminist concept) as their overarching goal, most included substantive elements consistent with other feminist theoretical frameworks. Several (11) projects might be categorized under multiple theories or even as consciously selecting a variety of approaches (postmodern). None built on an essentialist foundation; most implied that experiences girls have in our society because of their gender socialization (existentialist and psychoanalytic feminism) might be modified or developed to make science more attractive. Although several abstracts emphasized class (socialist) or race (ethnic) as primary factors deterring females, a substantial number implied that aspects of the nature of science teaching and practice themselves might have to be modified through more radical approaches.

Other individuals applying their conceptions of various feminist theories and reading the same abstracts, might categorize some of the projects differently than I did. I recognize that the decision about which aspects of a project, or words describing it in an abstract, to emphasize may have been somewhat arbitrary. In my opinion, the value of using feminist theories to categorize projects based on their descriptions in abstracts was that it demonstrated the influence of a variety of feminist theories on projects that appeared to state the singular liberal feminist goal of equity.

NOTES

1. The four projects were the 1988 E. Jo Baker project, the 1989–92 Daniels project, and the special projects by Keith and Skidmore (Dix).

2. The principal investigators of the 10 projects include the following individuals: Baker (Merl), Bendet, Cid, Dix, Ginorio, Kerr, Lindsley-Griffin, Marshall, Warren, and Zdravkovich.

3. The principal investigators of the 12 ethnic-centered projects include the following: Batra, Cid, Dix, George, Heller, Holland, Kerr, Marshall, Matute-Bianchi, Rodriguez, Walker (Sharon), and Warren.

4. The principal investigators of the 22 projects include the following: Chandrasekhar, Collins, Crissman, Diggelman, Fentiman, George, Gray, Gulari, Holland, Honey, Kishmere, Lambert, Manogue, McDonald, Onaral, Pagni, Rossi, Sanders, Teasdale, Walker (Ellen), Wall, and Whitney.

5. The principal investigators of the 27 projects include the following: Auchincloss, Baker (E. Jo), Blumstein/Targan, Brownstein, Cavin, Clark, De Francis, Frank, Franz, Gibb, Gulari, Johnson, Katkin (Model Project), Katkin (Experimental Project), Kebbekus, Kerr, Kimmel, Lancaster, Magill, Maki, Nekvasil, Scantlebury, Steinfeld, Sullivan, Tooney, Wetterhahn, and Wright.

6. The principal investigators of the 14 projects include the following: Bendet, Blumstein/Targan, Chandrasekhar, Crissman (Model Project and Information Dissemination Activity), Harrington, Honey, Kerr, Mappen, Morrow, O'Barr, Rosser, Sikes, Watson.

7. The principal investigators of the two projects are Pavone and Valyo.

CHAPTER 7

Evaluating Female Friendly Interventions

with Bonnie Kelly

Evaluation proves to be a difficult issue for most people who develop projects to attract, retain, and/or improve the performance of individuals or groups in education or within particular disciplines. As the project becomes increasingly complex and comprehensive, the difficulties associated with evaluation also increase.

Just as most of the interventions attempted to attract, retain, and improve the performance of individuals in science, engineering, and mathematics have not targeted women (Matyas & Malcom, 1991), very few of the interventions directed toward women and girls have been evaluated in substantive fashion (Davis & Rosser, 1996). Professional networks such as Women in Engineering Program Advocates Network and the Association for Women in Science report that some programs do some form of evaluation. Seldom, however, does this evaluation involve long-term studies of effect. Few programs use random assignment so that effect can be assessed reliably. Summative evaluations are rare; most evaluations are formative, looking only at participants, with no controls (Davis & Rosser, 1996). Evaluations most often are used in-house, to improve the next program. Results rarely appear in peer-reviewed journals; consequently, computerized library searches turn up little about evaluations of such programs.

In this chapter I will describe the evaluation of results from a federally funded multicampus faculty development project to bring about curricular and pedagogical changes for undergraduate students in SEM. I present the evaluation of the project as an example of one approach to examine some of the results of a relatively complex, multicampus, multiyear project, rather than as a model for emulation.

In Chapter 1 I described a National Science Foundation funded project, the University of South Carolina Model Project (Rosser & Kelly, 1994a), which attempted to inform faculty of female friendly (Rosser, 1990, 1993b) changes in curriculum content and pedagogy derived from research in women's studies and ethnic studies. An assumption and a major goal of the project was that an increase in instructor knowledge of ways to "warm up the classroom climate" (Hall & Sandler, 1982) for women and develop a more inclusive curriculum would enable instructors to evaluate and modify their own teaching to relate better to the needs of their women students. A secondary goal underlined the importance of applying these approaches in ways that continued to attract and retain male students in science, math, and engineering, while improving the retention and success of female students.

PROJECT PURPOSES AND OBJECTIVES

The overall purpose of the project was to make the participants aware of the differences that occur in the processes of instruction, learning, perception, and understanding due to the gender of the student. A hypothesis underlying the project was that increasing awareness of gender-related differences would lead to an improvement in the instructor's teaching performance. This improvement would increase the student's level of understanding and achievement, which in turn would raise the probability that the student would remain in college and continue through to postgraduate studies. Awareness of the new scholarship on women in science and mathematics curricula and pedagogy would aid faculty in attracting and retaining more women students in science/technology careers, thus meeting a national need and improving the women's access to more lucrative livelihoods.

The project's goals were met by certain objectives and strategies. A primary focus of the objectives included introducing the participants to new scholarly research, particularly from women's studies, which would enhance the participants' pedagogical techniques and in turn help to transform science and math college curricula. The underlying aim of the strategies was inclusive, both of the different viewpoints, conceptions, and perceptions among the faculty and of the diversity among students. It assumed that improved perception and information would lead to transformation.

Evaluation of the project centered on these questions:

- Does awareness of gender-related differences in learning and teaching produce a change in instruction?
- Does this awareness produce a change in learning?
- Does awareness of gender-related differences in learning and teaching help instructors to produce more successful students?
- More specifically, will more women be retained in math and science as a result of this project?

METHODS OF EVALUATION

In keeping with the strategies and applications recommended in the project, the evaluation methods incorporate both quantitative and qualitative approaches under cross-sectional and longitudinal studies. The methods of evaluation differed according to the objective being assessed. Pre- and postplenary attitudinal questionnaires (Rosser & Kelly, 1994a) measured shifts in perception of the participants before the project began and after the final plenary. The participants evaluated the overall effectiveness of the project. Confidence and interaction questionnaires assessed shifts in perception and confidence of the participants' students. Class averages of participants' students maintained before the project were compared with their averages after the project. Numbers of students retained by faculty before the project started and those retained after the project ended were tallied and compared with the class averages and retention of their departmental colleagues during the time frame of the project.

The Department of Institutional Research at the University of South Carolina established a student data set giving baseline figures and tracking mechanisms for analysis of performance shifts (grades) and retention shifts (continuing in science/math). The first plenary survey resulted in baseline figures for analysis of the participant attitude/perception shifts. Student survey results from preliminary participant courses gave baseline figures for analysis of the student confidence and perception shifts.

HEARING FROM THE FACULTY

ADDITIONAL QUESTIONNAIRE

An additional questionnaire (Rosser & Kelly, 1994a) consisted of 55 statements about which the participants rated their opinions on a scale of 1 (strongly disagree) to 5 (strongly agree). Research findings from women's studies (Hall & Sandler, 1982; Kahle, 1985; Rosser, 1990) were used to develop the statements for the questionnaire.

Participants responded to this questionnaire three times in the course of the project: immediately before and after the first plenary, and then immediately at the end of the last plenary. A portion of the questionnaire is shown in Figure 7.1. A complete version of the questionnaire has been published separately (Rosser & Kelly, 1994a, 1994b).

Since project participants agreed voluntarily to participate and probably were slightly biased toward the goals of the project, it was not certain how much shift in perception would occur. In fact, after 2 days of presentations by nationally known experts on women's studies, coupled with exposure to readings and

FIGURE 7.1. NSF Project: Faculty Attitudinal Questionnaire

Please respond by circling a number of preference:
1 for strongly disagree
2 for generally disagree
3 for neither disagree nor agree
4 for generally agree
5 for strongly agree

1. I think that women's speech patterns and other verbal and
nonverbal methods of communication cause their answers and
theories of science to be valued less than men's.
1 2 3 4 5

2. I think that teachers have a significant role in influencing
students.
1 2 3 4 5

3. I think that teachers/guidance counselors discourage
females from pursuing careers in science and mathematics.
1 2 3 4 5

4. I think that institutions of higher learning should develop
special programs to encourage and retain women in science
and mathematics.
1 2 3 4 5

5. I think that girls have a lower achievement rate and less
positive attitude than boys in science.
1 2 3 4 5

discussions, participants indicated a statistically significant shift on only two
statements (Rosser & Kelly, 1994a), using a one-tailed, paired difference t-test
with a significance level of $p = .05$.

Analysis of the data from the faculty questionnaire suggests that the information from the first plenary conference did affect significantly at least some
faculty attitudes regarding gender in the classroom. By matching pre- and postplenary responses, we found no reversals of opinion. More of the participants
had a stronger opinion as to the credence of the statements after the plenary.
Those who had given a less strong pre-plenary response (3 or below) increased
the most.

Comparison of the participant responses before the first plenary with those after the third plenary showed a dozen shifts that were strongly significant; 11 of these were in the positive direction correlated with project goals (see Table 7.1). The reversal on Statement 23 may have been due to the time of year when the plenaries took place. The first plenary was shortly after May graduation, whereas the third plenary was in January. The January date may have meant that faculty were less aware of graduation rates in general, and gender ratios of graduates in particular, than they would be in May.

The influence of the information gleaned from women's studies research shows up in most of the shifts of perception, especially in responses to Statements 36, 39, 40, and 46. After the third plenary, the participants more strongly considered possible racial biasing in text and curricular content (Statements 49 and 50). This corresponded with an ancillary but vitally important goal of the project—to focus on racial diversity as well as gender. In addition, the participants felt that the university system provides a good basis for networking and faculty support. This finding may be viewed as especially significant, given that one 4-year campus became independent from the system halfway through the project. All faculty participants from that campus elected to remain in the project, even though they were no longer a part of the University of South Carolina System.

Opinion Poll

At the end of the final plenary conference, we also ran an opinion poll to determine the effectiveness of the project (see Figure 7.2). We asked for the strengths and weaknesses of the project as perceived by the participants. Some comments included the following:

"I found the speakers to be very helpful to me. I especially enjoyed and profited from the reports of the participants."

"One strength of the project was the site visits. Rotating from campus to campus was good. Also the speakers are very dynamic. Sharing ideas at various stages was an excellent idea."

The last part of the opinion poll contained a rating (1 = poorly to 5 = well) as to whether participants thought the project met its goals. The average rating ranged between 3.9 and 4.7 (see Figures 7.3 to 7.8).

HEARING FROM THE STUDENTS

Student Questionnaire

Each participant gave students a pre- and postcourse questionnaire (Rosser & Kelly, 1994a) consisting of three parts. The first part asked for demographics

TABLE 7.1. Comparison of First Plenary to Third Plenary Group Mean Responses.

23. I know the gender ratio of female compared to male students that graduated from my department this past year.

Pre	Post	t-test	p-value
3.6	2.6	-2.6	< .01

24. I think that students are smarter or dumber than I was at the same age.

Pre	Post	t-test	p-value
3.2	2.6	-1.8	< .05

36. I think that the reason my department is underrepresented is because of the scarcity of qualified applicants from these groups.

Pre	Post	t-test	p-value
3.6	2.6	-2.9	< .005

38. I think that gender bias is reflected in the curricular content of my discipline.

Pre	Post	t-test	p-value
2.5	3.0	1.9	< .05

39. I consider possible gender bias in a text as one of the factors in selecting that text.

Pre	Post	t-test	p-value
2.7	3.8	3.8	< .001

40. I have worked to incorporate research, discoveries, and progress made by women in my lectures.

Pre	Post	t-test	p-value
3.2	4.0	3.0	< .005

45. I think that the curricular content of my field is gender-biased.

Pre	Post	t-test	p-value
2.8	3.2	1.9	< .05

46. I incorporate information and issues of particular interest to women in my course content.

Pre	Post	t-test	p-value
3.1	3.9	4.6	< .0005

48. I think that the USC system provides an excellent mechanism for communication among faculty from different campuses.

Pre	Post	t-test	p-value
2.7	3.2	1.7	< .05

49. I consider racial bias in a text as one of the factors in selecting a text.

Pre	Post	t-test	p-value
2.6	3.8	4.9	< .0005

50. I have worked to incorporate research, discoveries, and progress made by minorities in my lectures.

Pre	Post	t-test	p-value
2.9	3.7	3.9	< .001

52. I do not know how to adequately handle a student's inability to accept criticism.

Pre	Post	t-test	p-value
3.3	2.6	-2.3	< .02

FIGURE 7.2. Faculty Opinion Survey

We greatly appreciate your comments on the following:

1. What do you consider as strengths of the project, for example, the plenaries, site visits, speakers, etc. ?

2. What do you consider as weaknesses of the project, for example, the plenaries, site visits, speakers, etc.?

4. Please rate on a scale of *1=poorly* to *5=well* as to whether the following objectives of the project were met:

___Increase in participants' knowledge of current research findings regarding the reasons that women are not more prominently represented in science and mathematics.

___Improvement of participants' ability to relate to their women students through varying teaching approaches and applications.

___Improvement of participants' ability to relate to their men students through varying teaching approaches and applications.

___Development of teaching strategies and disciplinary applications tailored to each campus population and academic level.

___Establishment of a cooperative and mutually supportive network of faculty who share a commitment to increase the number of women in math and science.

such as gender, age, race, and number of science and math courses taken. The second asked the students to rate their own confidence regarding the course concepts on a scale of 1 (not confident) to 10 (highly confident). Each faculty participant decided which course concepts he or she wanted to know about. The third part of the questionnaire dealt with student perceptions of class interactions.

For correlation purposes each student was required to identify his or her questionnaire with a distinguishing number, symbol, or trademark, and was asked to remember it. Unfortunately, some trademarks were duplicated, and many students did not remember their trademarks. This resulted in loss of data.

Each participant was asked to teach the same course twice. Set 1 reflects the first time the course was taught; Set 2, the second time. The 18 participants

FIGURE 7.3. Increase in Participants' Knowledge of Current Research Findings

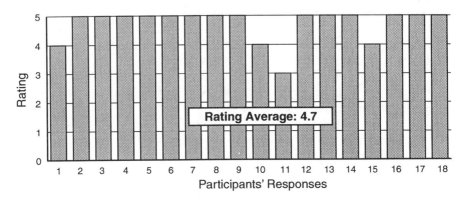

FIGURE 7.4. Improvement of Participants' Ability to Relate to Their Women Students

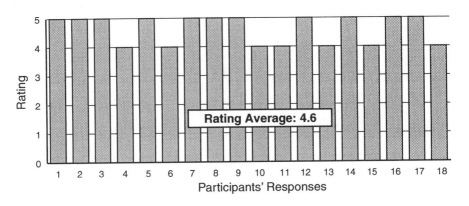

FIGURE 7.5. Improvement of Participants' Ability to Relate to Their Men Students

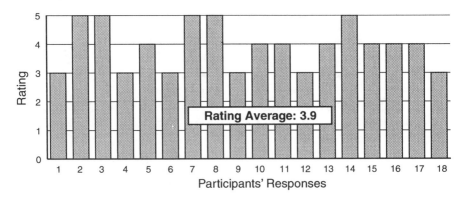

FIGURE 7.6. Development of Teaching Strategies Tailored to Campus Population

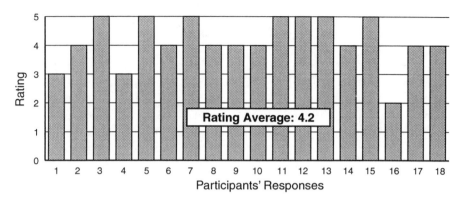

FIGURE 7.7. Establishment of a Cooperative and Supportive Network of Faculty

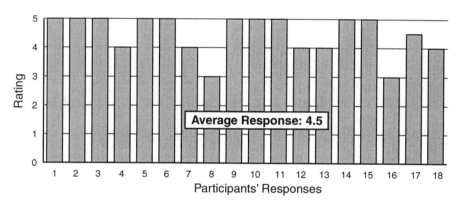

FIGURE 7.8. Overall Rating of the Project's Achievement of Goals

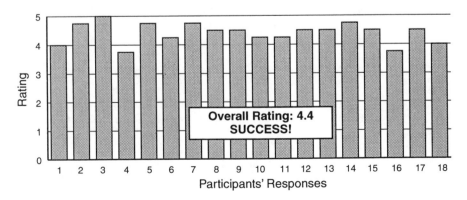

provided 32 courses, which could be matched by semester, type, and level. Four participants analyzed their own student questionnaires. The total correlated number of students involved in these courses was 257 in Set 1 (165 males, 92 females) and 218 in Set 2 (126 males, 92 females).

Female and Male Students' Confidence. Students responded to this part of the questionnaire at the beginning and end of a designated course taught by the participant. Participants received a synopsis of their students' means, standard deviations, and the tests with p-values; information as to how to read the synopsis; and some instruction as to how to interpret the results.

To see whether students became at least 70% confident of their subject matter before they went on to the next course, we compared the end mean scores for each course with an arbitrary mean of 7 out of a possible 10. A directional one-sample t-test, $p = .05$, was used each time to determine whether the mean achieved for that concept was the same or significantly better than the standard. If seven of the topics in the course had reached or surpassed the standard, then the course had students becoming at least 70% confident of their subject matter.

Of the 32 courses taught for Set 1 and Set 2:

- 40% did not increase to the 70% level in student confidence of course concepts with regard to both genders;
- 47% of the males and 40% of the females showed no significant increase in student confidence;
- 13% of the males and 20% of the females showed significant increase in confidence.

To see whether confidence had increased on the whole for the participants' students, we established a baseline using the surveys from the first course the participant taught. We compared the last course post surveys to the baseline figures. We ran a directional two-sample t-test on each matched course's correlated students, $p = .05$. If five or more topics had increased significantly from Set 1 to Set 2, then this constituted an increase in confidence.

Of the 16 correlated courses:

- 25% and 34% of the courses had no increase for male and female students, respectively;
- 25% and 31% of the courses had improvement with no significance;
- 50% and 35% of the courses had significant increase for males and females, respectively.

The third aspect of the confidence survey we called a gender-equitable or

TABLE 7.2. Pilot Course Responses for Question 8 of the Interaction in Classes Questionnaire

Responses Pre	Females	Males	Did Not Notice	Total
Females	9	6	4	19
Males	3	4	11	18
Total	12	10	15	37
Responses Post				
Females	0	18	1	19
Males	0	10	8	18
Total	0	28	9	37

gender-neutral level, that is, bringing everyone up to approximately the same level of confidence. On the whole, students' confidence increased from the beginning of a course to the end. In general, females had the larger increase, because their mean scores were lower at the beginning. The question we asked was this: Were their larger jumps in confidence due to the participants' awareness of gender differences in learning or due to randomness?

To see whether female students' increase in confidence was truly better than that of their male cohorts, we ran a two-tailed pooled variance t-test, $p = .05$, to determine whether female and male mean differences from Set 1 to Set 2 were significant. In 18% of matched courses taught during the project, we did find a significant positive shift in female confidence that was not due to randomness.

WOMEN'S AND MEN'S PARTICIPATION IN CLASS DISCUSSION

One of the participants helped develop this part of the questionnaire in a pilot course in summer 1992. A tally of Question 8 responses, given by female and male students in his course, follows in Table 7.2.

Analysis of the responses to Question 8 from this class suggests that females perceived females as the predominant interactors in previous science courses, while males did not notice. Males and females had different perceptions. By the end of the class (possibly due in part to this questionnaire), most students were aware of the gender of those interacting. In this class, females and males clearly had realigned their perceptions. Spurred by the information from this question, the instructor made a conscious commitment to call on female students more often and to involve them more in discussions the next time that he taught the course, which was in fall 1993. The results for this instructor at the end of that course were among the highest ratings with regard to confidence and positive student interaction responses.

TABLE 7.3. Responses for Questions 8, 13, and 17.

	Set 1 Male (165)	Set 1 Female (92)	Set 2 Male (126)	Set 2 Female (92)
Question 8				
Responses:				
(1)	65%	40%	44%*	30%
(2)	11%	25%	15%	27%
(3)	1%	0%	24%*	28%*
( )	23%	35%	17%	15%*
Question 13				
Responses:				
(1)	28%	12%	15%*	11%
(2)	10%	5%	5%	6%
(3)	1%	4%	51%**	46%**
( )	62%	78%	29%**	37%**
Question 17				
Responses:				
(1)	10%	12%	15%	20%
(2)	74%	55%	79%	72%*
( )	16%	33%	6%*	8%**

From the chosen pilot survey, we expanded the questionnaire to include 20 interaction responses based on perceptions by the students. We analyzed the responses to the Class Interactions section of the student questionnaire by using a directional z-test for comparing two proportions, at the .01 level. We wanted to know whether the change in percentage of responses was significant at the .01 level. The responses for Questions 8 and 13 could be one of these possibilities: (1) Male students, (2) Female students, (3) No discernible difference, and ( ) Leave blank if you did not notice. The responses for Question 17 could be: (1) No, (2) Yes, and ( ) Leave blank if course had no effect.

The results for Questions 8, 13, and 17 appear in Table 7.3. Change in percentage at the .01 level of significance is indicated with one asterisk.

Twenty-one percent fewer of the total proportion of males in the second set of courses said male students interact more in class. Fewer males and females took no notice of the interactions, which means that more students were aware of gender dynamics in class discussions.

This "sit up and take notice" attitude of the students, coupled with the fact that both male and female populations of the second set of courses saw *no discernible difference* in who interacted more gives credence to the belief that the project participants had transformed their teaching strategies to include everyone in class discussions and interplay.

The results for Question 8 are corroborated by those for Question 13. Again, we see no discernible difference as to who was called on more. In addition, considerably more students noticed the gender dynamics.

The responses for Question 17 dealt with student perception as to whether the course helped build their confidence in the subject matter. We had mixed results, with the response "(1) No" increasing, but not at the significance level. In contrast, more students felt that the course did have an effect on their confidence. Female students in particular felt that the course helped.

We ran a Chi-square test as well for this question to see whether the interdependence between confidence and gender had diminished in the second set of students. The Chi-square values for Set 1 and Set 2 were 11.4 and 2.88, respectively. These values indicate a relationship between gender and confidence for Set 2, although the degree of the relationship appears to have decreased. To verify further the results of the interaction responses, a log-linear analysis was performed using categorical modeling procedures. Analyses of the student perception shifts using these procedures gave supporting evidence that the course increased confidence, particularly for female students.

ASSESSMENT OF STUDENT RETENTION AND GRADES

THE DATABASE

The database set up by the Department of Institutional Research played a major part in determining whether student retention and performance of project participants increased compared with those of students taught by their colleagues, termed nonparticipants, who taught the same types and levels of courses. Two time frames were involved in this part of the evaluation process. The term "before" designates fall and spring semesters prior to the project (i.e., fall 1989 to spring 1992, excluding summer sessions). The term "during" defines the semesters in which the project courses were taught (i.e., fall 1992, spring 1993, and fall 1993). The spring 1994 semester also was taken into consideration when retention was assessed.

Participant courses used for the project were marked, and corresponding courses for nonparticipants were matched to these courses at all times. The level of courses was predominantly first-year undergraduate. Five courses were upper-level undergraduate courses, and these were matched in the groupings of participants and nonparticipants as well. Courses taught by a participant during the project frequently became designated as "treated" to distinguish them from nonparticipant, or "untreated," courses.

All students in such courses were tagged and denoted as participant *or* nonparticipant students. When grade means were compared, students who were in a participant course at any time during the project were *participant* students. If a student appeared in both a treated course and an untreated course at the same time, that student was eliminated from the database. Under the retention analysis, students were counted only once. Whenever a student *first* appeared in any course, that student was tracked to the next science course. Once tracked, that student no longer featured in the retention analysis.

The first statistical testing of the different data sets created by the above criteria was done by group (all students under consideration) and by gender (of all students under consideration), regardless of campus. In the second run of testing, the data sets were separated by campus. The five 2-year colleges were combined into one section called "regional campuses." The new partitions were then analyzed by group and by gender.

STUDENT'S STAY WITH THE PROJECT

Retention was defined as "taking at least one subsequent science course" during either the spring 1993, fall 1993, or spring 1994 semester. A "science course" was defined to include all science, engineering, mathematics, and nursing courses. Thus, a student who had taken, for example, a mathematics course would be defined as "retained" if that student went on to take, for example, a chemistry course at any other time during the project or immediately after the project, with either a participant or a nonparticipant. This could account for the high retention rates found for the 4-year and regional campuses, as shown in the tables. It should be noted that even if a student failed a required course for the discipline, that student could still take another "science" course.

As a group overall, as shown in Table 7.4, we found that approximately 98% of the students of participants took a subsequent science course, whereas approximately 96% of the students of the nonparticipants did. We had 98% versus 95% male students of participants and nonparticipants, respectively. We had 97% versus 96% female students of participants and nonparticipants, respectively. These were significant differences at the $p < .025$ level.

The retention of students from individual campuses, divided by gender, is shown in Table 7.4. The differences in participant compared with nonparticipant student retention for the two of the 4-year and the regional campuses were significant at $p = .025$, denoted by an asterisk. Only one of the participant student retention percentages was significantly lower, denoted by a double asterisk. The research campus nonparticipant female student retention was significantly higher than the participant female student retention. In the 4-year

TABLE 7.4. Student Retention Groups, Subsets, and Percentage.

Student Retention (Group)

	Participant	Nonparticipant
Group	97.89%	95.71%
Female	97.36%	95.52%
Male	98.37%	95.90%

*p<.025

Student Retention (Subset)

	Participant	Nonparticipant
Group	97.58%*	96.10%
Female	97.19%**	95.83%
Male	97.98%*	96.38%

*p<.05   **p=.1

Student Retention Percent (Group)

Campus	Participant		Nonparticipant	
	Male	Female	Male	Female
Research	97.6	91.7	97.2	97.4**
Three 4-Year	100.0*	100.0*	94.1	93.3
Campuses	100.0*	100.0*	96.8	94.8
	89.3	94.4	94.2	96.6
Regional	100.0*	100.0*	91.1	92.7

*p=.025   **p<.025

Student Retention Percent (Subset)

Campus	Participant		Nonparticipant	
	Male	Female	Male	Female
Research	95.7	90.4	98.5*	98.3*
Three 4-Year	100.0*	100.0*	94.1	93.3
Campuses	100.0*	100.0*	96.8	94.8
	89.3	94.4	94.2	96.6
Regional	100.0*	100.0*	91.1	92.7

*p<.05

campus that had a lower participant student retention, the number of participant students involved was too small for significance.

These high retention rates for 4-year and regional campuses may indicate that the parameter for "science" course was too broadly defined. In addition, there were three semesters in which a "science" course could be taken. (These same parameters were used for the nonparticipants as well.) Another reason for the higher retention could be that there were fewer courses for the students to choose from, but this applies to nonparticipant students at those campuses as well. It is even possible that participants may have overcompensated or reacted in order to improve the grades of their students. However, the participant student mean grades were not always better than those of the nonparticipant students. It could be that, since the smaller campuses have fewer faculty members, those faculty members who were project participants had a greater influence on their students and on their student retention. Reviewing the grades and the standard deviations of the student grades for these faculty members before and during the project revealed that the range of grades did not seem to change that much during the project. Even at the research campus, only the female retention showed a significant difference. Proportionately more participant than nonparticipant students continued to take a "science" course.

A Closer Look at Introductory Courses. Students who have persisted in their studies take upper-level courses. Although the project was designed to focus on introductory courses, three types of upper-level courses taught by participant faculty were included in the initial data set analyzed above. To examine the effect of the project on retention after introductory courses, the students in the upper-level courses were removed from the data set and a new subset of data was formed. The student retention of this subset was analyzed using similar methods to those employed in the combined data set.

The retention for project participants of the subset was less than that of the combined set, but still significant, primarily in favor of the participants (see Table 7.4). For the group and male retention, the difference was significant at $p < .05$ (one asterisk). The female student difference in retention was significant only at $p = .10$ (two asterisks). Because the upper-level course had only one nonparticipant course for comparison purposes during the project's time frame, the 100% retention rate versus 66.67% nonparticipant retention rate is not a valid comparison.

Both male and female student retention at the research campus had significant differences in favor of the nonparticipants at $p < .05$ as compared with before, where only female student retention was significant (see Table 7.4). The amount of difference in percentages increased in favor of the nonparticipants. This points out that the upper-level courses here had a positive impact for the project for both genders, particularly for males. No significantly different reten-

TABLE 7.5. Participants' Student Mean Grades.

Project	Group	Standard Deviation	Male	Standard Deviation	Female	Standard Deviation
Before	2.28	1.24	2.19	1.27	2.38	1.22
After	2.45*	1.27	2.49*	1.28	2.42*	1.26

*Differences are significant at p=.05.

tion rates were noted when the upper-level course in the 4-year campus was removed from the data set.

When student retention was broken down by campus, the analyses at times indicated that the Chi-square test may not have been valid due to 25% of the expected cell counts giving fewer than five observations. This occurred at the campuses that had upper-level courses.

BETTER GRADES THROUGH FEMINIST PEDAGOGY

We next asked whether project participants' students performed better due to participants' awareness of gender differences in teaching and learning. We obtained a data set of students blocked by participant versus nonparticipant, course, department, campus, and time. We adjusted for any duplication or overlap of student and course. Our criterion of performance was the mean class average of the science course types involved. We compared those courses taught by the participants before the project with those during it. We also compared courses participants taught during the project with courses taught by nonparticipants in the same time frame. We ran a nested ANOVA by general linear model procedures. The results are presented in Table 7.5.

Table 7.6 summarizes the mean grades of the courses taught by participants and nonparticipants during the project's time frame. The participant student grades were significantly higher than those of the nonparticipant students. The participant student grades also were compared with the nonparticipant student grades before the project began. The participants had 2.28 as their students' mean, whereas the nonparticipants had 2.19; the difference was significant. This suggested that the participants seemed to be better instructors before the project began. However, the degree of improvement in mean grades was significantly greater for the students of the participants during their involvement with the project.

In general, female students had higher grade averages than male students in the courses taught by participants before the project. The reverse situation occurred in the courses taught by participants during the project. The male students during the project's duration seem to have benefited more, in terms

TABLE 7.6. Student Grades During Project.

Student Grades During Project

	Participants		Nonparticipants	
	Mean	**Standard Deviation**	**Mean**	**Standard Deviation**
Group	2.46	1.27	2.22	1.32
Female	2.42	1.26	2.35	1.31
Male	2.49	1.28	2.09	1.33

Difference significant at p = .05.

Student Grades During Project (Subset)

	Participants		Nonparticipants	
	Mean	**Standard Deviation**	**Mean**	**Standard Deviation**
Group	2.33	1.26	2.22	1.33
Female	2.36	1.26	2.34	1.31
Male	2.30	1.27	2.09	1.33

of grades, from the instructors' changed pedagogy. One of the strategies to meet the goals of the project was to improve the participants' ability to relate to their men students as well as to their women students.

The difference in grades between the genders was significant before and during the project. The males had the steeper increase in grade average, almost half a grade, but the female student grade increase was significant as well.

Another Closer Look at Introductory Courses. Table 7.6 shows that when the upper-level courses were removed, the difference in grades for participant versus nonparticipant groups decreased to the point of insignificance. The participants had a grade mean of 2.33, whereas the nonparticipants had 2.22. However, when student gender was added as a variable, the differences between male and female student grades was significant ($p < .05$) for nonparticipants, specifically in favor of female students.

Between male and female students in the participant classes, there was a difference in grade mean of .06, which must be compared with an analysis of data for participants only in order to determine its significance. When this comparison was made, the analysis showed that there was no significant difference between the mean grades of male and female students of participants. For the upper-level courses, there was no significant difference between the 3.21 male student mean grade and the 2.97 female student mean grade. There was a difference of .02 between participant and nonparticipant female students, but this was not significant either. In addition, comparing participant with nonpartici-

TABLE 7.7. Student Grade Mean (Subset).

Campus	*Participant*		*Nonparticipant*	
	Male	**Female**	**Male**	**Female**
Research	2.62	2.65	2.17	2.17
Three 4-Year	2.41	2.57	2.64	3.00
Campuses	2.00	1.91	1.97	2.45
	2.27	2.15	1.61	1.93
Regional	2.24	2.31	2.41	2.43

pant male student mean grades, the 2.30 for participants was higher, but not significantly higher, than the 2.09 nonparticipant mean.

The introductory course participants improved their instructional performance during the project's time frame. When comparing student grade means during the project with previous grade means, the student grade means overall for participants were 2.33 and 2.26, respectively. This was significant at $p < .01$. The upper-level course participants also improved (3.16 compared with 2.63), but at a greater level of significance ($p < .01$).

When comparing female student grade means before and during the project, analysis indicated that the introductory course participant mean decreased by .02, whereas the nonparticipant mean increased by .10. Neither of these differences was significant. When comparing male student grade means before and during the project, analysis indicated that there was a significant difference in favor of participant male students. The nonparticipant male grade means decreased by .01, which was not significant.

When comparisons were made by campus, analyses indicated that the research campus participant student grades overall were significantly higher than respective nonparticipant student grades (see Table 7.7). They were not significant by gender; that is, it was definitely better to be in a participant's class, regardless of student gender.

At the first 4-year campus, being a participant or not was not significant, but gender, in favor of females for both participant and nonparticipant classes, was. Nonparticipant female student grades were higher than participant student grades, but not significantly so.

At the second 4-year campus, being a participant or not was significant in favor of nonparticipants, whose student grade mean was 2.22 versus the 1.97 participant student grade mean. Gender combined with participant or nonparticipant classification was significant, in favor of nonparticipant female student grade mean. Removal of upper courses here decreased female student grade mean by .02, but increased that of males by the same amount. These differences were not significant.

At the third 4-year campus, being a participant or not was significant in favor of participants, whose student grade mean was 2.21 as opposed to 1.77 for nonparticipants. Gender combined with participant or nonparticipant classification was significant for participant student grade mean, in particular male student grade mean.

For the regional campuses, being a participant or not was significant in favor of nonparticipants, whose student grade mean was 2.42 as opposed to 2.28 for participants. Gender did not make a difference nor did gender combined with participant or nonparticipant classification.

CONCLUSIONS

The findings of the evaluation and assessment indicate that female students of the participants became more confident of their own science and math ability. Both male and female students' confidence increased, and in some project courses female students' confidence increased to a significantly higher level than males. Participants under the aegis of the project seemed to produce more confident students.

Student performance for participants before and during the project with respect to grades was better for the project courses. Participant student grades, when compared with nonparticipant student grades during the project, were sometimes significantly lower and sometimes significantly higher, depending on the campus. This particular aspect of the analysis revealed that the project improved the grades of male more than female students. Females usually started with a higher grade mean than males, but males then surpassed the females at a significant level. Retention and student grade mean did not seem to have a positive relationship. Higher student grade mean did not necessarily produce higher retention. However, overall, participants under the aegis of the project appeared to have improved their instructional performance.

Student confidence and performance in subject matter help to foster student continuation in science/math. Although improvement in grades for female students in some participant courses was lower than increases in male student grades, their increased level of confidence may help females to continue their pursuit of a science/math degree. In percentages, retention of students was significantly higher in participant than in nonparticipant courses. It is felt that this was due primarily to the influence of the participants and student confidence rather than to the grades of the students, which were in some cases lower for participant students.

It appears that the introductory course participants did have a positive effect on both male and female students regarding retention, but not regarding student grades. The participants' improved instructional performance helped improve male student grades more than female student grades. Female student grades were higher than those of males, but it appears that male grades improved substantially on the average. Perhaps the project improved student performance regardless of gender in whatever area students were weak—confidence, grades, or retention. Upper-level courses helped increase project participants' influence on their students and contributed much to the success of the project regarding effects on both male and female students.

Participants under the aegis of the project did retain proportionately more students. The findings indicate that participants overall are producing more academically successful students. This group of college faculty changed their teaching strategies to the more inclusionary techniques recommended by the project. The results support the hypothesis that they are helping to reverse the trend of increasing student attrition, in particular female student attrition, in the sciences. The participants are beginning to transform the math, science, and engineering college classroom.

CHAPTER 8

Dangerous Times: Threats to Female Friendly Science Posed by the New Right and Tight Fiscal Resources

For more than a decade, I have used phase theories to evaluate progress toward inclusion of women, men of color, and other previously excluded groups. My initial introduction to phase theory came from participation in curriculum integration projects where women's studies scholars such as Mary Kay Tetreault (1985), Peggy McIntosh (1984), and Marilyn Schuster and Susan Van Dyne (1985) had developed these theories to chart the stages through which the curriculum was transformed to include the new scholarship from women's studies and ethnic studies.

Transformation toward inclusion represents a lengthy and difficult process that involves substantial work and resources. Indeed, it is probably necessary for most individuals involved in a program to pass through a stage before the program as a whole can reach the stage. Similarly, most programs or departments must pass through a stage before the division or college can reach that stage; most divisions, colleges, or other units must complete a stage before the agency or institution as a whole can reach it.

In addition to the recognition of the need for inclusion and the commitment to strive for inclusion, the willingness to rethink all previous knowledge and to devise different approaches for learning new information is required. Individuals find the process exciting, although challenging. It becomes increasingly difficult for departments, programs, divisions and colleges, and finally agencies and institutions. A critical mass is required at each stage before the unit as a whole can proceed to the next stage. Although considerable struggle, critical self-assessment, and willingness to reallocate resources may be necessary for the group to move to the next stage, the benefits derived from the diverse approaches, new information, and enlarged perspective are substantial for the unit or institution.

Substantive evaluations (Coulter & Vanfossen, 1995) of curriculum transformation efforts have documented the progress in revision and the sorts of efforts more likely to facilitate successful transformation for individual faculty, for departments, and for institutions as a whole. Such an evaluation does not serve as the primary focus of this chapter, although I have written evaluations of curriculum transformation projects in the sciences (Rosser & Kelly, 1994c). Instead, I would like to use the phase model of curriculum transformation to explore the superficial similarities between stage 2 and stage 6 and the ways in which tight resources and ideological backlash increase the chances that stage 2 progress will be labeled as stage 6.

Many pitfalls and problems prevent individuals, curricula, programs, and institutions from reaching stage 6, even when each individual accepts the basic overall goals and is committed to achieving them. A common phenomenon observed by those of us who have worked with phase theory in a variety of institutions over a considerable period of time is the mistaking of stage 2 transformation for stage 6. This error is easiest to perceive in the case of an individual teacher after a relatively brief exposure to phase theory and new scholarship in women's studies and ethnic studies, often provided by a one-week summer institute or a study group meeting once each week throughout a semester. Often such institutes and meetings achieve considerable success with their participants in raising awareness that women and men of color have been excluded from curriculum and pedagogy. During the institute or study group meetings, participants themselves may have experienced brief understandings of stages 3, 4, and 5 in their own personal development and understood the vision encompassing stage 6. Eager to translate their new awareness into inclusion in the curricular content and classroom interactions, participants often curtail true inclusion by the sort of scenario depicted in Chapter 1 involving Professor Alicia Smith. Despite her best intentions, Alicia mistook stage 2 for stage 6. She failed to focus sufficiently on race and gender, simply adding them to the course she previously had taught without rethinking the conception of the entire course.

These sorts of difficulties plague individuals' curricular and pedagogical attempts at inclusion. When these attempts occur within situations where guidance from experts with experience in transformation is available and within an overall context in which there is continued focus on race and gender, faculty may recognize the problems that arise from their stage 2 course and eventually develop courses at the next stage. Ultimately, they may reach and may teach a stage 6 course.

THREATS TO FEMALE FRIENDLY SCIENCE FROM THE NEW RIGHT

Moving the entire scientific enterprise to stage 6 would have been difficult even with a commitment to the importance of diversity in the science, engineering, and mathematics workforce, relatively abundant resources, and constant pressure from laws and judicial decisions supporting affirmative action. In the wake of the November 1994 elections in which 62% of white males voted Republican (Edsall, 1995) and federal spending and programs faced severe budget cuts, programs with gender and/or race as their central focus faced severe threats. In his February 5, 1995 appearance on NBC's Meet the Press, then Senate Majority Leader Robert Dole revealed that Republican lawmakers were studying whether federal affirmative action requirements should be dropped on the grounds that they discriminate against white men. "He has asked the Congressional Research Service to supply him with copies of all federal legislation that promotes affirmative action, or the use of racially oriented hiring preference in an effort to help minorities improve their economic status" (Swoboda, 1995, p. A1). In March 1995, President Clinton initiated his own review of affirmative action programs. All federal agencies had to provide him with information regarding affirmative action, including "NSF education programs that consider race, gender, or disability."

In June 1995, the U.S. Supreme Court ruled in the *Adarand Constructors, Inc.* v *Peña* decision that "federal affirmative action programs that use racial and ethnic criteria as a basis for decision making are subject to strict judicial scrutiny" (in Kole, 1995, p. 1). Affirmative action programs should be used to justify a compelling government interest in using race as a criterion for special treatment. Although past discrimination and diversity remain acceptable justifications, an affirmative action program will need to be narrowly tailored to meet the need.

On July 19, President Clinton held a press conference to reaffirm his support of affirmative action. During the course of the conference, he made the following statement:

> Based on the evidence, the job is not done. So here is what I think we should do. We should reaffirm the principle of affirmative action and fix the practices. We should have a simple slogan: Mend it, but don't end it. (Clinton, 1995a, p. 15)

The same day the President issued a memorandum for heads of executive departments and agencies on the subject of evaluation of affirmative action programs to bring them in line with the Supreme Court decision. The memorandum included the following directive:

> Accordingly, in all programs you administer that use race, ethnicity, or gender as a consideration to expand opportunity or provide benefits to members of groups that have suffered discrimination, I ask you to take steps to ensure adherence to the following policy principles. The policy principles are that any program must be eliminated or reformed if it:
> (a) creates a quota;
> (b) creates preferences for unqualified individuals;

(c) creates reverse discrimination; or
(d) continues even after its equal opportunity purposes have
been achieved. (Clinton, 1995b, p. 2)

On July 20, the University of California Board of Regents voted (14 to 10 with one abstention) to end the use of ethnicity or gender in student admissions and to use criteria related to economic and social need. In a separate 15 to 10 vote, Regents also eliminated the use of ethnicity and gender in the University of California's hiring and business practices, effective January 1996 (Wheeler, 1995, p. 1).

In June 1996, a blue-ribbon commission created by the American Association of University Professors released a report criticizing the decision of the University of California's Board of Regents to abolish the use of racial and ethnic preferences in the university system (Balch & Warren, 1996). A March 1996 court ruling in Texas prohibiting racial preferences as a basis for admissions to the university was followed quickly by a similar decision in Georgia in April 1996. In July 1996, the Supreme Court voted not to review the decision of the U.S. Court of Appeals for the Fifth Circuit (Texas), which barred the University of Texas law school from considering race in its admissions in *Texas* v. *Hopwood,* this plus the California vote on Proposition 209 leaves higher education in a quandary about the use of race in college and university admissions in particular, and about affirmative action in general (Lederman & Burd, 1996; Michaelson, 1996).

EFFECTS OF THE CURRENT POLITICAL AND ECONOMIC CLIMATES

The scientific and engineering community finds itself under siege from a combination of formidable problems. A very tight job market (Tobias & Chubin, 1996), shrinking grant funds from federal and foundation sources, and media attention to controversial cases of scientific misconduct and fraud (Kevles, 1996) create a difficult environment for scientists and engineers. Some scientists have resorted to parody and hoaxes to undercut the perceived threat of the cultural study of science. Alan Sokal's spoof of postmodern physics provides an example of such a caricature (McMillen, 1996). It would be most unfortunate if the conservative political climate and tight economic resources allowed the scientific community to ignore the significant positive contributions to science that may come from scholars, including feminist scholars, in the cultural study of science, and from increased gender and racial diversity within the pool of scientists.

What will be the stance of the scientific and engineering community and federal government toward programs they have recently developed for women and minorities? Will they abolish them outright, stating that they are yielding to political pressures from the right? Although this might be the honest response, it would be certain to incur the wrath of women and men of color, white women, and the many white men within the science, engineering, and mathematics community who understand the quality derived from a diverse workforce and support the goals of programs to increase inclusion.

More likely, the programs will be declared successful. Small gains in the numbers, acceptance of a diversity of approaches, and inclusion of information and achievements of women and minorities (all stage 2 efforts) will be promulgated as inclusion (stage 6). Against the recent backdrop where the absence of women and men of color was not noted (stage 1), these small increases will appear as progress and easily may be mistaken as stage 6, particularly by those unfamiliar with phase theory and the confusion between stage 2 and stage 6. Lacking parameters or benchmarks by which to measure true inclusion (stage 6), they may mistake minor improvements or increases as sufficient for success.

If programs to support inclusion are terminated, it is crucial to document where in their phase of development they were arrested. Superficial similarities in stage 2 and stage 6 efforts must not hide the reality that these programs were cut short in their infancy, well before the fruits of their maturity could be seen and measured.

Stage 2 efforts result in some additions of women and men of color to the pool of scientists, but fall short of reaching stage 6, where parity or benchmarks for representation of these groups equal their demographic characteristics in the overall population and would result in substantive changes in science research, practice, and teaching. Proportional diversity of race, class, and gender within the pool of scientists and within the scientific leadership should produce an inclusive curriculum (stage 6) in which flaws in research from androcentric and other biases due to race, class, and gender would have been corrected. Hypotheses held up for scrutiny to the scientific community would be refined by a continuing dialogue between a diverse community of scientists and laypeople. In the classroom and laboratory, the scientist-teacher would demonstrate and encourage students to use interdisciplinary approaches to problem solving that combine qualitative and quantitative methods, where appropriate (Rosser, 1990). She or he also would discuss the practical uses of scientific discoveries to help students place science in its social context and would communicate with nonscientists to eliminate any barriers that continued to separate scientists from laypeople (Bentley, 1985). As more people from different races, classes, ethnic backgrounds, and genders become scientists, the science they develop would be more accessible, varied, and humane.

Continued underrepresentation means that the improved quality of the science anticipated to result from a diverse scientific workforce, in which new and different perspectives and approaches to problems come from individuals of different races, genders, and cultural experiences, will not be fully realized. Even more disabling than its impact on the pool of scientists and the quality of science produced, may be the harmful effects on scientific literacy that result from failure to complete the phases of inclusion. Stage 4 programs aim to make both short- and long-term positive changes in the infrastructure of science, engineering, and mathematics education for women and girls. These programs recognize that the lack of inclusion results not only in many fewer women and men of color becoming scientists, but also in their taking fewer mathematics and science courses than they need to become scientifically literate in our increasingly technological and scientific world.

Men of color and women currently constitute two-thirds of the population and 57% of the workforce (Swoboda, 1995, p. A18). Between now and the year 2000, two-thirds of new entrants to the workforce will be women (U.S. Department of Labor, 1987). The failure to reach the majority of the population to ensure its scientific literacy damages more than the pool of scientists and the quality of science. It undercuts the effectiveness of the entire workforce in an increasingly competitive global economy. As faculty in science, mathematics, and engineering modify ideas originating from ethnic studies and women's studies that have been adopted by mainstream science education, they must remain vigilant in revisiting the impact on students, to ensure that the pedagogical techniques and curricular innovations continue to remain female friendly.

References

Adelman, C. (1991). *Women at thirtysomething: Paradoxes of attainment.* Washington, DC: U.S. Department of Education, Office of Educational Research and Development.

Alper, J. (1993). The pipeline is leaking women all the way along. *Science, 260,* 409–411.

American Association for the Advancement of Science. (1990). *Science for all Americans.* Washington, DC: Author.

American Association for the Advancement of Science. (1993). *Benchmarks for science literacy.* New York: Oxford University Press.

American Association of University Women. (1990). *Shortchanging girls, shortchanging America.* Washington, DC: Author.

American Association of University Women. (1992). *How schools shortchange girls.* Washington, DC: AAUW Educational Foundation.

American Women in Science. (1993). *A hand up: Women mentoring women in science.* Washington, DC: Author.

Arnold, K. (1987, June). *Retaining high achieving women in science and engineering.* Paper presented at the conference, Women in Science and Engineering: Changing Vision to Reality, University of Michigan, Ann Arbor. Sponsored by the American Association for the Advancement of Science.

Associated Press. (1995a, April 29). Appellate court refuses to rehear suit against VMI. *The State,* p. B6.

Associated Press. (1995b, June 3). Citadel would not require female cadet to shave head. *The Washington Post,* p. A2.

Associated Press. (1995c, August 19). Faulkner backs out of Citadel. *The Gainesville Sun,* pp. 1-A, 5-A.

Association for Women in Science. (1993). *A hand up: Women mentoring women in science* (D. Fort, Ed.). Washington, DC: Author.

Astin, A., & Astin, H. S. (1993). *Undergraduate science education: The impact of different college environments on the educational pipeline in the sciences.* Los Angeles: University of California, Higher Education Research Institute.

Astin, A. W., Green, K. C., Korn, W. S., & Riggs, E. R. (1991). *The American freshman: Twenty-year trends, 1966–1985.* Los Angeles: University of California, Higher Education Research Institute.

Astin, H., & Sax, L. (1996). Developing scientific talent in undergraduate women. In C-S. Davis, A. B. Ginorio, C. S. Hollenshead, B. B. Lazarus, P. M. Rayman, & Associates (Eds.), *The equity equation: Fostering the advancement of women in the sciences, mathematics, and engineering* (pp. 96–121). San Francisco: Jossey-Bass.

Baker, D. (1986). Sex differences in classroom interactions in secondary science. *Journal of Classroom Interaction, 22,* 212–218.

Baker, M. (1994). Abstract presented at Awardee Meeting for NSF Program for Women and Girls, July 7–8, 1994. Arlington, VA.

Balch, S., & Warren, P. (1996, June 21). A troubling defense of group preferences. *The Chronicle of Higher Education,* p. A44.

Barinaga, M. (1994). Surprises across the cultural divide. *Science, 263,* 1468–1472.

Belenky, M. F., Clinchy, B. M., Goldberger, N. R., & Tarule, J. M. (1986). *Women's ways of knowing.* New York: Basic Books.

Belitski, P. (1995). Girls + math = success. *Portfolio, IX*(8), 3.

Benbow, C., & Stanley, J. (1980). Sex differences in mathematical ability: Fact or artifact? *Science, 210,* 1262–1264.

Bentley, D. (1985). Men may understand the words, but do they know the music? Some cries de coeur in science education. In *Supplementary contributions to the third GASAT conference* (pp. 160–168). London: University of London, Chelsea College.

Billings, J. (1994). *Improving student learning in Washington State.* Olympia, WA: Superintendent of Public Instruction.

Biology and Gender Study Group. (1989). The importance of feminist critique for contemporary cell biology. In N. Tuana (Ed.), *Feminism and science* (pp. 172–187). Bloomington: Indiana University Press.

Birke, L. (1986). *Women, feminism, and biology: The feminist challenge.* New York: Methuen.

Blackwell, A. (1976). *The sexes throughout nature.* Westport, CT: Hyperion Press. (Original work published 1875)

Bleier, R. (1979). Social and political bias in science: An examination of animal studies and their generalizations to human behavior and evolution. In R. Hubbard & M. Lowe (Eds), *Genes and gender 2: Pitfalls in research on sex and gender* (pp. 49–70). New York: Gordian Press.

Bleier, R. (1984). *Science and gender: A critique of biology and its theories on women.* Elmsford, NY: Pergamon Press.

Bleier, R. (1986). Sex differences research: Science or belief? In R. Bleier (Ed.), *Feminist approaches to science* (pp. 147–164). Elmsford, NY: Pergamon Press.

Brown, A. L., & Campione, J. C. (1994). Guided discovery in a community of learners. In K. McGilly (Ed.), *Classroom lessons: Integrating cognitive theory and classroom practice* (pp. 229–270). Cambridge, MA: MIT Press.

Brown, S. V. (1995). Minority women in graduate science and engineering education [Abstract]. In *Unity in diversity* (p. 79). Atlanta, GA: AAAS Annual Meeting and Science Innovation Exposition.

Buffery, W., & Gray, J. (1972). Sex differences in the development of spatial and linguistic skills. In C. Ounsted & D. C. Taylor (Eds.), *Gender differences: Their ontogeny and significance* (pp. 5–19). Edinburgh: Churchill Livingstone.

Bureau of the Census. (1992). Series P-60, No. 174.

Burns, M. (1981, September). Groups of four: Solving the management problem. *Learning,* pp. 46–51.

Calkins, M. (1896). Community ideas of men and women. *Psychological Review, 3*(4), 426–430.

Career Pathways Report. (1993). *Briefing book on the School-to-Work Opportunities Act.* Washington, DC: The Independent Professional News Service for Educators in School-to-Work Transitions.

Career Pathways Report. (1994). *Briefing book on the School-to-Work Opportunities Act of 1994.* Washington, DC: The Independent Professional News Service for Educators in School-to-Work Transitions.

Champagne, A. B., & Newell, S. T. (1992). Directions for research and development: Alternative methods of assessing scientific literacy. *Journal of Research in Science Teaching, 29*(8), 841–860.

Chodorow, N. (1978). *The reproduction of mothering: Psychoanalysis and the sociology of gender.* Berkeley: University of California Press.

Cixous, H., & Clement, C. (1986). *The newly born woman.* Minneapolis: University of Minnesota Press.

Clewell, B. C., & Anderson, B. T. (1991). *Women of color in mathematics, science and engineering: A review of the literature.* Washington, DC: Center for Women Policy Studies.

Clewell, B. C., & Ginorio, A. B. (1996). Examining women's progress in the sciences from the perspective of diversity. In C-S. Davis, A. B. Ginorio, C. S. Hollenshead, B. B. Lazarus, P. M. Rayman, & Associates (Eds.), *The equity equation* (pp. 163–231). San Francisco: Jossey-Bass.

Clinton, W. (1995a). *Evaluation of affirmative action programs.* Memorandum for Heads of Executive Departments and Agencies. White House WorldWideWeb Page, p. 2.

Clinton, W. (1995b, July 19). Remarks by the President on Affirmative Action, White House Office of the Press Secretary.

Committee on Women in Science and Engineering. (1991). *Women in science and engineering: Increasing their numbers in the 1990s.* Washington, DC: National Academy Press.

Corea, G. (1985). *The mother machine: Reproductive technologies from artificial insemination to artificial wombs.* New York: Harper & Row.

Coulter, S., & Vanfossen, B. (1995). *Evaluation manual: How to incorporate evaluation into curriculum transformation projects and activities.* Towson, MD: National Center for Curriculum Transformation Resources on Women.

Crissman, S. (1994). Abstract presented at Awardee Meeting for NSF Program for Women and Girls. Arlington, VA. July 7–8, 1994.

Davis, C-S. (1993). Stepping beyond the campus, *Science, 260,* 414.

Davis, C-S., & Rosser, S. V. (1996). Program and curricular interventions. In C-S. Davis, A. B. Ginorio, C. S. Hollenshead, B.B. Lazarus, P. M. Rayman, & Associates (Eds.), *The equity equation* (pp. 232–264). San Francisco: Jossey-Bass.

Dawkins, R. (1976). *The selfish gene.* New York: Oxford University Press.

de Beauvoir, S. (1974). *The second sex* (H. M. Parshley, Trans. & Ed.). New York: Vintage Books.

Dinnerstein, D. (1977). *The mermaid and the minotaur: Sexual arrangements and human malaise.* New York: Harper Colophon Books.

Dinsmore, M. (1994). *Washington State School-to-Work Opportunities System: Final Report to the Governor.* Olympia, WA: Governor's Council on School to Work.

Dix, D. (1994). Abstract presented at Awardee Meeting for NSF Program for Women and Girls, Arlington, VA. July 7–8, 1994.

Dubois, E., Kelly, G. P., Kennedy, E., Korsmeyer, C., & Robinson, L. S. (1985). *Feminist scholarship: Kindling in the groves of academe.* Urbana: University of Illinois Press.

Dworkin, A. (1983). *Right-wing women.* New York: Coward-McCann.

Edsall, T. (1995, August 15). Pollsters view gender gap as political fixture: White men heed GOP call; women lean to Democrats. *The Washington Post* A-1.

Erhardt, J., & Sandler, B. (1990). *Rx for success: Improving the climate for women in medical schools and teaching hospitals.* Washington, DC: Association of American Colleges and Universities.

Etzkowitz, H., Kemelgor, C., Neuschatz, M., Uzzi, B., & Alonzo, J. (1994). The paradox of critical mass of women in science. *Science, 266,* 51–54.

Falconer, E. (1989). A story of success: The sciences at Spelman College. *SAGE, IV*(2), 34–38.

Fausto-Sterling, A. (1992). *Myths of gender* (Rev. ed.). New York: Basic Books.

Fear-Fenn, M., & Kapostasy, K. K. (1992). *Math + science + technology = vocational preparation for girls: A difficult equation to balance.* Columbus: Ohio State University, Center for Sex Equity.

Federal Register. (1993, February 3). 59(23), 5266-5291.

Federal Register. (1994, March 9). 59(46), 11154.

Fee, E. (1982). A feminist critique of scientific objectivity. *Science for the People, 14*(4), 8.

Firestone, S. (1970). *The dialectic of sex.* New York: Bantam Books.

Fossey, D. (1983). *Gorillas in the mist.* Boston: Houghton Mifflin.

Freud, S. (1924). The dissolution of the Oedipus complex. *Standard edition of the complete psychological works of Sigmund Freud.* London: Hogarth Press and the Institute of Psychoanalysis.

Friedan, B. (1974). *The feminine mystique.* New York: Dell.

Gardner, A. L. (1986). Effectiveness of strategies to encourage participation and retention of precollege and college women in science. Ph.D. thesis, Purdue University West Lafayette, IN.

General Accounting Office. (1992). *Apprenticeship training: Administration, use, and equal opportunity.* Washington, DC: Author.

George, Y. (1994). Abstract presented at Awardee Meeting for NSF Program for Women and Girls, Arlington, VA. July 7–8, 1994.

Giddings, P. (1984). *When and where we enter: The impact of black women on race and sex in America.* New York: Morrow.

Gilligan, C. (1982). *In a different voice: Psychological theory and women's development.* Cambridge, MA: Harvard University Press.

Gilligan, C., Ward, J. V., & Taylor, J. M. (1988). *Mapping the moral domain.* Cambridge, MA: Harvard University Press.

Goodall, J. (1971). *In the shadow of man.* Boston: Houghton Mifflin.

Goodfield, J. (1981). *An imagined world.* New York: Penguin Books.

Gorski, R., Harlan, R. E., Jacobson, C. D., Shryne, J. E., & Southam, A. M. (1980).

Evidence for the existence of a sexually dimorphic nucleus in the preoptic area of the rat. *Journal of Comparative Neurology, 193*, 529–539.

Goy, R., & Phoenix, C. H. (1971). The effects of testosterone propionate administered before birth on the development of behavior in genetic female rhesus monkeys. In C. H. Sawyer & R. A. Gorski (Eds.), *Steroid hormones and brain function* (pp. 193–201). Berkeley: University of California Press.

Grayson, D., & Martin, M. (1990). *GESA: Gender/ethnic expectations and student achievement.* Earlham, IN: Graymill.

Green, K. C. (1989a). A profile of undergraduates in the sciences. *The American Scientist, 78*, 475–480.

Green, K. C.. (1989b). Keynote address: A profile of undergraduates in the sciences. In National Advisory Group, Sigma Xi, the Scientific Research Society, *An exploration of the nature and quality of undergraduate education in science, mathematics and engineering.* Racine, WI: Wingspread Conference.

Griffin, S. (1978). *The death of nature.* New York: Harper & Row.

Grimshaw, J. (1986). *Feminist philosophers: Women's perspectives on philosophical traditions.* Sussex: Wheatsheaf.

Gunew, S. (1990). *Feminist knowledge: Critique and construct.* New York: Routledge.

Hall, R., & Sandler, B. (1982). *The classroom climate: A chilly one for women.* Washington, DC: Project on the Status and Education for Women, Association of American Colleges.

Haraway, D. (1978). Animal sociology and a natural economy of the body politic. *Signs, 4*(1), 21–60.

Haraway, D. (1989). *Primate visions: Gender, race, and nature in the world of modern science.* New York: Routledge.

Harding, J. (1985). Values, cognitive style and the curriculum. *Contributions to the Third Girls and Science and Technology Conference.* London: University of London, Chelsea College.

Harding, S. (1986). *The science question in feminism.* Ithaca, NY: Cornell University Press.

Hartman, M., & Banner, L. (Eds.). (1974). *Clio's consciousness raised.* New York: Bantam Books.

Hein, H. (1981). Women and science: Fitting men to think about nature. *International Journal of Women's Studies, 4*, 369–377.

Hennig, M., & Jardim, A. (1977). *The managerial woman.* New York: Anchorage-Doubleday.

Hollingsworth, L. S. (1914). Variability as related to sex differences in achievement. *American Journal of Sociology, 19*(4), 510–530.

Holloway, M. (1993). A lab of her own. *Scientific American, 269*(5), 94–103.

Honey, M. (1994). Abstract presented at Awardee Meeting at NSF Program for Women and Girls, Arlington, VA, July 7–8, 1994.

hooks, b. (1981). *Talking back: Thinking feminist, thinking black.* Boston: South End Press.

hooks, b. (1983). *Feminist theory from margin to center.* Boston: South End Press.

hooks, b. (1990). *Yearning: Race, gender, and cultural politics.* Boston: South End Press.

Hrdy, S. B. (1977). *The langurs of Abu: Female and male strategies of reproduction.* Cambridge, MA: Harvard University Press.

Hrdy, S. B. (1979). Infanticide among animals: A review, classification and examination of the implications for the reproductive strategies of females. *Ethology and Sociobiology, 1,* 3–40.

Hrdy, S. B. (1981). *The woman that never evolved.* Cambridge, MA: Harvard University Press.

Hrdy, S. B. (1984). Introduction: Female reproductive strategies. In M. Small (Ed.), *Female primates: Studies by women primatologists* (pp. 13–16). New York: Alan Liss.

Hrdy, S. B. (1986). Empathy, polyandry, and the myth of the coy female. In R. Bleier (Ed.), *Feminist approaches to science* (pp. 119–146). Elmsford, NY: Pergamon Press.

Hrdy, S., & Williams, G. C. (1983). Behavioral biology and the double standard. In S. K. Wasser (Ed.), *Social behavior of female vertebrates* (pp. 3–17). New York: Academic Press.

Hubbard, R. (1979). Introduction. In R. Hubbard & M. Lowe (Eds.), *Genes and gender 2: Pitfalls in research on sex and gender* (pp. 9–34). New York: Gordian Press.

Hubbard, R. (1990). *The politics of women's biology.* New Brunswick, NJ: Rutgers University Press.

Hynes, P. H. (1989). *The recurring silent spring.* Elmsford, NY: Pergamon Press.

Hynes, P. (1995). No classroom is an island. In S. V. Rosser (Ed.), *Teaching the majority: Breaking the gender barrier in science, mathematics, and engineering* (pp. 211–219). New York: Teachers College Press.

International Association for the Evaluation of Educational Attainment. (1988). *Science achievement in seventeen countries: A preliminary report.* Oxford: Pergamon Press.

Jaggar, A. (1983). *Feminist politics and human nature.* Totowa, NJ: Rowman & Allanheld.

Jaggar, A., & Rothenberg, P. (Eds.). (1984). *Feminist frameworks* (2nd ed.). New York: McGraw-Hill.

Johnson, D. W., & Johnson, F. (1994). *Joining together: Group theory and group skills* (5th ed.). Boston: Allyn & Bacon.

Jones, J. H. (1981). *Bad blood: The Tuskegee syphilis experiment—A tragedy of race and medicine.* New York: Free Press.

Kahle, J. B. (1985). *Women in science.* Philadelphia: Falmer Press.

Keller, E. F. (1982). Feminism and science. *Signs: Journal of Women in Culture and Society, 7*(3), 589–602.

Keller, E. F. (1983). *A feeling for the organism: The life and work of Barbara McClintock.* New York: W.H. Freeman.

Keller, E. F. (1985). *Reflections on gender and science.* New Haven, CT: Yale University Press.

Kerka, S. (1993). Trends and issues alerts. *Gender Equity in Vocational Education.* Columbus, Oh: ERIC Clearinghouse on Adult, Career, and Vocational Education.

Kerr, B., & Robinson, S. (1994). Abstract presented at Awardee Meeting for NSF Program for Women and Girls, Arlington, VA, July 7–8, 1994.

Keynes, H. B. (1989, Spring). University of Minnesota Talented Youth Mathematics Project: Recruiting girls for a more successful equation. *ITEMS,* University of Minnesota Institute of Technology.

Kole, A. (1995, August 3). Highlights of the Affirmative Action Review—Report to the President by the Office of the General Counsel, Department of Education.

Kramarae, C. (Ed). (1980). *The voices and words of women and men.* London: Pergamon Press.

Kramarae, C., & Treichler, P. (1986). *A feminist dictionary.* London: Pandora Press.

Kristeva, J. (1984). *The revolution in poetic language.* New York: Columbia University Press.

Kristeva, J. (1987). *Tales of love.* New York: Columbia University Press.

Lakoff, R. (1975). *Language and woman's place.* New York: Harper & Row.

Lancaster, J. (1975). *Primate behavior and the emergence of human culture.* New York: Holt, Rinehart and Winston.

Leavitt, R. (1975). *Peaceable primates and gentle people: Anthropological approaches to women's studies.* New York: Harper & Row.

Lederman, D., & Burd, S. (1996, July 12). High court refuses to hear appeal of rulings that barred considering race in admissions. *The Chronicle of Higher Education,* pp. A25–26.

Leibowitz, L. (1975). Perspectives in the evolution of sex differences. In R. Reiter (Ed.), *Toward an anthropology of women* (pp. 20–35). New York: Monthly Review Press.

Lie, S., & Bryhni, E. (1983). Girls and physics: Attitudes, experiences and underachievement. Contributions to the Second Girls and Science and Technology Conference. Oslo, Norway: University of Oslo, Institute of Physics, 202–211.

Light, R. (1990). *Explorations with students and faculty about teaching, learning, and student life.* Cambridge, MA: Harvard University Press.

Lloyd, G. (1984). *The man of reason: "Male" and "female" in western philosophy.* London: Methuen.

Lorde, A. (1984). *Sister outsider.* Trumansburg, NY: Crossing Press.

Lowry, M. (1995). *Working and learning together: Creating Washington's comprehensive School-to-Work Transition System.* Olympia: State of Washington.

MacKinnon, C. (1982). Feminism, Marxism, and the state: An agenda for theory. *Signs: Journal of Women in Culture and Society, 7*(3), 515–544.

MacKinnon, C. (1987). *Feminism unmodified: Discourses on life and law.* Cambridge, MA: Harvard University Press.

Malcom, S. M., Hall, P. Q., & Brown, J. W. (1976). *The double-bind: The price of being a minority woman in science.* Washington, DC: American Association for the Advancement of Science.

Martinez, M. E., & Mead, N. A. (1988). *Computer competence: The first national assessment.* Princeton, NJ: Educational Testing Service.

Massey, W. F., & Goldman, C. A. (1995). *The production and utilization of science and engineering doctorates in the United States.* Stanford, CA: Stanford University Press.

Matyas, M. L. (1985). Obstacles and constraints on women in science. In J. B. Kahle (Ed.), *Women in science* (pp. 77–101). Philadelphia: Falmer Press.

Matyas, M., & Malcom, S. M. (1991). *Investing in human potential: Science and engineering at the crossroads.* Washington, DC: American Association for the Advancement of Science.

McIntosh, P. (1984). The study of women: Processes of personal and curricular re-vision. *Forum for Liberal Education, 6*(5), 2–4.

McMillen, L. (1987, Sept. 9). More colleges and more disciplines incorporating scholarship on women into the classroom. *The Chronicle of Higher Education, 34*(2), pp. A15–A17.

McMillen, L. (1996, June 28). The science wars. *The Chronicle of Higher Education,* pp. A8, A9, A13.

Merchant, C. (1979). *The death of nature: Women, ecology and the scientific revolution.* New York: Harper & Row.

Michaelson, M. (1996, July 19). A time to increase public understanding of affirmative action. *The Chronicle of Higher Education,* p. A48.

Middlecamp, C. (1995). Culturally inclusive chemistry. In S. V. Rosser (Ed.), *Teaching the majority* (pp. 79–97). New York: Teachers College Press.

Milgram, D. (October 14, 1993). Testimony by Donna Milgram, Director of the Nontraditional Employment Training Project, Wider Opportunities for Women, on behalf of the Coalition on Women and Job Training before the Employment and Productivity Subcommittee of the Senate Labor and Human Resources Committee. Washington, DC: Displaced Homemakers Network.

Milgram, D., & Watkins, K. (1994). *Ensuring quality school-to-work opportunities for young women.* Washington, DC: Wider Opportunities for Women.

Mill, H. T. (1970). Enfranchisement of women. In A. S. Rossi (Ed.), *Essays on sex equality* (pp. 89–122). Chicago: University of Chicago Press.

Mill, J. S. (1970). The subjection of women. In A. S. Rossi (Ed.), *Essays on sex equality* (pp. 123–242). Chicago: University of Chicago Press.

Millett, K. (1970). *Sexual politics.* Garden City, NY: Doubleday.

National Advisory Group, Sigma Xi, the Scientific Research Society. (1989). *An exploration of the nature and quality of undergraduate education in science, mathematics and engineering.* Racine, WI: Wingspread Conference.

National Center for Education Statistics. (1990). *Vocational education in the United States: 1969–1990.* Washington, DC: Author.

National Research Council. (1994). Unpublished data.

National Research Council. (1996). *National Science Education Standards.* Washington, DC: National Academy Press.

National Research Council, Committee on Science, Engineering, and Public Policy. (1995). *Reshaping the graduate education of scientists and engineers.* Washington, DC: National Academy Press.

National Research Council, National Committee on Science Education Standards and Assessments. (1993, February & July). *National Science Education Standards working papers: An enhanced sampler* (Progress Report). Washington, DC: National Research Council.

National Science Foundation. (1986, 1988, 1990, 1992). *Report on women and minorities in science and engineering.* Arlington, VA: Author.

National Science Foundation. (1989). *Report on the NSF disciplinary workshops on undergraduate education.* Arlington, VA: Author.

National Science Foundation. (1991). *Survey on retention at higher education institutions.* Arlington, VA: Author, with the National Endowment for the Humanities, and the U.S. Department of Education.

National Science Foundation. (1991/1992/1993). *Undergraduate course and curriculum development program 1991, 1992, 1993 summary.* Arlington, VA: Author.

National Science Foundation. (1992). *Women and minorities in science and engineering: An update.* (NSF 92–303). Arlington, VA: Author.

National Science Foundation. (1993a). *Education and Human Resources Program for Women and Girls Program Announcement* (NSF 93–126). Arlington, VA: Author.

National Science Foundation. (1993b). *EHR activities for women and girls in science, engineering, and mathematics.* (NSF 93–126) Arlington, VA: Author.

National Science Foundation. (1993c). *The federal investment in science, mathematics, engineering, and technology education: Where now? What next?* Arlington, VA: Author.

National Science Foundation. (1994a). *NSF Visiting Professorships for Women.* (NSF 94–68) Arlington, VA: Author.

National Science Foundation. (1994b). *The Visiting Professorships for Women Program: Lowering the hurdles for women in science and engineering.* (NSF 94–88) Arlington, VA: Author.

National Science Foundation. (1994c). *Women, minorities, and persons with disabilities in science and engineering: 1994.* Arlington, VA: Author.

Neale, A., Gerhart, J., Hobbie, R. K., McDermott, L. C., Romer, R., & Thomas, B. R. (1991). The undergraduate physics major. *American Journal of Physics, 59,* 106–111.

Oakes, J. (1990). *Lost talent: The underparticipation of women, minorities, and disabled persons in science.* Washington, DC: National Science Foundation, with the Rand Corporation.

Oakes, J. T., Ormseth, R. B., & Camp, P. (1994). *Multiplying inequalities: The effect of race, social class, and tracking on students' opportunities to learn mathematics and science.* Santa Monica, CA: Rand Corporation.

O'Barr, J., & Wyer, M. (1990). *Women in science: A Duke University community initiative* [Abstract for NSF Grant HRD-95253431].

O'Brien, M. (1981). *The politics of reproduction.* Boston: Routledge & Kegan Paul.

O'Connell, A., & Russo, N. (1983). *Models of achievement.* New York: Columbia University Press.

Office of Technology Assessment. (1987). *New developments in biotechnology background paper: Public perceptions of biotechnology* (OTA-BP-BA-45). Washington, DC: Author.

Orenstein, P. (1994). *Schoolgirls: Young women, self-esteem and the confidence gap.* New York: Doubleday.

Project Kaleidoscope. (1991). *Volume I: What works: Building natural science communities.* Washington, DC: Independent Colleges Office.

Project Kaleidoscope. (1992). *Volume II: What works: Resources for reform.* Washington, DC: Independent Colleges Office.

Project Kaleidoscope. (1994). *Project Kaleidoscope Phase II: What works: Focusing on the future.* Washington, DC: Independent Colleges Office.

Project on the Status and Education of Women. (1988). *Evaluating courses for inclusion of new scholarship on women.* Washington, DC: Association of American Colleges.

Rayman, P., & Brett, B. (1993). *Pathways for women in the sciences: The Wellesley Report (Part I).* Wellesley, MA: Wellesley Center for Research on Women.

Rayman, P., & Brett, B. (1995). Women science majors: What makes a difference in persistence after graduation? *Journal of Higher Education, 66*(4), 388–414.

Rich, A. (1976). *Of woman born: Motherhood as experience.* New York: Norton.

Rosser, S. V. (1982). Androgyny and sociobiology. *International Journal of Women's Studies, 5*(5), 435–444.

Rosser, S. V. (1986). *Teaching science and health from a feminist perspective: A practical guide.* New York: Teachers College Press.

Rosser, S. V. (1988). Women in science and health care: A gender at risk. In S. V. Rosser (Ed.), *Feminism within the science and health care professions: Overcoming resistance* (pp. 3–15). New York: Teachers College Press.

Rosser, S. V. (1989). Teaching techniques to attract women to science: Applications of feminist theories and methodologies. *Women's Studies International Forum, 12*(3), 363–377.

Rosser, S. V. (1990). *Female friendly science: Applying women's studies, methods and theories to attract students.* New York: Teachers College Press.

Rosser, S. V. (1993a). Diversity among students—inclusive curriculum—improved science: An upward spiral. *Initiatives, 55,* 11–19.

Rosser, S. V. (1993b). Female friendly science: Including women in curricular content and pedagogy in science. *Journal of General Education, 42*(3), 191–220.

Rosser, S. V. (1993c). Gender bias in clinical research and the difference it makes. *Applied Clinical Trials, 2,* 44–52.

Rosser, S. V. (Ed.). (1995). *Teaching the majority.* New York: Teachers College Press.

Rosser, S. V., & Kelly, B. (1994a). *Educating women for success in science and mathematics* (NSF Project HRD 9053892). West Columbia: University of South Carolina Publications.

Rosser, S. V., & Kelly, B. (1994b). From hostile exclusion to friendly inclusion: University of South Carolina System model project for the transformation of science and math teaching to reach women in varied campus settings. *Journal of Women and Minorities in Science and Engineering, 1*(1), 29–44.

Rosser, S. V., & Kelly, B. (1994c). Who is helped by friendly inclusion? Final results from the USC System model project for the transformation of science and math teaching to reach women in varied campus settings. *Journal of Women and Minorities in Science and Engineering, 1*(13), 175–192.

Rossiter, M. W. (1984). *Women scientists in America: Struggles and strategies to 1940.* Baltimore, MD: Johns Hopkins University Press.

Rothfield, P. (1990). Feminism, subjectivity, and sexual difference. In S. Annew (Ed.), *Feminist knowledge: Critique and construct* (pp. 121–144). New York: Routledge.

Rowell, T. (1974). The concept of social dominance. *Behavioral Biology, 11,* 131–154.

Sadker, M., & Sadker, D. (1994). *Failing at fairness: How America's schools cheat girls.* New York: Scribner's.

Sanders, J. (1985, April). Making the computer neuter. *The Computing Teacher,* pp. 23–27.

Sanders, J. (1995). Girls and technology: Villain wanted. In S. V. Rosser (Ed.), *Teaching the majority* (pp. 147–159). New York: Teachers College Press.

Sax, L. (1994). Retaining tomorrow's scientists: Exploring the factors that keep male and female college students interested in science careers. *Journal of Women and Minorities in Science and Engineering, 1*(1), 45–62.

Sayre, A. (1975). *Rosalind Franklin and DNA: A vivid view of what it is like to be a gifted woman in an especially male profession.* New York: Norton.

Schuster, M., & Van Dyne, S. (1985). *Women's place in the academy: Transforming the liberal arts curriculum.* Totowa, NJ: Rowman & Allanheld.

Schwartz, A. T., Burrce, D., Silberman, R., Stanitsbi, C., Stratton, W., & Zipp, A. (1993). *Chemistry in context.* Dubuque, IA: William C. Brown.

Sebrechts, J. (1992, April). The cultivation of scientists at women's colleges. *The Journal of NIH Research, 4,* 22–26.

Sebrechts, J. (1995). The women's college difference. *Unity in diversity,* published abstract. AAAS Annual Meeting, Feb. 16–21, Atlanta, GA. Washington, DC: AAAS.

Sells, L. (1975). *Sex and discipline differences in doctoral attrition.* Unpublished Ph.D. dissertation, University of California at Berkeley.

Seymour, E. (1995). Guest comment: Why undergraduates leave the sciences. *American Journal of Physics, 63,* 199–202.

Seymour, E., & Hewitt, N. M. (1994). *Talking about leaving: Factors contributing to high attrition rates among science, mathematics, and engineering undergraduate majors* (Final Report to the Alfred P. Sloan Foundation on an Ethnographic Inquiry at Seven Institutions). Boulder, CO: Ethnography and Assessment Research, Bureau of Sociological Research.

Sharpe, N. R. (1995). Sisters spell success. *AWIS Magazine, 24*(5), 12–14.

Sigma Xi (1994). *Scientists, educators and national standards: Actions at the local level.* Research Triangle Park, NC: Sigma Xi.

Silverman, S., & Pritchard, A. (1993). *Building their future: Girls in technology education in Connecticut.* Hartford, CT: Vocational Equity Research, Training and Evaluation Center.

Skidmore (Dix), L. (1994). Abstract presented at Awardee Meeting for NSF Program for Women and Girls, July 7–8, 1994, Arlington, VA.

Slavin, R. E. (1990). *Cooperative learning, theory, research, and practice.* Englewood Cliffs, NJ: Prentice-Hall.

Smith, D. (1991). Classroom interaction and gender disparity in secondary vocational instruction. *Journal of Vocational Education Research, 16*(93), 35–58.

Smith-Rosenberg, C. (1975, Autumn). The female world of love and ritual: Relations between women in nineteenth century America. *Signs: Journal of Women in Culture and Society, 1,* 1–29.

Spalter-Roth, R., & Hartmann, H. (1991). *Improving women's status in the workforce: The family issue of the future.* Washington, DC: Institute for Women's Policy Research.

Spanier, B. (1982, April). Toward a balanced curriculum: The study of women at Wheaton College. *Change, 14,* 31–34.

Sperry, R. W. (1974). Lateral specialization in the surgically separated hemispheres. In F. O. Schmitt, & F. G. Wardon (Eds.), *The neurosciences: Third study program.* Cambridge, MA: MIT Press.

Steinmark, J., Thompson, V., & Cossey, R. (1986). *Family math.* Berkeley, CA: EQUALS Project, Lawrence Hall of Science.

Strenta, C., Elliott, R., Matier, M., Scott, J., & Adair, R. (1993). *Choosing and leaving science in highly selective institutions: General factors and the question of gender* (Report to the Alfred P. Sloan Foundation). Boulder: University of Colorado.

Swoboda, F. (1995, March 16). Glass ceiling firmly in place, panel finds. *Washington Post, 101,* A1, A18.

Tannen, D. (1990). *You just don't understand.* New York: Ballantine.

Tanner, A. (1896). The community of ideas of men and women. *Psychological Review, 3*(5), 548–550.

Tapper, M. (1986, June). Can a liberal be a feminist? *Supplement to the Australian Journal of Philosophy, 64,* 37–47.

Tetreault, M. K. (1985). Stages of thinking about women: An experience-derived evaluation model. *Journal of Higher Education, 5*(4), 368–384.

Thomas, V. (1989). Black women engineers and technologists. *Sage: Scholarly Journal on Black Women, 4*(2), 24–32.

Tidball, E. (1986, November/December). Baccalaureate origins of recent natural science doctorates. *Journal of Higher Education, 5*(7), 606–620.

To help girls keep up with boys: All-girl math and science classes. (1993, November 24). *New York Times,* pp. A1, B10.

Tobias, S. (1990). *They're not dumb, they're different.* Tucson, AZ: Research Corporation.

Tobias, S. (1992). *Revitalizing undergraduate science education: Why some things work and most don't.* Tucson, AZ: Research Corporation.

Tobias, S., & Chubin, D. (1996, July 12). New degrees for today's scientists. *The Chronicle of Higher Education,* pp. B1–B2.

Tong, R. (1989). *Feminist thought: A comprehensive introduction.* Boulder, CO: Westview Press.

Treisman, P. U. (1992). Studying students studying calculus: A look at the lives of minority mathematics students in college. *The College Mathematics Journal, 23*(5), 362–372.

Trivers, R. L. (1972). Parental investment and sexual selection. In B. Campbell (Ed.), *Sexual selection and the descent of man* (pp. 136–179). Chicago: Aldine.

U.S. Department of Education. (1995). *Application for grants under Women's Educational Equity Act Program.* Washington, DC: Author.

U.S. Department of Labor. (1987, June). *Workforce 2000.* Washington, DC: U.S. Government Printing Office.

Vetter, B. (1988). Where are the women in the physical sciences? In S. V. Rosser (Ed.), *Feminism within the science and health care professions: Overcoming resistance* (pp. 19–32). New York: Teachers College Press.

Vetter, B. M. (1989). *Professional women and minorities.* Washington, DC: Commission on Professionals in Science and Technology.

Vetter, B. M. (1992). *What is holding up the glass ceiling? Barriers to women in the science and engineering workforce* (Occasional Paper 92–3). Washington, DC: Commission on Professionals in Science and Technology.

Vetter, B. (1996). Women in science, mathematics and engineering: Myths and realities. In C-S. Davis, A. B. Ginorio, C. S. Hollenshead, B. B. Lazarus, P. M. Rayman, & Associates (Eds.), *The equity equation: Fostering the advancement of women in the sciences, mathematics, and engineering* (pp. 29–56). San Francisco: Jossey-Bass.

Wahl, E. (1993, April 16). Getting messy. *Science, 260,* 412–413.

Watanabe, M. (1995, September 18). Pressures wearing down researchers. *The Scientist,* pp. 1, 6–7.

Wheeler, E. J. (1995). *Regents vote on affirmative action.* Irvine: University of California.

Wheeler, P., & Harris, A. (1979). *Performance differences between males and females on the ATP physics test.* Berkeley, CA: Educational Testing Service.

Widnall, S. (1988). AAAS presidential lecture: Voices from the pipeline. *Science, 241,* 1740–1745.

Wilson, E. O. (1975). *Sociobiology: The new synthesis.* Cambridge, MA: Harvard University Press.

Wollstonecraft, M. (1975). *A vindication of the rights of woman* (C. Poston, Ed.). New York: Norton.

Women's Community Cancer Project. (1994, Winter). National Breast Cancer Coalition. *Women's Community Cancer Project Newsletter, 4,* 4.

Women's Community Cancer Project. (1992, Fall). A woman's cancer agenda: the demands. *Women's Community Cancer Project Newsletter, 2.*

Women's Educational Equity Act. (1993, November). *Women's Educational Equity Act Program Abstracts.* Washington, DC: Author.

Yentsch, C., & Sindermann, C. (1992). *The woman scientist: Meeting the challenges for a successful career.* New York: Plenum Press.

Yerkes, R. M. (1943). *Chimpanzees.* New Haven, CT: Yale University Press.

Zimmerman, D. H., & West, C. (1975). Sex roles, interruptions and silences in conversation. In B. Thorne & N. Henley (Eds.), *Language and sex: Difference and dominance* (pp. 105–129). Rowley, MA: Newbury House.

Bibliography: Selected Resources on Female Friendly Science

This bibliography updates an earlier one that Faye Chadwell compiled for Sue Rosser's *Female Friendly Science: Applying Women's Studies Methods and Theories to Attract Students* (New York: Teachers College Press, 1990). Therefore, most of the citations are for resources published after 1989. There are four parts to this bibliography—Part One: Achieving a Female Friendly Science— Resources on Pedagogy, Mentoring, and Recruitment; Part Two: Feminist Science; Part Three: Women in Science; and Part Four: Internet Resources.

Part One has a self-explanatory title. Part Two covers feminist critiques of science. It also includes some works by those who find feminist critiques of science problematic. Part Three provides some citations on women scientists. A bibliography published in *Teaching the Majority: Breaking the Gender Barrier in Science, Mathematics, and Engineering* (New York: Teachers College Press, 1995, pp. 231–251), edited by Sue Rosser, contains additional information on women in particular science fields. Because so much communication about female friendly science is available digitally or electronically, Part Four covers listservs and World Wide Web sites.

Faye A. Chadwell
Jill Holman
University of Oregon Libraries, Eugene

PART ONE: ACHIEVING A FEMALE FRIENDLY SCIENCE— RESOURCES ON PEDAGOGY, MENTORING, AND RECRUITMENT

Acker, S. (1994). *Gendered education: Sociological reflections on women, teaching, and feminism.* Philadelphia: Open University Press.

Adamu, A. U. (1990, June). Balancing the equation—Girls, tradition and science education in northern Nigeria. *Afhad Journal, 7,* 14–31.

Allen, N. (1992). A proposed course on women in science in an Australian university. *Feminist Teacher, 6*(3), 40–44.

Alper, J. (1993, April 16). The pipeline is leaking women all the way along. *Science, 260* (5106), 409–411.

American Association of University Women. (1994). *Shortchanging girls, shortchanging*

America: Executive summary: A nationwide poll that assesses self-esteem, educational experiences, interest in math and science, and career aspirations of girls and boys ages 9–15. (2nd ed.). Washington, DC: American Association of University Women Educational Foundation.

Anderson, B. T. (1992). Minority females in the science pipeline: Activities to enhance readiness, recruitment, and retention. *Initiatives, 55*(3), 31–38.

Aptheker, B. (1993). Introduction to feminism. *Women's Studies Quarterly, 21*(3–4), 63–68.

AWIS completes mentoring program. (1994). *Women's Research Network News, 5*(4), 7–8.

Baker, D., & Leary, R. (1995). Letting girls speak out about science. *Journal of Research in Science Teaching, 32*(1), 3–27.

Banziger, G. (1992). Women-in-the-sciences program at Marietta College: Focusing on math to keep women in science. *Journal of College Science Teaching, 21*(5), 279–281.

Beauchamp, R. S. (Ed.). (1991). Women in science: Options and intolerance [Special issue]. *Women's Education/Education Des Femmes, 9*(2).

Benditt, J. (Ed.). (1992). Women in science. First annual survey. *Science, 255*(5050), 1363–1388.

Berry, E., & Black, E. (1993). The integrative learning journal (or, getting beyond "true confessions" and "cold knowledge"). *Women's Studies Quarterly, 21*(3–4), 88–93.

Bianchini, J. (1993, April). *The high school biology textbook: A changing mosaic of gender, science, and purpose.* Paper presented at the annual meeting of the American Educational Research Association, Atlanta. (ERIC Document Reproduction Service No. ED 363 513)

Bickel, J. (1995). Women in U.S. academic medicine: 1994 status report. *AWIS Magazine, 24*(2), 6–9, 15.

Bird, S. J. (1993). *Mentoring means future scientists: A guide for developing mentoring programs based on the AWIS Mentoring Project.* Washington, DC: Association for Women in Science.

Bird, S. J., & Didion, C. J. (1992). Retaining women science students: A mentoring project of the Association for Women in Science. *Initiatives, 55*(3), 3–12.

Birke, L., & Barr, J. (1994). Women, science, and adult education: Toward a feminist curriculum? *Women's Studies International Forum, 17* (5), 473–483.

Blosser, P. E. (1990). *Procedures to increase the entry of women into science-related careers.* Washington, DC: Office of Educational Research and Improvement.

Bonsangue, M. V., & Drew, D. E. (1995). Increasing minority students' success in calculus. *New Directions for Teaching and Learning, 61*, 23–33.

Borman, S. (1991, November 4). College science studies: Women, minority recruitment lags. *Chemical & Engineering News, 69*(44), 6–7.

Breaking anonymity: The chilly climate for women faculty. (1995). (ERIC Document Reproduction Service No. ED 388 209)

Brennan, M. B. (1993, June 14). Programs seek to draw more women into engineering & science. *Chemical & Engineering News, 71*(24), 43–44.

Brickhouse, N. W., et al. (1990, February). Women and chemistry: Shifting the equilibrium toward success. *Journal of Chemical Education, 67*(2), 116–118.

Bright, C. (1993). Teaching feminist pedagogy: An undergraduate course. *Women's Studies Quarterly, 21*(3–4), 128–132.

Brodsky, S. M. (1990). *Campus seminars/workshops to improve recruitment and retention of women and minorities in associate degree science and engineering technology programs. Final report.* Albany: New York State Education Department. (ERIC Document Reproduction Service No. ED 325 197)

Burroughs, C. B. (1990). The immediate classroom: Feminist pedagogy and Peter Brook's *The Empty Space. Feminist Teacher, 5*(2), 10–14.

Burton, L. (1995). Moving towards a feminist epistemology of mathematics. *Educational Studies in Mathematics, 28*(3), 275–291.

Campbell, P. B. (1992). *Math, science, and your daughter: What can parents do?* Encouraging Girls in Math and Science Series. Washington, DC: Women's Educational Equity Program. (ERIC Document Reproduction Service No. ED 350 172)

Campbell, P. B. (1992). *Nothing can stop us now: Designing effective programs for girls in math, science, and engineering.* Encouraging Girls in Math and Science Series. Washington, DC: Women's Educational Equity Program. (ERIC Document Reproduction Service No. ED 350 173)

Campbell, P. B. (1992). *What works and what doesn't? Ways to evaluate programs for girls in math, science, and engineering.* Encouraging Girls in Math and Science Series. Washington, DC: Women's Educational Equity Program. (ERIC Document Reproduction Service No. ED 350 171)

Campbell, P. B. (1992). *Working together, making changes: Working in and out of school to encourage girls in math and science.* Encouraging Girls in Math and Science Series. Washington, DC: Women's Educational Equity Program. (ERIC Document Reproduction Service No. ED 350 170)

Castenell, L. A., Jr. & William F. P. (Eds.). (1993). *Understanding curriculum as racial text: Representations of identity and difference in education.* Albany: State University of New York Press.

Chomicka, D., Truchan, L., & Gurria, G. (1992). The "Women In Science Day" at Alverno College: Collaboration that leads to success. *Journal of College Science Teaching, 21*(5), 306–309.

Clair, R. (1995). Introduction: Birth of a project. In *The scientific education of girls: Education beyond reproach* (pp 1–7)? Bristol, PA: Jessica Kingsley, Publishers, LTD, UNESCO.

Clewell, B. C., & Anderson, B. T. (1991). *Women of color in mathematics, science and engineering: A review of the literature.* Washington, DC: Center for Women Policy Studies. (ERIC Document Reproduction Service No. ED 347 222)

Clewell, B. C., et al. (1992). The prevalence and nature of mathematics, science, and computer science intervention programs serving minority and female students in grades four through eight. *Equity and Excellence, 25*(2–4), 209–215.

Collea, F. P. (1990). Increasing minorities in science and engineering: A critical look at two programs. *Journal of College Science Teaching, 20*(1), 31–34, 41.

Culotta, E., Kahn, P., Koppel, T., & Gibbons, A. (1993, April 16). Women struggle to crack the code of corporate culture. *Science, 260*(5106), 398–404.

Dain, J. (1991). Women and computing: Some responses to falling numbers in higher education. *Women's Studies International Forum, 14*(3), 217–225.

Damarin, S. K. (1990). Unthinking educational technology. In *Proceedings of selected paper presentations at the convention of the Association for Educational Communications and Technology.* (ERIC Document Reproduction Service No. ED 323 925)

Damarin, S. K. (1991). Rethinking science and mathematics curriculum and instruction: Feminist perspectives in the computer era. *Journal of Education, 173*(1), 107–123.

Davis, C. (1996). *The equity equation: Fostering the advancement of women in the sciences, mathematics, and engineering.* San Francisco: Jossey-Bass.

Davis, F. (1993). *Feminist pedagogy in the physical sciences.* Quebec: Ministere de l'enseignement superieur et de la science, Programme d'aide a la recherche sur l'enseignement et l'apprentissage.

Davis, F., & Steiger, A. (1993). *Feminist pedagogy in the physical sciences.* (ERIC Document Reproduction Service No. ED 372 781)

Davis, F., et al. (1989). *A practical assessment of feminist pedagogy* (Research Report). (ERIC Document Reproduction Service No. ED 327 502)

Deats, S. M. & Lenker, L. T. (1994). *Gender and academe: Feminist pedagogy and politics.* Lanham, MD: Rowman & Littlefield.

Didion, C. J. (1993, May). Attracting graduate and undergraduate women as science majors. *Journal of College Science Teaching, 22*(6), 336, 368.

Didion, C. J. (1993, September). Letter of reference: An often-deciding factor in women's academic or career advancement. *Journal of College Science Teaching, 23*(1), 9–10.

Didion, C. J. (1993, October). Making teaching environments hospitable for women in science. *Journal of College Science Teaching, 23*(2), 82–83.

Didion, C. J. (1995). Mentoring women in science. *Educational Horizons, 73*(3), 141–144.

Dix, L. S., Matyas, M. L., & Dresselhaus, M. S. (Eds.). (1992). *Science and engineering programs: On target for women?* Washington, DC: National Academy Press.

Dresselhaus, M. S. (1991). (Ed.). *Women in science and engineering: Increasing their numbers in the 1990s: A statement on policy and strategy.* Washington, DC: National Academy Press.

Dumais, L. (1992). Impact of the participation of women in science—On rethinking the place of women especially in occupational health. *Women and Health, 18*(3), 11–25.

Dunn, K. (1993). Feminist teaching: Who are your students? *Women's Studies Quarterly, 21*(3–4), 39–45.

Eldredge, M., et al. (1990). Gender, science, and technology: A selected annotated bibliography. *Behavioral & Social Sciences Librarian, 9*(1), 77–134.

Falconer, E. Z. (1989, Fall). A story of success—The sciences at Spelman College. *Sage: A Scholarly Journal on Black Women, 6,* 36–39.

Farmer, H. S., et al. (1995). Women's career choices: Focus on science, math, and technology careers. *Journal of Counseling Psychology, 42*(2), 155–170.

Feldberg, G. (1992). From anti-feminine to anti-feminist? Students' reflections on women and science. *Women and Therapy, 12*(4), 113–125.

Fisher, B. (1993). The heart has its reasons: Feeling, thinking, and community-building in feminist education. *Women's Studies Quarterly, 21*(3–4), 75–88.

Fort, D. C., Bird, S. J., & Didion, C. J. (1995). *A hand up: Women mentoring women in science* (2nd ed.). Washington, DC: Association for Women in Science.

Fox, M. F., & Firebaugh, G. (1992). Confidence in science: The gender gap. *Social Science Quarterly, 73*(1), 101–113.

Franklin, U. (1993). Letter to a graduate student. *Canadian Woman Studies, 13*(2), 12–15.

Friedman, B. (1990). Bringing knowledge of women mathematicians into the mathematics classroom. *Mathematics and Computer Education, 24*(3), 250–253.

Gabriel, S. L., & Smithson, I. (Eds.). (1990). *Gender in the classroom: Power and pedagogy.* Urbana: University of Illinois Press.

Giese, P. A. (1992). Women in science: 5000 years of obstacles and achievements. *Appraisal: Science Books for Young People, 25*(2), 1–20.

Ginorio, A. B. (1995). *Warming the climate for women in academic science.* Washington, DC: Association of American Colleges and Universities.

Girls in schools: A bibliography of research on girls in U.S. public schools, kindergarten through grade 12 (3rd ed.). (ERIC Document Reproduction Service No. ED 360 241)

Gore, J. (1993). *The struggle for pedagogies: Critical and feminist discourses as regimes of truth.* New York: Routledge.

Gough, A. G. (1995, April). *Recognising women in environmental education pedagogy and research: Toward an ecofeminist poststructuralist perspective.* Paper presented at the annual meeting of the American Educational Research Association, San Francisco. (ERIC Document Reproduction Service No. ED 385 447)

Gray, P. E., & McBay, S. M. (1990, Summer). Breaking the barriers: Women and minorities in the sciences. *On the Issues, 15,* 7–9.

Hall, C. (Ed.). (1989). Toward a more inclusive curriculum: The integration of gender, race, and class. In *Selected proceedings from a Regional Conference Held at Ursinus College* (Collegeville, PA, October 21, 1988; Vol. I, No. 1). (ERIC Document Reproduction Service No. ED 315 005)

Hammonds, E. M. (1991, August 23). Underrepresentations. *Science, 253*(5022), 919.

Handler, B. S., & Shmurak, C. B. (1991). Rigor, resolve, religion: Mary Lyon and science education. *Teaching Education, 3*(2), 137–142.

Hanson, S. L. (1996). *Lost talent: Women in the sciences.* Philadelphia: Temple University Press.

Harding, S. (1989). Women as creators of knowledge: New environments. *American Behavioral Scientist, 32*(6), 700–707.

Hayes, D. W. (1993). Making inroads: Women in science and technical research: Environmental change slow and difficult. *Black Issues in Higher Education, 10*(17), 34–38.

Hesse-Biber, S., & Gilbert, M. K. (1994). Closing the technological gender gap: Feminist pedagogy in the computer-assisted classroom. *Teaching Sociology, 22*(1), 19–31.

Hirsh, E., & Olson, G. A. (1995). Starting from marginalized lives: A conversation with Sandra Harding. *JAC: A Journal of Composition Theory, 15*(2), 193–225.

Holland, J., Blair, M., & Sheldon, S. (Eds.). (1995). *Debates and issues in feminist re-*

search and pedagogy: A reader. Philadelphia: Multilingual Matters, in association with the Open University.

hooks, b. (1994). *Teaching to transgress: Education as the practice of freedom.* New York: Routledge.

Hughes, K. P. (1995). Feminist pedagogy and feminist epistemology: An overview. *International Journal of Lifelong Education, 14*(3), 214–230.

Illman, D. (1993, August 2). Research for women, minority undergrads. *Chemical & Engineering News, 71*(31), 31.

Jansen, S. C. (1989, May). *Mind machines, myth, metaphor, and scientific imagination.* Paper presented at the annual meeting of the International Communication Association, San Francisco. (ERIC Document Reproduction Service No. ED 311 522)

Jennings, P. (1992, November–December). New opportunities in science. *New Directions for Women, 21*(6), 10.

Jipson, J., et al. (1995). *Repositioning feminism and education: Perspectives on educating for social change.* Westport, CT: Bergin & Garvey.

Kalinowski, J., & Buerk, D. (1995). Enhancing women's mathematical competence: A student-centered analysis. *NWSA Journal, 7*(2), 1–17.

Kelly, G. J., et al. (1993). Science education in sociocultural context: Perspectives from the sociology of science. *Science Education, 77*(2), 207–220.

Kleinfeld, J., & Yerian, S. (1991). *Preparing prospective teachers to develop the mathematical and scientific abilities of young women: The development of teaching cases. Final report.* Fairbanks: Alaska University. (ERIC Document Reproduction Service No. ED 346 025)

Koch, J. (1992). Elementary science education: Looking through the lens of gender. *Initiatives, 55*(3), 67–71.

Koritz, H. (Ed.). (1992, March/April). Women and science [Special issue]. *Journal of College Science Teaching, 21*(5).

Koshland, D. E., Jr. (1992, November 15). Minorities in science. *Science, 258*(5085), 1067.

Lanzinger, I. (1993). Toward feminist science teaching. *Canadian Woman Studies, 13*(2), 95–99.

Lather, P. A. (1991). *Getting smart: Feminist research and pedagogy with/in the postmodern.* New York: Routledge.

Laws, P. W., et al. (1995). Women's responses to an activity-based introductory physics program. *New Directions for Teaching and Learning, 61*, 77–87.

Linder, R. (1995). Exploring cultural diversity in an undergraduate science program. *Transformations: The New Jersey Project Journal, 6*(1), 76–84.

Lloyd, B. W. (Ed.). (1994). The art of teaching chemistry. *Journal of Chemical Education, 71*(11), 925–928.

Luke, C., & Gore, J. (Eds.). (1992). *Feminisms and critical pedagogy.* New York: Routledge.

Lurkis, E. (1994, March). *Gender and the rhetoric of reproduction in popular science texts.* Paper presented at the annual meeting of the Conference on College Composition and Communication, Nashville, TN. (ERIC Document Reproduction Service No. ED 374 447)

Maher, F., & Tetreault, M. K. T. (1994). *The feminist classroom: An inside look at how professors and students are transforming higher education for a diverse society.* New York: Basic Books.

Mahood, L. (1993). Reconstructing girlhood: Putting "clever" girls in science. *Canadian Woman Studies, 13*(2), 91–94.

Mahood, L. (1994). "Typical" girls paint their nails, "clever girls" go into science. *Connexions: An International Women's Quarterly, 45,* 20–22.

Malcom, S. (1989). Increasing the participation of black women in science and technology. *Sage: A Scholarly Journal on Black Women, 6*(2), 15–17.

Matthews, C. M. (1990). *Underrepresented minorities and women in science, mathematics, and engineering: Problems and issues for the 1990s* (CRS Report for Congress). Washington, DC: Library of Congress. (ERIC Document Reproduction Service No. ED 337 525)

Matyas, M. L., & Dix, L. S. (Eds.). (1992). *Science and engineering programs: On target for women?* Washington, DC: National Academy Press.

McCartney, A. (1991, Spring–Summer). The science and technology careers workshop—integrating feminist approaches in residential science education. *Resources for Feminist Research, 20,* 50–51.

McCormick, M. E., & Wold, J. S. (1993). Intervention programs for gifted girls. *Roeper Review, 16*(2), 85–88.

McKenna, E. (1996). Some reflections concerning feminist pedagogy. *Metaphilosophy, 27*(1–2), 178–192.

McWilliam, E. (1994). *In broken images: Feminist tales for a different teacher education.* New York: Teachers College Press.

Meschel, S. V. (1992). Teacher Keng's heritage: A survey of Chinese women scientists. *Journal of Chemical Education, 69*(9), 723–730.

Middleton, S. (1993). *Educating feminists: Life histories and pedagogy.* New York: Teachers College Press.

Morgan, C. S. (1992). College students' perceptions of barriers to women in science and engineering. *Youth and Society, 24*(2), 228–236.

MWIS develops local chapters. (1994, Fall). *Women's Research Network News, 6*(2), 19–20.

National Association for Women in Education. (1993). *Gender equity in math and science.* Washington, DC: Author.

National Research Council (U.S.). Committee on Women in Science and Engineering. (1991). *Women in science and engineering: Increasing their numbers in the 1990s: A statement on policy and strategy.* Washington, DC: National Academy Press.

National Research Council (U.S.). Committee on Women in Science and Engineering. Ad hoc Panel on Industry. (1994). *Women scientists and engineers employed in industry: Why so few?: A report based on a conference.* Washington, DC: National Academy Press.

Ng, R., Staton, P., & Scane, J. (Eds.). (1995). *Anti-racism, feminism, and critical approaches to education.* Westport, CT: Bergin & Garvey.

Oakes, J. (1990). *Lost talent: The underparticipation of women, minorities, and disabled persons in science.* Washington, DC: National Science Foundation with the Rand Corporation.

Oglov, V., & Ching, H. (1993). Voices of women on science. *Canadian Woman Studies,* *13*(2), 48–50.

Otto, P. B. (1991). One science, one sex? *School Science and Mathematics, 91*(8), 367–372.

Parker, L. H., Rennie, L. J., & Fraser, B. J. (Eds.). (1996). *Gender, science, and mathematics: Shortening the shadow.* Boston: Kluwer Academic Press.

Parsons, S., et al. (1995, April). *The art of reflecting in a two-way mirror: A collaborative autobiographical study by three science educators.* Paper presented at the annual meeting of the National Association for Research in Science Teaching, San Francisco. (ERIC Document Reproduction Service No. ED 381 376)

Peltz, W. H. (1990). Can girls + science − stereotypes = success? *Science Teacher, 57* (9), 44–49.

Perry, R., & Greber, L. (1990). Women and computers: An introduction. *Signs: Journal of Women in Culture and Society, 16*(1), 74–101.

Phillips, P. S., & McKay, R. (1994). Women in science: A brief history within chemistry. *School Science Review, 76*(274), 132–137.

Pollina, A. (1995). Gender balance: Lessons from girls in science and mathematics. *Educational Leadership, 53*(1), 30–33.

Pope, L. M. (1995). Advising women considering nontraditional fields of study. *New Directions for Teaching and Learning, 62,* 71–77.

Quimbita, G. (1991). *Preparing women and minorities for careers in math and science: The role of community colleges.* Los Angeles: ERIC Clearinghouse for Junior Colleges. (ERIC Document Reproduction Service No. ED 333 943)

Raloff, J. (1990, December 14). Science: Recruiting nontraditional players. *Science News, 140*(24), 396–398.

Ramsden, J. M. (1990). All quiet on the gender front? *School Science Review, 72*(259), 49–55.

Rayman, P., & Brett, B. (1995). Women science majors: What makes a difference in persistence after graduation? *Journal of Higher Education, 66*(4), 388–414.

Raymond, C. (1991, December 11). Continuing shortage of women in science decried: Many drop out. *Chronicle of Higher Education, 38*(16), A31–A32.

Reynolds, A. J. (1991). The middle schooling process: Influences on science and mathematics achievement from the longitudinal study of American youth. *Adolescence, 26,* (101), 133–158.

Rogers, P., & Kaiser, G. (1995). *Equity in mathematics education: Influences of feminism and culture.* Bristol, PA: Falmer Press.

Rogers, S. J., & Menaghan, E. G. (1991, December). Women's persistence in undergraduate majors—The effects of gender-disproportionate representation. *Gender & Society, 5,* 549–564.

Rose, H. (1994, May 13). Science and environment. *New Statesman Society, 7*(302), 29.

Ross, N. (1990). Exploring ecofeminism. *Journal of Experiential Education, 13*(3), 23–28.

Rosser, S. V. (1988). *Feminism within the science and health care professions: Overcoming resistance.* New York: Teachers College Press.

Rosser, S. V. (1989). Teaching techniques to attract women to science: Applications of feminist theories and methodologies. *Women's Studies International Forum, 12* (3), 363–377.

Rosser, S. (1990). *Female friendly science: Applying women's studies methods and theories to attract students to science.* New York: Teachers College Press.

Rosser, S. V. (1992). Diversity among scientists—inclusive curriculum—improved science: An upward spiral. *Initiatives, 55* (2), 11–19.

Rosser, S. V. (1993). Female friendly science: Including women in curricular content and pedagogy in science. *Journal of General Education, 42* (3), 191–220.

Rosser, S. V. (Ed.). (1995). *Teaching the majority: Breaking the gender barrier in science, mathematics, and engineering.* New York: Teachers College Press.

Roychoudhury, A., Tippins, D., & Nichols, S. (1993). An exploratory attempt toward a feminist pedagogy for science education. *Action in Teacher Education, 15* (4), 36–46.

Sanders, J. (1994). *Lifting the barriers: 600 tested strategies that really work to increase girls' participation in science, mathematics and computers.* Port Washington, NY: Jo Sanders.

Saunders, J., & Platt, L. (1992). *Brains on toast: The inexact science of gender* [Videorecording]. Brooklyn, NY: Liss Platt & Joyan Saunders.

Schniedewind, N. (1993). Teaching feminist process in the 1990s. *Women's Studies Quarterly, 21* (3–4), 17–30.

Schuerich, J. (1992, April). Methodological implications of feminist and poststructuralism views of science. Paper presented at the annual meeting of the American Educational Research Association, San Francisco. (ERIC Document Reproduction Service No. ED 364 421)

Science and technology [Special issue]. (1989, Fall). *Sage: A Scholarly Journal on Black Women, 6* (2).

Science in the U.S.—With one hand tied behind us. (1989). *Hood on the Issues, 1,* 3–14.

Scott, L. U., & Heller, P. (1991). Team work works! Strategies for integrating women and minorities into the physical sciences. *Science Teacher, 58* (1), 24–28.

Sebrechts, J. S. (1992). Cultivating scientists at women's colleges. *Initiatives, 55* (2), 45–51.

Seymour, E. (1995). The loss of women from science, mathematics, and engineering undergraduate majors: An explanatory account. *Science Education, 79* (4), 437–473.

Shea, S. L., & Wright, M. H. (1994). The Women in Science model program at Southern Illinois University at Carbondale. *Initiatives, 56* (1), 29–36.

Shrewsbury, C. M. (1993). What is feminist pedagogy? *Women's Studies Quarterly, 21* (3–4), 8–16.

Siebert, E. (1992). Women in science? *Journal of College Science Teaching, 21* (5), 269–271.

Sloat, B. F. (1990). Perspectives on women and the sciences. *AWIS Newsletter, 19* (6), 4–5.

Sloat, B. F. (1992). Undergraduate women in the sciences: Removing barriers. *Initiatives, 55* (2), 5–10.

Sonnert, G. (1995). *Who succeeds in science?: The gender dimension.* New Brunswick, NJ: Rutgers University Press.

Staberg, E. (1994). Gender and science in Swedish compulsory school. *Gender and Education, 6*(1), 35–45.

Steiger, A., & Davis, F. (1992, May). *Feminist pedagogy and the teaching of science: An experiential workshop.* Description of a workshop conducted at the annual conference of the Association of Canadian Community Colleges, Montreal. (ERIC Document Reproduction Service No. ED 348 116)

Stolte-Heiskanen, V., & Furst-Dilic, R. (Eds.). (1991). *Women in science: Token women or gender equality?* New York: St. Martin's Press.

Stone, L. (Ed.). (1994). *The education feminism reader.* New York: Routledge.

Strenta, A. C., et al. (1994). Choosing and leaving science in highly selective institutions. *Research in Higher Education, 35*(5), 513–547.

Thompson, A., & Gitlin, A. (1995). Creating spaces for reconstructing knowledge in feminist pedagogy. *Educational Theory 45*(2), 125–150.

Thompson, M. E. (1993). Diversity in the classroom: Creating opportunities for learning feminist theory. *Women's Studies Quarterly, 21*(3–4), 114–121.

Tilghman, S. (1993). The status of science: Male versus female scientists. *WIN* [*Women's International Network*] *News, 19*(2), 73–74.

Tobias, S. (1992). Women and science. *Journal of College Science Teaching, 21*(5), 276–278.

Tolmie, A., & Howe, C. (1993, June). Gender and dialogue in secondary school physics. *Gender and Education, 5*(2), 191–209.

Travis, J. (1993, April 16). Making room for women in the culture of science. *Science, 260*(5106), 412–415.

Tsuji, G., & Ziegler, S. (1990). *What research says about increasing the numbers of female students taking math and science in secondary school.* Toronto: Toronto Board of Education. (ERIC Document Reproduction Service No. ED 317 417)

Turkle, S., & Papert, S. (1990). Epistemological pluralism: Styles and voices within the computer culture. *Signs: Journal of Women in Culture and Society, 16*(1), 128–157.

United States Congress. House Committee on Science, Space, and Technology. Subcommittee on Energy. (1994). *Women and K–12 science and mathematics education hearing before the Subcommittee on Energy.* Washington, DC: U.S. Government Printing Office.

Vetter, B. (1992). Ferment: yes—progress: maybe—change: slow. *Mosaic, 23*(3), 34–41.

Wallsgrove, R. (1993). The shopping cart of knowledge [science]. *off our backs, 23* (10), 9.

Warren, K. J. (1989, Fall). Rewriting the future—The feminist challenge to the malestream curriculum. *Feminist Teacher, 4,* 46–52.

Weiler, K. (1995). Revisioning feminist pedagogy. *NWSA Journal, 7*(2), 100–106.

Wilson, M., & Snapp, E. (1992). *Options for girls: A door to the future: An anthology on science and math education.* Austin, TX: Pro-Ed.

Wingspread Conference. (1991). *Improving career access to science and engineering for women.* Racine, WI: Johnson Foundation.

Women in science project at Dartmouth gains momentum. (1994, Spring). *Women's Research Network News 6*(1), 11.

Worthley, J. S. (1992, March). Is science persistence a matter of values? *Psychology of Women Quarterly, 16,* 57–68.

Yarrison-Rice, J. M. (1995). On the problem of making science attractive for women and minorities: An annotated bibliography. *American Journal of Physics, 63*(3), 203–211.

Yentsch, C. M., & Sindermann, C. J. (1992). *The woman scientist: Meeting the challenges for a successful career.* New York: Plenum Press.

Zuckerman, H., Cole, J. R., & Bruer, J. T. (1991). *The outer circle: Women in the scientific community.* New York: Norton.

PART TWO: FEMINIST SCIENCE

Adams, C. J., & Donovan, J. (Eds.). (1995). *Animals and women: Feminist theoretical explorations.* Durham, NC: Duke University Press.

Alcoff, L., & Potter, E. (1993). *Feminist epistemologies.* New York: Routledge.

Altman, I., & Ts'erts'man, A. (1994). *Women and the environment.* New York: Plenum Press.

Antony, L. M., & Witt, C. (Eds.). (1993). *A mind of one's own: Feminist essays on reason and objectivity.* Boulder, CO: Westview Press.

Barinaga, M., & Gibbons, A. (1993, April 16). Feminists find gender everywhere in science. *Science, 260* (5106), 392–393.

Bedard, M. E. (1991). Weird science and the God machine: The technological reproduction of the mind/body split. *NWSA Journal, 3*(1), 20–37.

Benjamin, M. (Ed.). (1993). *A question of identity: Women, science, and literature.* New Brunswick, NJ: Rutgers University Press.

Benjamin, M. (Ed.). (1994). *Science and sensibility: Gender and scientific enquiry, 1780–1945.* Cambridge, MA: Basil Blackwell.

Birke, L. I. A. (1991). Science, feminism, and animal natures II: Feminist critiques and the place of animals in science. *Women's Studies International Forum, 14*(5), 451–458.

Birke, L. I. A. (1994). *Feminism, animals, and science: The naming of the shrew.* Philadelphia: Open University Press.

Bleier, R. (1991). *Feminist approaches to science.* New York: Teachers College Press.

Brière, P. (1989, September). Du savoir des femmes à la science des hommes. *Resources for Feminist Research, 18,* 62–66.

Brown, R. B. (1994). Knowledge and knowing: A feminist perspective. *Science Communication, 16*(2), 152.

Byrne, E. M. (1993). *Women and science: The snark syndrome.* Washington, DC: Falmer Press.

Cancian, F. M. (1992). 1991 Cheryl Miller lecture: Feminist science—Methodologies that challenge inequality. *Gender & Society, 6*(4), 623–642.

Cancian, F. M. (1993). Reply to Risman, Sprague, and Howard. *Gender & Society, 7* (4), 610.

Cantrell, C. (1990). Analogy as destiny: Cartesian man and the woman reader. *Hypatia, 5*(2), 7–19.

Christiansen-Ruffman, L. (1993). Community base and feminist vision: The essential grounding of science in women's community. *Canadian Woman Studies, 13*(2), 16–20.

Clifford, A. M. (1992). Feminist perspectives on science: Implications for an ecological theology of creation. *Journal of Feminist Studies in Religion, 8*(2), 65–90.

Crasnow, S. (1993). Can science be objective? Longino's science as knowledge. *Hypatia, 8*(3), 194–201.

Curthoys, A. (1991). The three body problem—Feminism and chaos theory. *Hecate, 17*(1), 14–21.

Dagg, A. I., & Beauchamp, R. S. (1991, Spring). Is there a feminist science? Perceived impact of gender on research by women scientists. *Atlantis, 16,* 77–84.

Donawerth, J. (1990). Utopian science: Contemporary feminist science theory and science fiction by women. *NWSA Journal, 2*(4), 535–557.

Donini, E. (1994). Feminisms, contextualization, and diversity: A critical perspective on science and development. *Women's Studies International Forum, 17*(2–3), 249–256.

Dugdale, A. (1990). Beyond relativism: Moving on—Feminist struggles. *Australian Feminist Studies, 12,* 51–63.

Fausto-Sterling, A. (1989). Life in the XY corral. *Women's Studies International Forum, 12*(3), 319–331.

Fausto-Sterling, A. (1992). Building two-way streets: The case of feminism and science. *NWSA Journal, 4*(3), 336–349. (Comments on this essay by S. Harding, R. Hubbard, S. Rosser, & N. Tuana follow in the Spring 1993 issue of *NWSA Journal.* Fausto-Sterling responds to these comments in the same issue.)

Feldberg, G. (1992). How different? New essays on gender and science. *Women and Therapy, 12*(4), 47–60.

Findlen, P. (1991). Gender and the scientific "civilizing process." *Journal of the History of Biology, 24,* 331–338.

Gay, H. (1993). Saving the phenomena and saving conventions: A contribution to the debate over feminist epistemology. *Canadian Woman Studies, 13*(2), 37–42.

Goode, S. (1995). Do men do weird science? *Insight on the News, 11*(8), 15–18.

Gorham, G. (1995). The concept of truth in feminist sciences. *Hypatia, 10*(3), 99–116.

Grint, K., & Woolgar, S. (1995). On some failures of nerve in constructivist and feminist analyses of technology. *Science, Technology, & Human Values, 20*(3), 286–330.

Haack, S. (1992). Science "from a feminist perspective." *Philosophy, 67*(259), 5–18.

Halberstam, J. (1991, Fall). Automating gender—Postmodern feminism in the age of the intelligent machine. *Feminist Studies, 17,* 439–460.

Halpin, Z. (1989). Scientific objectivity and the concept of "The Other." *Women's Studies International Forum, 12*(3), 285–294.

Halyes, N. K. (1992). Gender encoding in fluid mechanics: Masculine channels and feminine flows. *Differences, 4*(2), 16–44.

Hamner, J. (1990). Men, power, and the exploitation of women. *Women's Studies International Forum, 13*(5), 443–456.

Haraway, D. (1989). Monkeys, aliens, and women: Love, science, and politics at the intersection of feminist theory and colonial discourse. *Women's Studies International Forum, 12*(3), 295–312.

Haraway, D. (1989). *Primate visions: Gender, race, and nature in the world of modern science.* New York: Routledge.

Haraway, D. (1991). *Simians, cyborgs, and women: The reinvention of nature.* New York: Routledge.

Haraway, D. (1994). A game of cat's cradle: Science studies, feminist theory, cultural studies. *Configurations: A Journal of Literature and Science, 2*(1), 59.

Harding, S. (1989). How the women's movement benefits science: Two views. *Women's Studies International Forum, 12*(3), 271–283.

Harding, S. (1989). Women as creators of knowledge: New environments. *American Behavioral Scientist, 32*(6), 700–707.

Harding, S. (1990). Feminism and theories of scientific knowledge. *Women: A Cultural Review, 1*(1), 87–98.

Harding, S. (1991). *Whose science? Whose knowledge?* Ithaca, NY: Cornell University Press.

Harding, S. (Ed.). (1993). *The "racial" economy of science: Toward a democratic future.* Bloomington: Indiana University Press.

Hirschauer, S., & Mol, A. (1995). Shifting sexes, moving stories: Feminist/constructivist dialogues. *Science, Technology, & Human Values, 20*(3), 368+.

Holmes, H. B. (1989). Can clinical research be both ethical and scientific? *Hypatia, 4* (2), 156–168.

Hosek, C. (1991). Coming together. *Women and Environments, 12*(3–4), 14–16.

Hrdy, S. B. (1990). Sex bias in nature and in history: A late 1980s reexamination of the "biological origins" argument. *American Journal of Physical Anthropology,* (Suppl. 11), 25–37.

Hubbard, R. (1990). *The politics of women's biology.* New Brunswick, NJ: Rutgers University Press.

Hubbard, R. (1995). *Profitable promises: Essays on women, science, and health.* Monroe, ME: Common Courage Press.

Hubbard, R., & Wald, E. (1993). *Exploding the gene myth.* Boston: Beacon Press.

Hughes, D. M. (1991, August). Transforming science and technology: Has the elephant yet flicked its trunk? *NWSA Journal, 3,* 382–401.

Jackson, A. (1989). Feminist critiques of science. *Notices of the American Mathematical Society, 36*(6), 669+.

Jacobus, M., Keller, E. F., & Shuttleworth, S. (Eds.). (1990). *Body/politics: Women and the discourses of science.* New York: Routledge.

Jamison, P. K. (1992). No Eden under glass: A discussion with Donna Haraway. *Feminist Teacher, 6*(2), 10–15.

Johnson, A. (1989, August–September). New research on women and science. *off our backs, 19*(8), 12.

Jordanova, L. J. (1989). *Sexual visions: Images of gender in science and medicine between the eighteenth and twentieth centuries.* Madison: University of Wisconsin Press.

Keller, E. F. (1992). *Secrets of life, secrets of death: Essays on science and culture.* New York: Routledge.

Keller, E. F., & Longino, H. E. (Eds.). (1995). *Feminism and science.* New York: Oxford University Press.

Kirkup, G., & Keller, L. S. (Eds.). (1992). *Inventing women: Science, technology, and gender.* Cambridge, MA: Basil Blackwell.

Koertge, N. (1994). Do feminists alienate women from the sciences? *The Education Digest, 60*(4), 49–52.

Lakomski, G. (1989). Against feminist science: Harding and the science question in feminism. *Educational Philosophy and Theory, 21*(2), 1–11.

Larson, E. J. (1995). *Sex, race, and science: Eugenics in the Deep South.* Baltimore, MD: Johns Hopkins University Press.

Lederman, M. (1993). Structuring feminist science. *Women's Studies International Forum, 16*(6), 605–613.

Lich, H. T. (1994). The Vietnamese woman in scientific creation and technological transference. *Isis International/Women in Action, 2–3,* 16–19.

Lomperis, L., & Stanbury, S. (Eds.). (1993). *Feminist approaches to the body in medieval literature.* Philadelphia: University of Pennsylvania Press.

Longino, H. (1989). Feminist critiques of rationality: Critiques of science or philosophy of science? *Women's Studies International Forum, 12*(3), 261–269.

Longino, H. (1990). *Science as social knowledge.* Princeton, NJ: Princeton University Press.

Lorber, J. (1993). Believing is seeing: Biology as ideology. *Gender & Society, 7*(4), 568–581.

Lorrigan, G. (1995). Science—Whose knowledge? *Broadsheet: New Zealand Feminist Magazine, 205,* 24–25.

Lykke, N., & Braidotti, R. (Eds.). (1996). *Between monsters, goddesses and cyborgs: Feminist confrontations with science, medicine and cyberspace.* Atlantic Highlands, NJ: Zed Books.

Mackinnon, A. (1993). "Crossing borders, redefining boundaries, traversing centuries: From Linnaeus to cyberspace": Sex/gender in techno-science worlds conference. *Australian Feminist Studies, 18,* 247–249.

MacKinnon, M. H., & McIntyre, M. I. (Eds.). (1995). *Readings in ecology and feminist theology.* Kansas City, KS: Sheed & Ward.

Marsden, C., & Omery, A. (1992). Women, science, and a women's science. *Women's Studies, 21*(4), 479–489.

Martin, E. (1991). The egg and the sperm: How science has constructed a romance based on stereotypical male–female roles. *Signs, 16,* 485–501.

Martinez, L. M. (1994). If you like knitting, why are you talking about engineering? *Isis International Women in Action, 2–3,* 13–15.

McCaughey, M. (1993). Redirecting feminist critiques of science. *Hypatia, 8*(4), 72–84.

McGowan, T. D. (1992). The metaphysical science of Aristotle's generation of animals and its feminist critics. *The review of metaphysics, 46*(2), 307–342.

McIlwee, J. S., & Robinson, J. G. (1992). *Women in engineering: Gender, power, and workplace culture.* Albany: State University of New York Press.

McIntosh, A. (1996). The emperor has no clothes . . . let us paint our loinclothes rainbow: A classical and feminist critique of contemporary science policy. *Environmental Values, 5*(1), 3–30.

Meece, J., & Jones, G. (1996). Girls in mathematics and science: Constructivism as a feminist perspective. *The High School Journal, 79*(3), 242.

Menzies, H. (1993). Science through her looking glass. *Canadian Woman Studies, 13* (2), 54–58.

Merchant, C. (1989). *Ecological revolutions: Nature, gender, and science in New England.* Chapel Hill: University of North Carolina Press.

Merchant, C. (1990). *The death of nature: Women, ecology, and the scientific revolution.* San Francisco: Harper & Row.

Mies, M. (1990). Women's studies—Science, violence, and responsibility. *Women's Studies International Forum, 13*(5), 433–441.

Mies, M. (1993). *Ecofeminism.* Atlantic Highlands, NJ: Zed Books.

Morse, M. (1995). *Women changing science: Voices from a field in transition.* New York: Insight Books.

Morton, S. (1990). Philosophical feminism: A bibliographic guide to critiques of science. *Resources for Feminist Research, 19*(2), 2+.

Mura, R. (1991). *Searching for subjectivity in the world of the sciences: Feminist viewpoints.* Ottawa: Canadian Research Institute for the Advancement of Women.

Nadeau, R. (1996). *S/he brain: Science, sexual politics, and the feminist movement.* Westport, CT: Praeger.

Nelson, L. (1991). Feminist science criticism and critical thinking. *Transformations, 2* (1), 26–35.

Nelson, L. (1995). A feminist naturalized philosophy of science. *Synthese, 104*(3), 399.

Noble, D. F. (1992). *A world without women: The Christian clerical culture of western science.* New York: Knopf.

Oglov, V. (1993). Voices of women on science. *Canadian Woman Studies, 13*(2), 54–58.

Olson, R. (1990, June). Historical reflections on feminist critiques of science: The scientific background to modern feminism. *History of Science, 28*(80, Pt. 2), 125–148.

Oudshoorn, N., & van den Wijngaard, L. (1991). Dualism in biology: The case of sex hormones. *Women's Studies International Forum , 14*(5), 459–471.

Pinnick, C. L. (1994). Feminist epistemology: Implications for philosophy of science. *Philosophy of Science, 61*(4), 646–657.

Politics of genetics: A conversation with Anne Fausto-Sterling and Diane Paul. (1994, July). [Interview]. *Women's Review of Books 11*(10), 17–18.

Pool, R. (1994). *Eve's rib: The biological roots of sex differences.* New York: Crown.

Potter, E. (1995). Good science and good philosophy of science. *Synthese, 104*(3), 422–440.

Price, J. S. (1993). Guest comment: Gender bias in the sciences—Some up-to-date information on the subject. *American Journal of Physics, 61*(7), 589–590.

Risman, B. J., Sprague, J., & Howard, J. (1993). Comment on Francesca M. Cancian's "Feminist Science." *Gender & Society, 7*(4), 608.

Rose, H. (1989). Talking about science as a socialist-feminist. *Rethinking Marxism, 2* (3), 26–30.

Rose, H. (1994). *Love, power, and knowledge: Towards a feminist transformation of the sciences.* Bloomington: Indiana University Press.

Rose, S. (1989). Women biologists and the "old boy" network. *Women's Studies International Forum, 12*(3), 349–354.

Rosser, S. V. (1988). *Feminism within the science and health care professions: Overcoming resistance.* New York: Teachers College Press.

Rosser, S. V. (1989). Re-visioning clinical research: Gender and the ethics of experimental design. *Hypatia, 4*(2), 125–139.

Rosser, S. V. (1989). Ruth Bleier: A passionate vision for feminism and science. *Women's Studies International Forum, 12*(3), 249–252.

Rosser, S. V. (1992, September–December). Are there feminist methodologies appropriate for the natural sciences and do they make a difference? *Women's Studies International Forum, 15*(5–6), 535–550.

Rosser, S. V. (1992). *Biology & feminism: A dynamic interaction.* New York: Twayne.

Rosser, S. V. (1994). *Women's health—Missing from U.S. medicine.* Bloomington: Indiana University Press.

Rundblad, G. (1990). Feminism and the constructions of knowledge: Speculations on a subjective science. *Women and Language, 13*(1), 53–55.

Russett, C. E. (1989). *Sexual science: The Victorian construction of womanhood.* Cambridge, MA: Harvard University Press.

Saunders, J. (1991). *Non-human nature and feminism: Towards a green feminist theory.* Worcester, MA: Worcester College of Higher Education.

Scheinin, R. (1989). Women as scientists: Their rights and obligations. *Journal of Business Ethics, 8*(2–3), 131–155.

Schiebinger, L. (1989). *The mind has no sex?: Women in the origins of modern science.* Cambridge, MA: Harvard University Press.

Schiebinger, L. (1990). The anatomy of difference: Race and gender in eighteenth-century science. *Eighteenth-Century Studies, 23,* 387–406.

Schiebinger, L. (1993). *Nature's body: Gender in the making of modern science.* Boston: Beacon Press.

Sheets-Johnstone, M. (1992). Corporeal archetypes and power: Preliminary clarifications and considerations of sex. *Hypatia, 7*(3), 39–76.

Shepherd, L. J. (1993). *Lifting the veil: The feminine faces of science.* Boston: Shambhala.

Sileo, C. C. (1995). Science. *Insight on the News, 11*(26), 36–37.

Soper, K. (1995). Feminism and ecology: Realism and rhetoric in the discourses of nature. *Science, Technology, & Human Values, 20*(3), 311–331.

Spanier, B. (1991). Gender and ideology in science: A study of molecular biology. *NWSA Journal, 3*(2), 167–198.

Spanier, B. (1995). Biological determinism and homosexuality. *NWSA Journal 7*(1), 54–71.

Spanier, B. (1995). *Im/partial science: Gender ideology in molecular biology.* Bloomington: Indiana University Press.

Stark, S. (1992). Overcoming Butlerianobstacles: May Sinclair and the problem of biological determinism. *Women's Studies, 21*(3), 265–283.

Steinberg, D. L. (1994). Power, positionality and epistemology: Towards an anti-oppressive feminist standpoint approach to science, medicine and technology. *Women: A Cultural Review, 5*(3), 295.

Swedberg, L. (1993). Fallible or lovable: Response to Anne Fausto-Sterling's "Building Two-Way Streets." *NWSA Journal, 5*(3), 389–391.

Theriot, N. M. (1993, August). Women's voices in nineteenth-century medical discourse: A step toward deconstructing science. *Signs, 19*(1), 1–31.

Tobach, E., & Rosoff, B. (Eds.). (1994). *Challenging racism and sexism: Alternatives to genetic explanations.* New York: Feminist Press.

Tomaselli, S. (1991, June 1). Reflections on the history of the science of woman. *History of Science, 29* (84, Pt. 2), 185–205.

Tripp-Knowles, P. (1993). Margaret Benston's feminist science critique: A review and tribute. *Canadian Woman Studies, 13*(2), 25–27.

Tripp-Knowles, P. (1994). Androcentric bias in science? *Women's Studies International Forum, 17*(1), 1–8.

Tripp-Knowles, P. (1995). A review of the literature on barriers encountered by women in science academia. *Resources for Feminist Research, 24*(1/2), 28–34.

Tuana, N. (Ed.). (1989). *Feminism and science.* Bloomington: Indiana University Press.

Tuana, N. (1993). *The less noble sex: Scientific, religious, and philosophical conceptions of woman's nature.* Bloomington: Indiana University Press.

Tuana, N. (1995). The values of science: Empiricism from a feminist perspective. *Synthese, 104*(3), 441+.

United Nations Commission on Science and Technology for Development. Gender Working Group. (1995). *Missing links: Gender equity in science and technology for development.* Ottawa, Canada: International Development Research Centre, in Association with Intermediate Technology Publications and UNIFEM.

van Wingerden, I. (1993, July–August). Once you have seen how scientific knowledge is made, you give up the idea that what you are "discovering" may actually be "nature." *Women's Studies International Forum, 16*(4), 379–380.

Wagner, I. (1994). Connecting communities of practice: Feminism, science, and technology. *Women's Studies International Forum, 17*(2–3), 257–265.

Wertheim, M. (1995). *Pythagoras' trousers: God, physics, and the gender wars.* New York: Times Books/Random House.

Windholz, G. (1989). Three researchers in Pavlov's laboratories. *NWSA Journal, 1*(3), 491–496.

Witt, P. L., Bauerle, C., Derouen, D., Kamel, D., Kelleher, P., McCarthy, M., Namenwirth, M., Sabatini, L., & Voytovich, M. (1989). The October 29th Group: Defining a feminist science. *Women's Studies International Forum, 12*(3), 253–259.

Wolffensperger, J. (1993). Science is truly a male world: The interconnectedness of knowledge, gender, and power within university education. *Gender and Education, 5*(1), 37–54.

Wylie, A., Okruhlik, K., Thielen-Wilson, L., & Morton, S. (1989). Feminist critiques of science: The feminist epistemological and methodological literature. *Women's Studies International Forum, 12*(3), 379–388.

Wylie, A., Okruhlik, K., Thielen-Wilson, L., & Morton, S. (1990). Philosophical feminism: A bibliographic guide to critiques of science. *Resources for Feminist Research/Documentation Sur La Recherche Feministe, 19*(2), 2–38.

Zack, N. (1996). *Bachelors of science: Seventeenth-century identity, then and now.* Philadelphia: Temple University Press.

PART THREE: WOMEN IN SCIENCE

Ainley, M. G. (1993). "Women's work" in Canadian chemistry. *Canadian Woman Studies, 13*(2), 43–46.

Allen, N. (1992). Australian women in science: Two unorthodox careers. *Women's Studies International Forum, 15*(5/6), 551–562.

Bailey, M. J. (1994). *American women in science: A biographical dictionary.* Santa Barbara, CA: ABC–CLIO.

Bindocci, C. G. (1993). *Women and technology: An annotated bibliography.* New York: Garland.

Bonta, M. (1991). *Women in the field: America's pioneering women naturalists.* College Station: Texas A & M University Press.

Brush, S. G. (1991). Women in science and engineering. *American Scientist, 79*(5), 404–419.

Clewell, B. C., & Anderson, B. T. (1991). *Women of color in mathematics, science and engineering: A review of the literature.* Washington, DC: Center for Women Policy Studies. (ERIC Document Reproduction Service No. ED 347 222)

Cobb, J. P. (1989). A life in science: Research and service. *Sage, 6*(2), 39–43.

Cummins, H., McDaniel, S. A., & Beauchamp, R. S. (1990, Spring). Becoming inventors: Women who aspire to invent. *Atlantis, 15,* 90–93.

Erinosho, S. Y. (Ed.). (1994). *Perspectives on women in science and technology in Nigeria.* Ibadan, Nigeria: Sam Bookman.

Gallop, N. (1994). *Science is women's work: Photos and biographies of American women in the sciences.* Windsor, CA: National Women's History Project.

Gibson, M. (1990). On the insensitivity of women: Science and the woman question in liberal Italy, 1890–1910. *Journal of Women's History, 2*(2), 11–41.

Gornick, V. (1990). *Women in science: 100 journeys into the territory* (rev. ed.). New York: Simon & Schuster.

Herzenberg, C. L. (1990). The participation of women in science during antiquity and the middle ages. *Interdisciplinary Science Reviews, 15*(4), 294–297.

Herzenberg, C. L., Meschel, S. V., & Altena, J. A. (1991, February). Women scientists and physicians of antiquity and the middle ages. *Journal of Chemical Education, 68,* 101–105.

Hoyrup, E. (1989, June). Women of science, technology, and medicine: A bibliography. *Resources for Feminist Research, 18*(2), 82–83.

Kass-Simon, G., & Farnes, P. (Eds.). (1990). *Women of science: Righting the record.* Bloomington: Indiana University Press.

King, R. C. (1989). Becoming a scientist: An important career decision. *Sage, 6*(2), 47–50.

McGrayne, S. B. (1993). *Nobel Prize women in science: Their lives, struggles, and momentous discoveries.* Secaucus, NJ: Carol Publishing Group.

Morse, M. (1995). *Women changing science: Voices from a field in transition.* New York: Insight.

Mozans, H. J. (1991). *Woman in science.* South Bend, IN: University of Notre Dame Press.

Ogilive, M. B. (1990). *Women in science: Antiquity through the nineteenth century: A biographical dictionary with annotated bibliography.* Cambridge, MA: MIT Press.

Outram, D. (1991, September). Fat, gorillas, and misogyny: Women's history in science. *British Journal for the History of Science, 24*(82), 361–368.

Phillips, P. (1990). *The scientific lady: A social history of women's scientific interests, 1520–1918.* New York: St. Martin's Press.

Rossiter, M. (1995). *Women scientists in America: Before affirmative action, 1940–1972.* Baltimore, MD: Johns Hopkins University Press.

Rudolph, E. D. (1990, May). Women who studied plants in the pre-twentieth century United States and Canada. *Taxon, 39*(2), 151–205.

Science and technology [Special issue]. (1989, Fall). *Sage: A Scholarly Journal on Black Women, 6*(2).

Searing, S. (Compiler). (1991). *Women and science: Issues and resources* (4th ed.). Madison: University of Wisconsin System Women's Studies Librarian.

Sime, R. L. (1996). *Lise Meitner: A life in physics.* Berkeley: University of California Press.

Sluby, P. C. (1989, Fall). Black women and inventions. *Sage: A Scholarly Journal on Black Women, 6*(2), 33–35.

Stanley, A. (1990). Invention begins at forty—Older women of the 19th century as inventors. *Journal of Women and Aging, 2*(2), 133–151.

Tanio, N. (1991). Gendering the history of science. *Nuncius, 6*(2), 295–305.

Thompson, P. J. (1994, April). *Ellen Swallow Richards (1842–1911): Ecological foremother.* Paper presented at the annual meeting of the American Educational Research Association, New Orleans. (ERIC Document Reproduction Service No. ED 374 014)

Troemel-Ploetz, S. (1990). Mileva Einstein-Marić—The woman who did Einstein's mathematics. *Women's Studies International Forum, 13*(5), 415–432.

Warren, R. L. (1994). *The scientist within you: Experiments and biographies of distinguished women in science: Instructor's guide for use with students ages 8–13.* Eugene, OR: ACI.

Warren, R. L. (1995). *The scientist within you: Women scientists from seven continents: Biographies and activities: Instructor's guide for use with students ages 10–15.* Eugene, OR: ACI.

Weisbard, P. H., & Apple, R. D. (Eds.). (1993). The history of women and science, health, and technology: A bibliographic guide to the professions and the disciplines (2nd ed.). Madison: University of Wisconsin System Women's Studies Librarian. (Also available on the Internet at this URL: gopher://gopher.adp.wisc.edu:70/11/.browse/.METAGLSHW).

Yount, L. (1995). *Twentieth-century women scientists.* New York: Facts on File.

PART FOUR: INTERNET RESOURCES

LISTSERVS

We compiled this list of listservs from the World Wide Web. The descriptions were supplied by the owners of the listserv or by others. In some cases, the owner supplied two addresses. If one does not work, try the other. Unless otherwise stated, subscribe by sending an e-mail message consisting of SUBSCRIBE, the list name, and your full name to the address indicated. For example, Marie Curie could send an e-mail message to LISTSERV@CMSUVMB.CMSU.EDU saying SUBSCRIBE EDUCOM-W Marie Curie.

Please remember that addresses do change on the Web. If you are unable to subscribe to one of these, be sure to try a WWW search for more up-to-date information or ask a librarian for assistance.

CCWEST is a list (and a site of resources) for women and girls in science and technology in Canada. Send the subscription message to LISTPROCESSOR@ CUNEWS.CARLETON.CA

CSWA for women in astronomy. Try contacting the owner at elmegreen@vassar.edu or AASWOMEN@vaxsar.vassar.edu

EDUCOM-W is a moderated list to facilitate discussion of issues in technology and education that are of interest to women. Send subscription request to LISTSERV@ BITNIC.EDUCOM.EDU or LISTSERV@CMSUVMB.CMSU.EDU or LISTSERV@CMSUVMB

EWM is a list for European women in mathematics. Send subscription message to LISTSERV@VM.CNUCE.CNR.IT

FAB focuses on feminist approaches to bio-ethics. To subscribe, send a message containing your full name and e-mail address to FAB-REQUEST@PHIL.RUU.NL

FIST Feminism in Science and Technology is an unmoderated list for discussion of feminism, science, and technology. Send subscription request to LISTSERV@ DAWN.HAMPSHIRE.EDU or fist-request@family.hampshire.edu. Also can try sending a message with just "subscribe" on the Subject line to FIST-REQUEST@NIESTU.COM

GENDER-SET is a list for discussion of research on gender, science, engineering, and technology (SET). To subscribe, send the message JOIN GENDER-SET Your Name to MAILBASE@MAILBASE.AC.UK

LIS stands for Lesbians in Science and is a list for lesbians in industry, universities, government labs, etc. Send message SUBSCRIBE LIS Your Name Your e-address to LIS-REQUEST@KENYON.EDU

MRSWOMEN is a list for women in materials science and related fields. Send subscription message to LISTSERV@CMSA.BERKELEY.EDU

MWCF is the Metro Women Chemists Forum, sponsored by the American Chemical Society. It gives women in the chemical professions an opportunity to discuss and share information on job and personal issues such as dealing with advisors and coworkers, harassment on the job, unemployment, and managing career and family. To subscribe, send the message "subscribe MWCF" (include the quotation marks) to juzak@aecom.yu.edu

The National Organization of Gay and Lesbian Scientists and Technical Professionals operates NOGLSTP. Send subscription requests to NOGLSTP-REQUEST@ ELROY.JPL.NASA.GOV

SYSTERS provides a forum for female computer scientists for the exchange of research and career information. (Restricted membership.) Send subscription request to SYSTERS-REQUEST@PA.DEC.COM or systers-request@ decwrl.dec.com or try sending an e-mail message to SYSTERS-ADMIN@

SYSTERS.ORG with "subscribe" on the Subject line or fill out the form at URL:http://www.systers.org:80/mecca/cgi-bin/new-req.tcl

SYSTERS-STUDENTS is a student-oriented version of the SYSTERS list (see above). It is for female graduate and undergraduate students in computer science. To subscribe, send a brief introduction to SYSTERS-STUDENTS-REQUEST@MARIA. WUSTL.EDU explaining why you'd like to join (or asking for more information).

WAM exists to help members of Women and Mathematics keep in touch and share information. To subscribe, send the message SUBSCRIBE WAM to MAJOR-DOMO@MYSTERY.COM

WEBWOMEN-TECH is a list for women involved in the technical side of managing web sites. To subscribe, send a message with just the word SUBSCRIBE in the Subject header toWEBWOMEN-TECH-REQUEST@NIESTU.COM

WEPAN-L Women in Engineering Program Advocates Network. Send subscription request to LISTSERV@VM.CC.PURDUE.EDU

WIPHYS is a moderated list for issues of concern to women in physics. Send subscription request to LISTSERV@NYSERNET.ORG or LISTSERV@APS.ORG

WISENET is a list for women in science, mathematics, and engineering. Send subscription request to LISTSERV@UICVM.UIC.EDU

WMST_L serves academic and professional needs of people interested in women's studies teaching, research, libraries, and programs. Send subscription request to LIST-SERV@UMDD.UMD.EDU

World Wide Web Sites

Please remember that Web sites may disappear or change addresses without warning. The Internet is not as stable as traditional books and journals. Try a Web search or ask a librarian if these URLs do not work. Also, don't forget all the punctuation marks and to use capital letters if the URL has them.

The Ada Project: Tapping Internet resources for women in computer science. (Updated frequently). URL: http://www.cs.yale.edu/HTML/YALE/CS/HyPlans/tap/

David, B. G., Wood, L., & Wilson, R. (1993, May). UC Berkeley compendium of tips for teaching with excellence. URL: gopher://infocal.berkeley.edu/11/.p/otherdepts/ttips/GD

DesJardins, M. (1994, December). How to succeed in graduate school: A guide for students and advisors. In Crossroads ACM Student Journal. URL (Parts 1 and 2): http://www.acm.org/crossroads/xrds1-2/advice1.html http://www.acm.org/crossroads/xrds1-3/advice2.html

Etzkowitz, H. (1994). Barriers to women in academic science and engineering. Also in W. Pearson, Jr. & I. Fechter (Eds.), *Who will do science? Educating the next generation*. Baltimore, MD: Johns Hopkins University Press. URL: http://www.ai.-mit.edu/people/ellens/Gender/EKNU.html

Gender Issues in Technology. (dates vary for individual articles). [gopher site]. The Ontario Institute for Studies in Education. URL: gopher://porpoise.oise.on.ca/11/resources/IRes4Ed/resources/gender/Gender%20Issues%20in%20Technology

Koch, M. (1996, February 13). No girls allowed! Originally published in *TECHNOS*

Quarterly for Education and Technology (Fall 1994). (Describes how girls are excluded from technology and offers suggestions for improvement.) URL: http://gnn.com/gnn/meta/edu/features/archive/gtech.html#reading

Logged On or Left Out? (1996, January). Sacramento Bee special report: Women in computing. URL: http://www.nando.net/sacbee/women/

Matyas, M., & Dix, L. S. (1992). Science and engineering programs: On target for women? URL: http://web.mit.edu/ethics/www/ecsel/abstracts/sci-engprog-links.html

Moses, L. E. (1993, September). Our computer science classrooms: Are they "friendly" to female students? Also published in *SIGCSE Bulletin*. URL: http://www.muc.edu/cwis/person/moses/comments/paper.html

Nine Steps to Achieving Gender Equity in Science Classrooms. (1995, November). Compiled by Women Science Students and Science Faculty and Staff at the New England Consortium for Undergraduate Science Education Colleges and based on initial work by students at Brown University. Published by the Office of the Dean of the College at Brown University. URL: http://www.brown.edu/ Administration/Dean_of_the_College/homepginfo/Equity_handbook.html

O'Rourke, J. (1995, November 16). Statistics on women in computer science and engineering. Committee on the Status of Women, Computer Research Association. URL: http://cs.smith.edu/~orourke/fstats.html

Rayman, P., & Brett, B. (1995). Women science majors: What makes a difference in persistence after graduation? Also published in *Journal of Higher Education* (July/August 1995). URL: http://web.mit.edu/ethics/www/ecsel/abstracts/academenv3.html

Spertus, E. (1996, March). Women and computer science. URL: http://www.ai.mit.edu/people/ellens/gender.html

Spertus, E. (1996, March). Women and minorities in science and engineering. URL: http://www.ai.mit.edu/people/ellens/Gender/wom_and_min.html

Tapping the Talent—An Agenda for Action for Business to Increase the Talent Available to Them by Encouraging More Young Women into Science, Engineering and Technology. (1996, March). Opportunity 2000. URL: http://info.lut.ac.uk/orgs/opp2000/

University of Wisconsin–Madison Draft of an Action Plan for Women in Science, Engineering, and Mathematics. (1993). Submitted by the CIC/UW–Madison Women in Science Planning Group to the CIC and to Chancellor David Ward, Interim Vice Chancellor Richard Barrows, the Deans and Department Chairs in the Divisions of Biological and Physical Sciences, and the Deans of the Graduate School and School of Education. URL: gopher://gopher.adp.wisc.edu/11/.browse/.METACOMWS

Weisbard, P. H., & Apple, R. D. (1993). The history of women and science, health, and technology: A bibliographic guide to the professions and the disciplines (2nd ed.). Madison: University of Wisconsin System Women's Studies Librarian. URL: gopher://infolib.lib.berkeley.edu/11/eres/resdbs/womstu/womenbib or gopher://gopher.adp.wisc.edu:70/11/.browse/.METAGLSHW (better)

Women in Computing: The Newsletter for the Top Women in IS. (Ongoing). URL: http://www.wcmh.com/oc/wic/

Women, Minorities, and Persons with Disabilities in Science & Engineering. (1994). National Science Foundation. NSF 94-333. URL: http://www.qrc.com:80/nsf/srs/wmpdse94/

Index

About the Author

Sue V. Rosser earned a Ph.D. in zoology from the University of Wisconsin–Madison. She currently serves as Director of the Center for Women's Studies and Gender Research at the University of Florida in Gainesville, where she is also Professor of Anthropology and holds affiliate appointments in Zoology and the School of Medicine. In 1995 she was Senior Program Officer for Women's Programs at the National Science Foundation. Author of more than 70 journal articles on theoretical and applied issues surrounding women in science and women's health, her books include *Teaching Science and Health from a Feminist Perspective: A Practical Guide* (1986); *Feminism Within the Science and Health Care Professions: Overcoming Resistance* (1988); *Female Friendly Science: Applying Women's Studies Methods and Theories to Attract Students* (1990); *Feminism and Biology: A Dynamic Interaction* (1992); *Women's Health: Missing from U.S. Medicine* (1994); and *Teaching the Majority: Breaking the Gender Barrier in Science, Mathematics, and Engineering* (1995).